Ethics and Organizational Communication

Communication and Social Organization
Gary L. Kreps, series editor

Conflict and Diversity
  Claire Damken Brown, Charlotte C. Snedeker, and Beate D. Sykes (eds.)

Ethics and Organizational Communication
  Matthew W. Seeger

forthcoming

Organization Means Communication
  Ruggero Cesaria and Pamela Shockley-Zalabek (eds.)

Creating and Sustaining Community in Organizational Life
  Patricia Kay Felkins

Communication and Social Action Research
  Joseph Pilotta

Organizational Communication and Change
  Philip Salem (ed.)

Communicating with Customers
  Wendy S. Zabava-Ford

Ethics and Organizational Communication

Matthew W. Seeger
Wayne State University

HAMPTON PRESS INC.
CRESSKILL, NEW JERSEY

Copyright © 1997 by Hampton Press, Inc.

Printed in the United States of America

Library of Congress Cataloging-in-Publication Data

Seeger, Matthew W. (Matthew Wayne), 1957-
    Ethics and organizational communication / Matthew W. Seeger.
        p.   cm. -- (The Hampton Press communication series.
Communication and social organization)
    Includes bibliographic references and indexes
    ISBN 1-57273-118-4 (cloth). -- ISBN 1-57273-119-2 (pbk.)
    1. Communication in organizations--Moral and ethical aspects.
I. Title. II. Series.
HC30.3.S43   1997
175--DC21   97-21693
                                                            CIP

Hampton Press, Inc.
23 Broadway
Cresskill, NJ 07626

Contents

Acknowledgments

This book, as with all efforts to survey broad bodies of theory and research, is the product of many hands. I thank Gary Kreps for both his insights into the Weickian model and for his support of this project. The editorial staff at Hampton Press, in particular Barbara Bernstein, provided excellent support. Jack Kay provided encouragement throughout this project. The Wayne State University Graduate School provided economic assistance. My research assistant, Tim Borchers, provided an important second set of eyes. My friend Steven J. Hipfel provided specialized research assistance. Matt Sikora did the hard work of changing edited copy into clean copy. My ideas and my interests in ethics have been greatly influenced by the SCA Commission on Communication Ethics and many of its members including Richard Johannesen, Jim Jaksa, and Mike Pritchard. Most important to this project, however, are the doctoral students here at Wayne State University who have been interested in the ethics of organizational communication; Michele Simms, Debra Kernisky, Tony McGill, Barbara King, and Betsy Stevens, to name a very few.

My personal sense of right and wrong, good and bad was instilled by my parents Reverend Melvin R. Seeger and Jeannette Seeger and made material by my family, my wife Beth, and my children Maggie and Henry. I dedicate this work to them.

I would also like to gratefully acknowledge the following individuals and organizations who granted permission for use of their materials:

Professor Karl Weick for his use of the Model of Enactment in Chapter 2; The General Motors Corporation for use of John E. Smith's "Letter to Our Stockholders and Friends," from the 1994 Annual Report, in Chapter 2; the Chrysler Corporation for use of sections from the Chrysler Corporation Code of Ethical Behavior in Chapter 13. Also, thanks to Louis Clark and the Government Accountability Project (810 First Street N.E., Suite 630, Washington, DC 20002-3633; http://www.accessone.com.gap/) for for use of "Felix Smith: Defending the Public Trust" and "Sonja Anderson: Environmental Sacrifice Zones" in Chapter 6.

Preface

Ethical and value-based perspectives occupy an increasingly prominent place in organizational studies. The organizational context is complex, chaotic, and often illogical. Organizational, stakeholder, and individual values inevitably come into conflict creating moral dilemmas and ethically suspect outcomes. Organizational studies have developed a diverse body of theory and research focusing on these issues. The study of ethics also has a long and rich tradition in communication extending back to the classical Greeks. The primary focus has been on ethics in public communication, however, as one of the primary links between rhetorical theory and philosophy. Communication ethics has recently been reinvigorated as an area of scholarship and pedagogy and begun systematic examination of broader contexts of human communication.

This text seeks to integrate many divergent themes related to organizational communication ethics, grounding them in Karl Weick's rich notion of equivocality and organizing. In the first section of this book, I argue that a form of ethical equivocality arises in organizations due to the inherent value-based nature of ethical questions, and because conflicting perspectives and stakeholders usually interpret ethical questions in very different ways. Ethical equivocality, as with all forms of equivocality, is reduced through rules and cycles. Communication, as the basis of a cycle, is particularly critical in reducing ethical equivocality. Communication is both an issue of organizational communication ethics, and the process whereby ethical issues are resolved in organizational contexts. The second section of this book deals with a set of issues that concern micro-organizational communication ethics. These relate primarily to the individual or group level and include responsibility and accountability, privacy and employee rights, free speech and employee voice, and whistleblowing. The third section focuses on macro-organizational communication ethics. These issues relate to the organizational level of analysis and include legitimacy, organizational responsibility, advertising, and stakeholder interests and concerns. The final section of this book focuses on special concerns including ethics and organizational change, ethics and leadership, and suggestions for making ethics part of the agenda.

Ethical questions, issues, and dilemmas are inherent to our humanness. That includes human constructions such as organization. Any comprehensive model of organization must incorporate an understanding of the role of values and ethics. Although it is easy to adopt an ethically neutral approach when discussing organizations and communication, this is simply not an option. My hope is that this text will assist in the process of putting ethics on the agenda.

—Matthew W. Seeger

1

Ethical Issues in Communication and Organization

The most powerful force in modern society is the organization. In fact, organizations can be thought of as complex sociotechnological systems designed specifically to accomplish large and complex goals. Whether in its not-for-profit mode (the Methodist Church, United Way, or Department of Health and Human Services) or in a profit-making form (General Motors, Ben and Jerry's, or the Kmart Corporation), the modern organization commands great human, physical, and technological resources. Cheney (1991) observed that the messages produced by organizations dominate society. The largest and most diverse organizational form, the multinational corporation, extends beyond national boundaries taking advantage of geographic variations in labor, raw materials, and markets to increase efficiency and effectiveness. All of our lives, and the development of society as a whole, are profoundly influenced by these large, complex structures called *organizations.*

Despite this unprecedented level of influence, surprisingly little is known about the impact of organizations. Does the modern organizationally dominated society increase individual freedom and human dignity? Do organizational influences promote good social consequences? Do organizations expand choices and the opportunity to make rational,

1

informed decisions? Do organizational messages contribute to full and complete debate of complex social problems and issues? Are organizational influences conducive to the free exchange of information, perspectives, and ideas? Although these questions strike at the heart of the organization's role in society, and the outcomes they create, they are fundamentally questions of values and ethics. In fact, a majority of the judgments made about organizations, their processes, products, and outcomes are largely ethical judgments.

ETHICS AND VALUES

Ethics and ethical questions are fundamental to organizations and to all of human experience. They are concerned with essential judgments of good–bad, right–wrong, desirable–undesirable, acceptable–unacceptable, legitimate–illegitimate, worthy–unworthy. These judgments, in turn, influence all manner of perceptions, decisions, attitudes, choices, and actions (Conrad, 1993). Ethics are also associated with the general standards of moral conduct in a given society or social context. Taken together, these standards and judgments are central features in the development and maintenance of social relations, structures, and institutions. Lying, for example, is not only ethically unjustifiable, it undermines the fundamental ability of humans to interact in a meaningful and predictable manner (Bok, 1979). These ethical judgments are based on values; the more specific oughts, ideals, norms, and goals that permeate all aspects of a society (Beyer & Lutze, 1993; Johannesen, 1990; Rokeach, 1973). In Western society, for example, the idea of the individual and her or his right to free expression and self-determination is a fundamental value on which judgments of what is and is not ethical are made. Similarly, the values of democracy, free speech, and access to information are basic ideals that are used to make ethical judgments in a variety of contexts.

Several characteristics of values are critical to understanding how they function in making ethical judgments. First, values exist in a hierarchical relationship to one another. Society generally seeks to protect young children from certain forms of television programming (i.e., explicit sex and violence) even at the cost of the broadcaster's rights to complete freedom of communication. In this case, the values associated with protecting young children outweigh the values of free and uncensored mass communication. The process of making ethical judgments involves sorting out and balancing the various hierarchical relationships of values. Ethical dilemmas develop when these conflicting values or ethical positions are relatively equal, forcing a choice between two comparatively desirable–undesirable, good–bad, right–wrong choices.

Because of the complexities and dynamics of value systems, such ethical dilemmas are common, particularly in situations where a number of values interact, such as in organizations.

A second characteristic of values is that no single value or set of values is always accepted as universal. Rather, they vary widely from individual to individual, context to context, and culture to culture. The bitter and divisive debate over abortion, for example, pits two sets of competing values (values of "choice" and values of "life") against one another. Some traditional cultures do not place equal value on both men and women. Efforts to pressure some countries to adopt policies that value human rights and environmentalism have sometimes resulted in charges of cultural imperialism as these cultures do not share the environmental and civil liberty ethics that are consistent with those of Western countries. This characteristic accounts for the fact that values are so often the basis of disagreement and conflict.

A third feature of values concerns their dynamic character. Values are not static, but change over time in response to changing social needs and perceptions. Environmentalism, as a strong social value, for example, is a very recent development. Only since the turn of the century has environmental degradation and even the extinction of species been of more than passing concern. In fact, the extinction of "nuisance species," such as the wolf, coyote, bear, and cougar was seen as desirable and actively promoted. The green revolution of corporations responding to a new environmental ethic and featuring their environmental responsibility in corporate image campaigns is a more recent phenomenon. Similarly, affirmative action and equal representation for minority groups are comparatively recent developments in the history of organizations. Many organizations now actively seek diversity in their workforces and feature this fact in their advertising and public relations campaigns.

A final feature of values concerns their role in individual and group identity. Values are a central component in individual self-concepts and in the development of social collectivities (Beyer & Lutze, 1993). Individuals see themselves through the lens of their personal value systems. These values are instilled at a young age, usually by family and cultural groups, and are a core feature of individuality. Collectivities in the form of groups, organizations, and cultures also take much of their identity and cohesion from common value systems. This helps not only in identifying who is and is not a member of a particular group, but also assists members in crafting a homogeneous perception of the world. Because values are such intimate and closely held components of identity at both the individual and group level, questioning of values is sometimes interpreted as questioning an individual's basic identity. This often makes discussions of ethics particularly volatile.

ORGANIZATIONAL VALUES

In addition to these four general characteristics of values, a complex set of values exists that define, justify, and legitimize organizations. Rieke and Sillars (1993) identified five general values manifest in business discourse. These include future orientation, success orientation, cost–benefit orientation, production orientation, and competition orientation. These values are both internally directed, concerning the internal operations of the organization, and externally directed, concerning the organization's role in society.

Organizations, both profit-making and not-for-profit, value success and a positive cost–benefit ratio as part of the larger goal of economic integrity. For the profit making organization, this means not only creating wealth for the owners but doing so at a level that is competitive with other organizations in the industry and with other industries. If, for example, an organization consistently performs at a level lower than other organizations in the industry, investors pursue other opportunities. Even the not-for-profit organization must demonstrate some basic level of fiscal integrity in order to justify its activities. This *profit motive* or *economic reality* of organizational life is one of the most constant themes of the modern organization and one that organizational leaders often complain is misunderstood by the general public (Drucker, 1981). The phrases "there is no crime in making a profit" and "making an honest profit" supports the generally accepted notion that profit-making per se is not unethical. Moreover, success, as judged by the ability to compete and maintain economic integrity is necessary for the organization's future orientation. Without some basic level of economic viability, an organization has no future.

Organizations also value stability and predictability as part of their future and production orientations and promote internal norms that assist in maintaining stability among employees. Loyalty, cooperation, commitment, faithfulness, predictability, and identification are promoted by organizations because they asset in maintaining order, consistency of effort, and continued productivity. They also represent a form of unobtrusive and understood control over employees often manifest in organizational messages (Tompkins & Cheney, 1985). Organizations reward loyalty, commitment, and faithfulness, and use these values for making ethical judgments about member activities. Whistleblowers, for example, are often criticized as unethical because they have violated basic values of loyalty and faithfulness to the organization. The loyal employee is usually held up as a model for others to emulate.

Organizations also have their own unique set of values, norms, and ideals encoded into a corporate culture (Deal & Kennedy, 1982;

Peters & Waterman, 1982). These are the unique social structures and processes that are manifest in part because of the industry, technology, physical context, and history of the organization (Smirich, 1983). These processes are "largely defined by the communication practices members use to create subjective and inter subjective interpretations of organizational life" (Sypher, Applegate, & Sypher, 1985, p. 14). Cultural values represent a particular organization's unique adaptation to contingencies and opportunities and helps clarify the shoulds and oughts of organizational life for members. Culture also clarifies what it means to be part of a particular organization (Putnam & Cheney, 1985). New members are socialized into the culture so that myths, norms, and values are passed on. These shoulds and oughts are used to make ethical judgments of both individual and organizational activities and outcomes. Myths and stories may help new members learn the norms for interacting with organizational clients or customers. Some critics have also suggested that part of the enculturation process involves abandoning individual morals and values as the basis of ethical judgments and replacing them with an organizationally based collective ethic (Jackall, 1988).

Externally related organizational values derive from the products, services, and consequences organizations create and the various audiences for the messages they produce. Organizational spokespersons, for example, often argue that their companies create jobs, support the tax base, and promote general economic development and that these are necessary for the stability of society. Profit-making companies engage in philanthropy in part to further expand their base of external support. The specific goods and services organizations produce also have associated values. Computers, for example, may enhance the ability of individuals to access and process information, educate themselves, solve problems, and make rational choices. Pharmaceutical companies are quick to point out that their products save lives. In fact, modern life clearly could not exist without the vast array of goods, services, and supports produced by organizations. The efficiency and scale of productivity created by organizations allow for a wide array of inexpensive consumer goods, cheap energy, and the diversity of services that most Western societies have come to expect.

Because they permeate all aspects of human activity yet are subject to change, various interpretations, and conflict, values and ethical judgments are critical points of examination. In particular, communication is necessary to identify the various values inherent in a situation and to sort out the various relationships between values. Conrad (1993) noted:

> It is through discourse that individuals develop their own views of
> morality; through discourse that organizations develop and inculcate
> core values and ethical codes; and through discourse that incon-
> gruities within individual and organizational value-sets are managed
> and contradictions between the value sets of different persons are
> negotiated. (p. 2)

Discussing, debating, challenging, and seeking clarification, are necessary in making informed ethical judgments. Without such talk, values
remain confused and equivocal, little consensus develops about which
ethics are appropriate in which context and the probabilities of making
an ethically suspect judgment are significantly enhanced.

ETHICS AND ORGANIZATIONAL COMMUNICATION

From the perspective of communication, ethical questions arise whenever a message has the potential to impact another person (Jaksa &
Pritchard, 1988; Johannesen, 1990). Inside organizations, such communicative exchanges occur continuously as part of the ongoing process of
organizing. Conducting appraisal interviews with employees; sending
and receiving job instructions; interacting with coworkers; and processing orders, forms, and applications all involve ethics. Often, these ethical
questions only have limited weight because the potential impact on others is comparatively slight and because the values are not central.
Moderately inflating an employee's job evaluation because it is easier
than providing a more honest and critical evaluation, for example, usually has a modest impact. Moreover, moderate distortions in the form of
small life management untruths or "white lies" are necessary to the
smooth and congenial day-to-day interactions with others (Bok, 1979).
Seriously downgrading an employee's evaluation because he or she is
suspected of being a corporate whistleblower, however, represents a
much more serious ethical question. Not only is the potential harm
greater, but the values of free speech and dissent, central to democratic
society, are threatened.

Communication between organizations and larger external audiences or publics also has the potential for impacting others and, consequently, also raises ethical questions and dilemmas. The decision to use
puffery in describing a product as "new, improved, and miraculous" in
advertising, for example, may mislead a consumer. Because most consumers have learned not to take advertising as fact, the potential harm
for such modest distortions is relatively slight. The warning "*caveat emptor:* let the buyer beware" is firmly ingrained as part of our consumer cul-

ture. Withholding, downplaying, or distorting information about the potential deadly consequences of a product, however, not only has the potential of creating serious harm but may violate fundamental values concerning free and informed choice and free access to critical information. From this perspective, the decades long campaign by the tobacco industry to downplay the risks of smoking and to withhold important information from the public can only be described as fundamentally unethical.

Questions about the ethics of organizational communication, in many ways, are consistent with the general ethical questions that face all of society. Many of the values manifest in organizations, including freedom of choice, honesty, accuracy, rights of self-determination, rights to privacy, and free speech, exist throughout society. In other ways, however, ethical questions in organizational communication function in very different ways from questions in other contexts. The rights of individuals to privacy, free speech, and self-determination, for example, must be balanced against the rights of the organization. Free speech generally does not extend to the organization's proprietary information otherwise, profit-making organizations could not protect trade secrets. The individual's right to privacy is also somewhat diminished in the organizational context. Supervisors and managers often monitor activities of workers on the job to ensure that they are complying with policy and procedures.

In addition to the continual need to balance the individual's rights against the rights of the organization, the ethics of organizational communication are also somewhat unique because of the way organizational outcomes are created. Specifically, organizational outcomes are not the product of individuals working alone. Rather, cooperative, individual contributions to organizational outcomes usually occur through a structure of hierarchy, division of labor, communication networks, technology, and a set of policies and procedures. Whenever many hands are involved in some process, it is difficult, if not impossible, to identify a particular individual or set of individuals who are morally responsible for the outcome. Individual managers, supervisors, or employees may have little or no control over some product or process that is later judged unethical. Leaders may have little information about the operation of far flung divisions or facilities. Some ethicists, however, have argued that only individuals can be moral agents and only individuals can be held responsible for unethical conduct. Werhane (1985), for example, noted that in a majority of cases, individuals are the sole moral agents responsible for outcomes. Responsibility for unethical organizational actions accrues to the individual managers or leaders even in those instances where they may not be directly responsible for the outcomes. Others, such as French (1984), argued that organizations as collectivities do indeed cause outcomes and must also be held responsible for unethical decisions and outcomes. Nicotera and Cushman (1992) stated unequivocally that "corporations receive rewards, pay taxes and fines, make charitable contributions obey and disobey laws and can be held accountable" (p. 438).

This controversy has been hotly debated in the organizational ethics literature and continues to be a source of much disagreement (see also Garrett, Bradfords, Meyers, & Becker, 1989; Jackall, 1988; Redding, 1990). On one hand, viewing the individual as the only moral agent tends to release the organization from an ethical obligation. Only human agents have the capacity to make ethical judgments of right–wrong, good–bad. Organizations are free to scapegoat and blame individual managers or decision makers for any wrongdoing. The organization per se escapes any ethical responsibility. A logical extension of this position is that organizations are by definition amoral, or as Redding (1990) asked, "To what extent (if at all) are organizations, qua organizations inherently unethical (or immoral or evil)?" (p. 17). On the other hand, a view of the organization as a moral agent downplays the significance of humans as the agents of moral reasoning and decision making. Individuals are then free to act in unethical ways with the knowledge that they will not be held responsible for the outcomes and that ethical responsibility resides with the organization. This view reinforces the legal concept of a *corporate veil* that may shield individual managers from any personal legal responsibility for the harms caused by the organization. Petress and King (1990) suggested that society has reached a point where responsibility has become a matter of rival interpretations where individuals argue about their level of personal responsibility for outcomes.

Perhaps it is this disagreement that has contributed to the notion of the organization as morally neutral. From this perspective, business should be solely concerned with the economic well-being of its owners and operating within the strict confines of the law. There is no room for good works in profit-making organizations. In its most extreme form, the morally neutral position suggests that "business and business decisions" should not take ethical questions into account. Rather, the only moral imperative for profit-making organizations is to make a profit. The noted economist Friedman (1962) is perhaps the most well-known proponent of this view. His often quoted phrase from *Capitalism and Freedom* "there is one and only one social responsibility of business—to use its resources and engage in activities designed to increase its profits" (p. 133) is grounded in this profit-making value and supports the argument that only individuals can be socially responsible.

Although this view has traditionally dominated many discussions of business ethics, it is increasingly seen by both critics and practicing managers as narrow, short-sighted, and contributing to much of the vitriolic criticism of profit-making organizations. Avoiding discussions of right and wrong does not remove these questions from the organizational context. If anything, such avoidance simply ensures that values and ethi-

cal issues will remain equivocal and that organizations will act unethical-
ly. It is also clear that organizations create outcomes that are judged as
good or bad. The courts have increasingly extended rights most often
associated with individuals to organizations. The Supreme Court's doctrine of "commercial speech," for example, extended limited rights of free
speech to organizations. Further, organizations no longer exist only for
the benefit of making profit for the owners. Organizations also provide
jobs, support the tax base, use society's resources, and generally benefit from the larger society within which they exist. Increasingly, managers
and chief executive officers (CEOs) seem willing to acknowledge these
larger benefits as they seek to expand the organization's base of support. CEOs argue that their organizations provide jobs, support families,
contribute to the tax base, and engage in philanthropy. From this perspective, the organization is grounded in a wide array of social values
and has a responsibility and ethical obligation to that larger society.
Simply making a profit is not adequate. In order to be successful in the
long run, the modern organization must also operate in a socially
responsible and ethical manner.

ORGANIZATION AND ORGANIZATIONAL COMMUNICATION

Definitions of organization have evolved as society has sought new roles
and responsibilities for organizations, and as organizations and theory
and research about organizations has became more diverse and complex. Traditionally, organizations are seen as complex machine-like
structures that employ resources (human, physical, informational, raw
materials) and technology in a functional relationship to one another to
produce some outcomes (Putnam, 1982). These views developed as the
industrial revolution and mass production assembly lines revolutionized
human work and life. They derive from classical/scientific management
theorists such as Taylor, Galbraith, Fayol, and Weber. The organization
is a rational, goal-directed entity characterized by a structure of hierarchy, division of labor, policy, procedures, and rules. Communication, in
the form of networks, is part of this structure and necessary for coordination. When communication breaks down, the machine loses efficiency.
Workers are viewed primarily extensions of the machine who operate in
standardized, predictable, and routine ways (Putnam, 1982).

Much of the attraction of classical/scientific management was
due to the resulting increases in organizational productivity and profitability. Critics, however, were quick to judge this approach as fundamentally unethical because it violated basic values of human dignity.
The physical and psychological harm inflicted on many workers in the

pursuit of greater efficiency and profitability cheapened human life. During the early 1900s, casualty figures for assembly line workers ran into the hundreds of thousands. Treating workers like machines is clearly unethical because it violates fundamental values of human dignity. Despite a number of subsequent developments and new perspectives, however, this machine-like view of organizations continues to dominate many organizations.

The shift toward a more humane view of organizations occurred as social science began systematically investigating human behavior and as workers sought more meaningful work. The view of organizations propagated by human resources theorists such as Lewin, Argyris, and McGregor emphasized human interactions and the creativity, ingenuity, and commitment innate to humans. These theorists recognized humans as unique social beings rather than as extensions of machines. This thinking dominates much of current organizational theory and many of the popular programs of organizational effectiveness such as Japanese management, teams, and quality programs. Communication is central to both the process of human interaction and the contributions workers make to the organization. These human approaches have generally been judged as more consistent with the values of self-determination, human dignity, and human capacity for rational decision making and creativity than the machine-like notions of classical and scientific management.

Most current conceptualizations of organizations are much broader than either the classical scientific management theory or the human resources concepts. Current views emphasize the organization as a system and social context, where communicators exchange symbols to create social reality and share meaning. Pfeffer (1981), for example, suggested that organizations be viewed as "a set of beliefs, attitudes and values which impose order on goal directed behavior" (p. 3). These cultural or interpretive approaches to organization view communication as a central process in the creation, maintenance, and extension of a collective corporate meaning (Putnam, 1982; Smirich, 1983). In this sense, the organization develops its own unique culture that uses sets of symbols, myths, norms, and values to effectively and efficiently accomplish goals. The organization as a social collectivity exists because participants hold these elements in common. These conceptualizations of organizations as cultures have also reinvigorated research into the value-based and normative aspects of organizational life.

Beyond these general notions, however, the concept of organization is quite variable. Organizations vary greatly in size and complexity from small close-knit groups working on simple tasks to multinational conglomerates dealing with hundreds of thousands of employees and billion dollar budgets. Structures of organizational coordination range from machine-like, explicit control, as in the military, to much more symbolic and cultural forms of implicit control. Technology, the way in which organizations transform inputs into outputs, ranges from low-tech animal and human energy, to the high-tech use of computer systems, nuclear processes, and genetic engineering. The goals and outcomes organizations pursue are similarly variable. Religious organizations, such as the Catholic Church, have as a formal goal the salvation of souls and the spiritual well-being of members. Activists groups like Mothers Against Drunk Driving and Earth First! seek to change public policy and social conduct. Profit-making organizations, including IBM and NBC, have as goals the creation of wealth for the owners of the organization. In addition, organizations have subsidiary goals that derive from their primary goals. These subsidiary goals often overlap and are sometimes in conflict. Profit-making organizations, for example, are also interested in the well-being of their members and seek to change public policy and social practice. Religious organizations also seek to change public policy and must keep an eye on the economics of the bottom line.

From the perspective of general systems theory, this variation and complexity in organizations is quite natural and reflects the diverse and changing contexts within which organizations exist. Organizations, as systems, must continually receive resources (raw materials, energy, information) from their environment and return goods and services to that environment. The larger economic, political, physical, technological, and legal environment, to a large measure, determines how an organization functions, what designs and structures will be successful, what products and services will be viable, and what markets will be profitable (Pfeffer & Salancik, 1978).

From this social systems perspective, organizations are ongoing processes as opposed to static entities with material, substantive character. Rather than an organization existing, organizations are more appropriately seen as an ongoing series of exchanges and interactions between individuals inside and outside the symbolic boundaries of the organization. Communication is the process that allows this ongoing organizing to occur. Probably the best know proponent of the process view of organization is Karl Weick. His theory of organizing is grounded in a systems viewpoint where the process of communication is seen as inexorably linked to the ongoing and evolving process of organizing.

THE STUDY OF ETHICS

Ethics is an ancient area of study, tracing its origins at least to the ancient Greeks who saw a link to communication. Plato's rejection of Sophistry was based largely on his judgment that such "base popular speaking" does not "endeavor to make the souls of the citizens as good as possible. . . " nor does the sophist strive to "speak what is best, whether it be pleasant or unpleasant to the hearers" (Plato, *Gorgias*, 1854, 1, 12–13). For Plato, Truth was a constant and universal ethic. Rhetoric, as cookery, obscured the Truth. In contrast, Aristotle, made a very close connection between ethics and his systems of rhetoric. In particular, Aristotle was interested in the means for discovery of truth, which he saw as more situational and in need of discovery. Rhetoric was seen as the process for revealing the truth and the means whereby truth was made clear to the audience. In addition, Aristotle built upon the Greek ideal of perfection in balance and symmetry to emphasize moderation and temperance in all things. His "Golden Mean" saw virtue in harmony and balance between the excesses of extreme positions. In rhetoric, for example, the virtuous speakers sought to balance the use of strict logic and emotional appeals (Golden, Berquist, & Coleman, 1983). Rather than bland compromise, however, the Golden Mean, requires the virtuous person to find the correct or appropriate balance (Christians, Rotzoll, & Fackler, 1991, p.13).

Similarly, religion has profoundly impacted the development of ethics. Questions of good–bad, right–wrong and desirable–undesirable are central features of most religious doctrines. The Old Testament injunctions of "Thou shall not lie," and "Thou shall not bare false witness" are ethics of communication as well as part of a code conduct for the faithful. The New Testament concept of stewardship, the Christian parable of the talents, and the admonishment against usury have implications for the ethical conduct of profit-making organizations (Pemberton & Finn, 1985). Christians, Rotzoll, and Fackler (1991) argued that the Judeo-Christian injunction "Love your neighbor as yourself," has ramifications for the humane treatment of individuals as unique persons as opposed to ends or objects. Such a perspective also has implications for organizations treating individuals merely as markets and consumers rather than as unique individuals.

Several contemporary Christian theologians have examined the role of profit-making organizations and have sometimes concluded that capitalistic business practices are inconsistent with Christianity. The well-known liberation theologian, Gustavo Gutierrez, for example, has argued that severe poverty such as that in Central America can be attributed to multinational profit-making organizations. Christian theologies of liberation have become popular throughout Latin and Central America, Africa, Asia, and with some North American christian groups. These views link christianity and socialism and seek to empower the poor in their struggle with oppressive capitalist systems (Tabb, 1986). Other critics, such as theologian Michael Novak (1982) argued that profit-making multinational corporations are the best hope for resolution of poverty in developing countries. Poverty, he argued, can only be overcome through the creation of wealth and the capitalist system has proven most successful in creating wealth, expanding the middle class, and reducing poverty.

One comprehensive relationship between organizational ethics and religion developed out of the Protestant doctrines of John Calvin. This "Protestant work ethic" was first examined by the organizational theorist Weber. Weber proposed a close connection between Protestant ideas of hard work as a means for spiritual salvation and the development of capitalism. Economic success, according to this tenet, was a sign of individual virtue. The person in poverty had reaped the rewards of laziness and lack of initiative. The Protestant work ethic is closely tied to early development of capitalism including Smith's writings and the development of the Horatio Alger myths of economic success through "pluck and luck." The ethic was also used as a moral justification of the fabulous wealth accrued by the early "Robber Barons," the Carnegies, Fords, and Rockefellers. Critics have pointed out that these justifications are distortions of Calvin's original tenets and his emphasis on a deep commitment to the health and well-being of the entire community. Although the extremes of wealth and poverty have reduced the viability and universality of the Protestant work ethic, it remains a powerful ethical justification for the modern corporation.

It is in the area of philosophy, however, that commentaries on ethics have developed in very rich and complex ways. Philosophers have wrestled with many of the fundamental characteristics of humanity, morality, and ethics. One such issue concerns the notions of universality versus relativism of ethics. In the former area, philosophers and ethicists sought to identify the fundamental moral truths or universal ethical principles; those ethics that were manifest universally, without regard to variations of context or culture. The best known proponent of such universalism in ethics is the 16th-century philosopher Immanual Kant. Kant's "categorical imperative" enjoined humans to "Act only on that maxim whereby you can, at the same time will that it would be a universal law" (Christians et al., 1991, p. 14). Kant's reasoning derived in part from his belief in a higher truth, which is manifest through the human conscience. Some actions, according to Kant, are always and unconditionally wrong, whereas others are always categorically right. Although Kant's dictums appear dogmatic, their universality has much appeal in providing clear moral constants in various contexts. These and related efforts, however, have often been criticized on the grounds that they are intolerant, inflexible and insensitive to contingencies of context (Jaksa & Pritchard, 1988, p. 11). Although the universalists' position has failed to generate complete agreement about specific fundamental moral truths, such basic ethical principles as respect for human life, the rights of self-determination, and honesty and truthfulness are widely accepted. These principles vary little from culture to culture and although there are exceptions to each, these exceptions represent rare cases rather than common practice.

In contrast, the relativist perspective, sometimes referred to as *situational ethics*, emphasizes the unique circumstances of any event or decision. Even the moral imperative against taking another life, for example, can be justified in times of war or during self-defense. Lying is often defended on the grounds of protecting others from the harsh truth. Stealing to support the poor has been popularized as moral in the Robin Hood myths. Relativism in the extreme suggests that no principles of ethical conduct exist and that each situation must be judged as unique. In individualist relativism, the only acceptable ethical judgment is that made by the individual of his or her own conduct and the only morality is being true to oneself (Jaksa & Pritchard, 1988). The most recent manifestation of extreme moral relativism is found in postmodern theory that argues that there are no general standards for making ethical judgments (Hoover, 1994). These positions are often criticized, on the grounds that they allow for the defense of all activities and decisions, regardless of the moral dimensions.

One well known relativist position was popularized by the 17th-century British philosopher and political economist, John Stewart Mill. Mill's principle of utility may be loosely summarized as seeking the greatest good (defined as *pleasure*) for the greatest number of people. This utilitarian perspective requires that one assess the situation and weigh the possible good versus harm that may occur. Although Mill's work was essentially hedonistic, subsequent work has focused on "good" more broadly defined as the "greatest public good." Good in this case is assessed by outcome or consequence, not by some inherent quality of an act or position. This principle has much appeal in its relationship to democracy where the majority of the citizens determine policy.

Interestingly, much of the modern attention directed toward ethics focuses on the problems of organizational ethics. This attention is often traced to the Nixon Administration and the Watergate scandal in the early 1970s (Carroll, 1975; Jackall, 1988; Jaksa & Pritchard, 1988). This vivid event was striking both in the centrality of the values and norms that were violated and in the level of news coverage given the event. The Committee to Re-elect the President not only violated the law, it compromised the fundamental values of democracy and norms of fairness. This harm was compounded with deception as the Nixon Administration sought to cover up the scandal and avoid responsibility. Nixon's public admissions of wrongdoing and resignation shook the confidence of most Americans as well as the moral foundations of Western democratic institutions and the faith of many in elected leadership. Watergate vividly demonstrated the ethical problems that often develop in institutional contexts. The ethical decay of the 1970s was followed by widespread scandal in the 1980s. The insider trading scandals of Michael Millkin and Ivan Boesky demonstrated the ethical decay so often associated with unrestrained pursuit of profit. The collapse of almost the entire savings and loan industry in the late 1980s also featured unrestrained greed leading to deception. In this case, the "victimless" crime of insider trading was replaced by thousands of small investors who lost their life savings to corporate leaders such as William Keating. Iran-gate featured another presidential administration engaged in the moral morass of lying, deception, and fraud frighteningly reminiscent of Watergate. Unlike Watergate, however, executive privilege, the shredding of documents, and arguments about "national security" proved effective in protecting the major figures from personal accountability (Petress & King, 1990).

These, and equally compelling if not as well-publicized scandals, revitalized the study of ethics. Much of this rebirth focuses on the area of applied ethics; the effort to use principles of ethical conduct to address the day-to-day dilemmas faced in a number of contexts. Organizations and professional associations have been particularly central in this effort. Professional groups such as physicians, engineers, and public relations practitioners, among others, have sought to carefully examine the ethical dilemmas associated with their professions. Organizations have rushed to create codes of conduct to provide moral guidelines for members. Although pessimists often reject these efforts as self-serving window dressing, designed more to avoid lawsuits than to stem the tide of moral decay, they have at least elevated the level of discussion regarding ethics and forced individuals and groups to consider the values associated with their activities.

A TAXONOMY OF ORGANIZATIONAL COMMUNICATION ETHICS

Ethical issues concerning organizations and organizational communication have been classified in a variety of different ways. In 1987, for example, the Conference Board surveyed 300 practicing executives about organizational ethics. Four major ethical areas emerged from these results. First, equity, or fairness included the issues of executive pay, comparable worth, and pricing. The second category, concerning rights, included due process, privacy issues, sexual harassment, employment at will, and whistleblowing. Third was honesty and included conflict of interests, questionable payments, advertising content, confidentiality of records, and procedures for cash management. Finally, the exercise of corporate power, defined as *organizational influence*, included political action committees (PACs), corporate contributions, plant/facility downsizing and closing, and workplace safety.

It is also possible to group ethics according to the various perspectives with which they are associated. Johannesen (1990) has identified seven ethical perspectives that are relevant to the study of communication ethics. Each perspective is "a major ethical viewpoint or 'lens' . . . used to examine specific issues and instances of ethics. Each perspective derives from particular value premises and tradition" (p. 19–20). The political perspective, for example, derives from particular systems of government. Western political ethics are grounded in the ideals and values of democracy, including the various rights and responsibilities outlined in the U.S. Constitution and Declaration of Independence. In addition to freedom, dignity of the individual, fairness and the rights of democratic participation, the U.S. Constitution protects property rights. A second perspective identified by Johannesen concerns human nature. This perspective is grounded in the essential characteristics of humanness including the ability to make rational informed decisions and use language. Dialogue, the third perspective, has emerged from work in interpersonal communication. It emphasizes the elements of mutual exchange, authenticity, openness, and inclusion. Dialogue as a mutual sharing among communicators, is often contrasted with monologue, one person speaking to a passive audience of many persons. Johannesen's fourth perspective is situational, which "focuses regularly and specifically on the specific communicative situation at hand" (p. 79). This perspective gives particular attention to the needs, interests, values, standards, and goals of the audience in assessing ethics. Religious perspectives draw on the morals, standards and rules of various religious traditions in making ethical judgments. Similarly, legal perspectives draw on the formal injunctions of legal codes. Finally, utilitarian perspectives "emphasize usefulness, pleasure, and happiness to assess communication ethics" (p. 97).

From the perspective of communication, the ethical questions organizations face can also be categorized by their audiences. Communication theorists often suggest that communicators have a special obligation to their audiences. Evan and Freeman (1993) called these audiences *organizational stakeholders*—"groups and individuals who benefit from or are harmed by and whose rights are violated or respected by, corporate actions" (p. 259). Stakeholders may include owners, suppliers, management, employees, the local community, and customers. In examining communication practices in public relations, researchers have recognized two general sets of audiences for organizational messages. These are internal audiences and external audiences. Internal audiences include employees, managers, and other active and regular participants who are closely affiliated with the organization (Newsom, Scott, & Turk, 1989). These groups usually have close ties and regular interaction with the organization. External publics are those audiences within the organization's larger environment who have less regular interaction and usually more specialized interests in the organization.

These two sets of audiences have particular needs and interests and create particular types of ethical issues and dilemmas for the organization. External audiences are interested in more macroscopic issues and values. Internal audiences are concerned about more microscopic issues and values. The ethical issues associated with internal and external audiences are presented in Table 1.1. For example, on the microlevel of internal audiences and stakeholders, issues and dilemmas often arise when the perceived rights, values, and needs of employees come into conflict with perceived rights, values, and needs of the organization.

Table 1.1. Issues of Organizational Communication Ethics.

Micro Issues of Organizational Communication Ethics: Relating to the responsibilities, values, and rights of internal publics or audiences, often in conflict or inconsistent with the organizations values and goals:

> *Responsibility/Accountability*: Issues and dilemmas related to determining who is responsible and accountable for outcomes.
> *Privacy and Employee Rights*: Issues and dilemmas related to the rights of employees usually in conflict with the organization's goals.
> *Free Speech/Employee Voice*: Issues and dilemmas related to the values of free speech and the relative level of employee input into decisions.
> *Whistleblowing*: Issues and dilemmas related to the rights and ability of employees to speak out in response to some perceived ethical wrongdoing or to ethically dissent.

Macro Issues of Organizational Communication Ethics: Relating to the responsibilities, values, and rights of external publics or audiences, often in conflict or inconsistent with the organization's values and goals:

> *Legitimacy*: Issues and dilemmas related to judgments of the organization's overall social worth and its fundamental right to exist.
> *Organizational Responsibility*: Issues and dilemmas related to the organization's activities and outcomes
> *Advertising*: Issues and dilemmas related to the messages organizations produce about products, services, and issues.
> *Stakeholder concerns*: Issues and dilemmas related to the organization's response to the concerns and interests of diverse external stakeholder groups.

The rights of the employee to speak out and blow the whistle when he or she perceives some wrongdoing, for example, is often in conflict with the right of the organizations to maintain confidentiality. Similarly, the rights of the employee for privacy are often in conflict with the goals of the organization to control and supervise its workforce. In these cases, the organization has close ties, substantial control over, and regular contact with these internal audiences. Internal audiences are more likely to share core organizational values and require fewer justifications and explanations for its activities (Cheney & Fernette, 1993). This level of control and opportunity for communication leads to particular ways of approaching these issues and dilemmas. Organizations often require that employees behave in certain ways.

Macro issues and dilemmas develop when the responsibilities, values, and rights of external publics or audiences are in conflict or inconsistent with the organization's values and goals. An organization's effort to market its product to particular groups, for example, may be seen as inconsistent with the well-being of these groups. With the case of external audiences, the organization has less control over the stakeholder group, less frequent contact with the group as a potential audience, and the ties between the stakeholder group and the organization are much looser. This suggests a different set of contingencies for approaching these issues and dilemmas than might be appropriate for internal stakeholders. Cheney and Fernette suggested that organizations may have to provide more detailed accounts and explanations of their actions to external audiences than they do to internal audiences.

Each of these general ethical issues is examined in detail in subsequent chapters beginning with the micro issues. Each is discussed as an issue of both organizing and communicating under conditions of ethical uncertainty or equivocality. Because of the relationship between internal and external audiences or stakeholders and the organization, these issues require a constant balancing of the values and ideals of various groups and the goals and values of the organization. In this sense, they represent common ethical dilemmas members must attend to, discuss, and ultimately resolve.

SUMMARY

The ethics of organization and communication are not distinct from ethics in other contexts. Organizations and organizational communication, however, present some unique problem and emphasize some ethical issues over others. This includes competing organizational and individual values, the tendency to diffuse responsibility, and the competing demands, interests and values of the various organizational audiences. These audiences or stakeholders have their own unique values, needs, and norms that are sometimes in conflict with the organization. The particular conflicts between internal and external stakeholders result in different types of ethical issues and dilemmas. These characteristics of organizations and values contribute to very high levels of ethical uncertainty of equivocality in organizations. Reduction of this equivocality and resolution of ethical issues requires communication.

CASE: COMPETING ORGANIZATIONAL VALUES

The University of Northeastern Michigan (UNM) is a mid-size state supported institution. UNM is situated in a small town that is well known for its conservative religious climate and institutions. The community is home to several large and successful conservative Christian congregations, and two small affiliated seminaries. Local politicians regularly run on platforms of conservative Christian ideology including strong opposition to abortion, birth control, sex education, and teaching morality in the public schools. The community traditionally has had an excellent relationship with the university. Seminarians often attend classes at the university and roughly half the students are commuters, living at home while attending classes at UNM.

Conflicts began when one seminarian attending classes enrolled in a sociology course entitled "Human Sexuality." The course was taught by a new assistant professor who, throughout the course, was a vocal advocate of abortion rights, birth control, and sex education. At one point, the professor distributed condoms to the class and lectured on their proper use in preventing disease and pregnancy.

The seminarian reported this to his church, which in turn took the matter to the local council of churches. Within a week, protesters were picketing the sociology department, local ministers had taken up the cause and were asking, from their pulpits, why premarital sex was being advocated by tax-supported institutions. The university's Office of Community Relations was receiving 50 phone calls a day protesting the course in human sexuality. In the meantime, the local chapter of the American Association of University Professors had also taken up the issues as one of academic freedom and run full-page ads in the student paper defending the sociology department, the professor, and comparing the community response to the Inquisition.

Discussion Questions

1. What are the primary values that are in competition? How are these values related to various contexts or domains? 3, 4
2. What responsibility, if any, does the university have to take into account the religious values of the community in matters of curriculum and instruction?
3. What right does the community have, if any, to seek to influence matters of curriculum and instruction?
4. What suggestions can you offer for addressing this value conflict?

2) College - Students choose classes

2

Modeling Organizations and Organizational Ethics

Questions of ethics, communication, and organizing are complex and interdependent. Modeling is useful in sorting out the relationships between these concepts and in understanding why ethical issues are, or are not, taken into account in organizations. Weick's system-based theory of organizing is particularly fruitful in this regard because it is grounded in the relationship between communicating and organizing. This chapter reviews Weick's model and applies it to issues of organizational ethics. Weick's model is used to identify several of the difficulties organizations have in talking about and attending to ethical issues and clarifying why organizations so often are accused of being unethical. This framework also implies specific activities that may enhance the ability of organizations to make sense out of ethical issues.

GENERAL SYSTEMS THEORY

One of the most widely accepted paradigms for examining organizations is general systems theory (Katz & Kahn, 1966; Knight & McDaniel, 1979;

Kreps, 1990). Systems theory initially grew out of biology and physics in the 1940s and 1950s. It was a response to the dominant reductionist approaches that examined components of a system in isolation and ignored interaction between the components. In contrast, systems theory emphasizes the organization as a whole as it functions to accomplish goals. This emphasis includes the connections between internal subsystems and connections between the system and the larger environment or suprasystem. This emphasis on holistic views of organizations makes systems theory particularly useful for discussions of values and ethics.

The organization's environment, from this view, is a source of critical resources (inputs) that are processed by technology and throughput into outputs, which are then returned to the environment. More inputs are acquired from the environment and the cycle begins again. The ongoing cyclical process of input–throughput–output allows the organization to postpone the natural process of entropy, or disorganization and decay. Should the process be interrupted for any reason (strikes, shortages of resources, lack of markets), the organization begins to decay. In addition to the connections between subsystems and suprasystems, systems theory also emphasizes the concept of synergy, the notion that the system as a whole is somehow different than the sum of its individual parts. Often, synergistic outcomes are much greater than the sum of the individual parts, whereas sometimes these outcome are less. Systems theory sees communication as a mechanism for connecting and regulating internal subsystems and as a critical mechanism linking the organization to its larger environment.

Systems theory has several other features that are important for the study of organizations, communication, and ethics. First, its general character allows researchers to apply the systems paradigm to various contexts. Systems theory has been used in biology, economics, physics, medicine, political science, psychology, sociology, and organizational theory. The general nature of systems theory also allows organizational researchers to examine a wide range of system components including departments, divisions, employees, technologies, policies, and resources, as well as values, ideas, norms, and ethics. Researchers employing systems perspectives, for example, often discuss the organization as a sociotechnical system combining human and social elements with technology to create organizational synergy.

Second, the systems concepts of process and dynamic homeostasis emphasize the ongoing, developmental character of organizations. The common view of organization as a stable structure is inconsistent with the reality of organizational life. Organizations, according to the systems viewpoint, are always changing as they continually adapt to the larger environment. They must adapt to ensure access to scarce human, physical, technical, and economic resources. The resources themselves also change, requiring further adaptation. Because the environment is a source of scarce and changing resources that might be used in other ways, the organization must continually justify and legitimize its use of resources to a larger environment of changing expectations, shifting values, and alternating needs. Social support for public education, for example, is contingent on the belief that education is using scarce economic resources in appropriate ways.

Third, systems theory suggests that it is inappropriate to view organizational elements or processes in isolation from one another. Rather, the essential character of the organizational system is found in interactions and the resulting synergy. According to this view, questions of values and ethics cannot be isolated from questions of organizational efficiency, effectiveness, personnel, products, services, design, and so on. Conrad (1993) argued that values are inculcated into all aspects of organizational life including defining and solving problems, searching for and using information, and scanning the informational environment. Values systems and ethics can be seen as subsystems, interconnected with all aspects of organizational operation.

Finally, the emphasis placed on context or organizational environment has directed researcher attention to the external factors that influence the organization. This is, in part, due to the fact that organizations are more dependent on their environments than ever before. An increasingly global economy has dramatically extended these dependencies in complex and unpredictable ways. Constituent, special interest, and watchdog groups are more active and vocal in talking about organizational activities and outcomes. An ever hungry press is more willing to publicize accusations of organizational and managerial wrongdoing. In a world of declining resources and greater demand on those resources, organizations must be sensitive not only to their bottom line profitability, but also to their larger social value. Systems theory is a reminder that organizations are not merely economic structures concerned with profit, but are part of a larger social, cultural, and value context.

ORGANIZATIONAL ENVIRONMENTS

Organizational environments have been conceptualized in a variety of ways. Early efforts focused on the degree of interconnectivity and the amount of change. Emery and Trist (1965), for example, suggested that environments could be classified on a continuum of placid–random, placid–clustered, disturbed reactive, and turbulent field. The placid random environment is relatively stable with little interconnection between the various environmental components. On the other end of the continuum, the disturbed reactive environment is both dynamic and unpredictable. Some models attempt to segment the environment into distinct domains. Goldhaber (1993) identified five broad environmental contingencies: economic, technological, legal, sociopolitical, and environmental (p. 288). The economic contingencies concern market stability and its impact on critical resources. Technological contingencies include technological processes, information, and equipment. Legal contingencies are associated with the parameters of organizational behaviors outlined in formal codes, statutes, and regulations at all levels of government. The sociopolitical contingencies involve a broad set of cultural, political, and social conditions including norms, values, customs, and political alignments that affect the organization. Finally, environmental contingencies associated with the physical context of the organization include such things as climate, population, and the organization's physical context. Each of these contingencies has associated audiences or publics with their own value and normative contingencies and constraints. The values important to one audience are often in conflict with the values of another audience.

    Other efforts have focused on the way in which the environment is actually manifest and affects the organization. Duncan (1972), for example, argued that the environment is primarily a source of perceived uncertainty for organizational decision makers. Uncertainty relates to the organization's ability to predict future environmental states and control outcomes. Organizations seek to reduce this uncertainty in order to make more informed and successful decisions. Duncan also suggested that this perceived environmental uncertainty directly affected the organization's internal operations and ultimately its success.

    Most current conceptualizations also emphasize the power of the environment to influence the organization's basic processes, structures, and activities. Some theorists have suggested a Darwinian view of organization whereby the environment determines the organization (Pfeffer & Salancik, 1978). Through a process of "natural selection," those organizations that are best able to adapt to the changing conditions of the larger environment or who are able to modify the environment in some strategic way, survive. Those organizations that are poorly matched to the environment, or that are unable to adapt to changes, die (Wholey & Brittain, 1986). Most observers also suggest that organizational environments are evolving toward greater complexity, interconnectivity, and dynamism.

    A model of the elements of the environment that influence the organization's internal subsystems through connections between the environment and the system is presented in Fig. 2.1. As this model indicates, organizational boundaries are not symmetrical, but are amoeba-like due to their continual interaction with the shifting and dynamic contingencies of the external environment. Weick (1979) argued that environments are neither "clear-cut or stable" but "shift, disappear and are arbitrarily drawn" (p. 132). Environments and their relationship to organizations, are chaotic, dynamic, unpredictable, and subject to widely differing interpretations. The dotted lines and arrows indicate that not all issues and elements are attended to by the environment. In many instances, they do not penetrate the semantic, psychological, and physical boundaries surrounding the organization. The interlocking circles and arrows in Figure 2.1 depict the various subsystems that process organizational inputs, including those informational inputs that penetrate the organization's boundaries. Various elements of the organization also send messages to the environment seeking to influence external conditions.

The environment itself is composed of a number of different symbolic and material elements including resources, a physical context, technologies, social conditions, regulations, competitors, values, norms, myths, and beliefs. From this perspective, values, norms, and beliefs are particularly important environmental factors because they are used in answering fundamental questions about the organization's larger social role and value. Individuals and groups also use judgments about the ethics of organizations in determining whether they should interact with

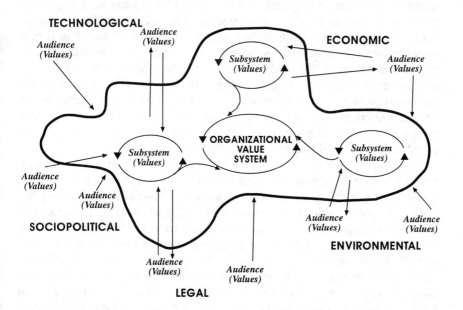

Figure 2.1. A model of organizing and environments

organizations. In 1990, for example, *Shopping for a Better World* was published as a guide to organizations with responsible records of environmentalism, community involvement, and affirmative action. In the last few years, several mutual funds, such as the College Retirement Equities Fund Social Choice Account, have been created that invest in companies meeting a set of social criterion. Following the Exxon Valdez spill of crude oil in Alaska, thousands of consumers returned their Exxon credit cards. A variety of special interest groups and watchdog agencies publicly criticize and pressure organizations to operate in ethical and responsible ways.

It is also important to emphasize that the organization's relationship to its environment is one of mutual exchange and influence. In examining the role of the organizational boundary agent, for example, Aldrich and Herker (1977) suggested two broad sets of activities. The first is a representative function where boundary agents send organizational messages to the environment and serve as spokespersons for the organization. The second is a receiving function where the boundary agent collects messages from the environment, brings them into the organization, and interprets the environment for the organization. Similarly, Pfeffer and Salancik (1978) observed that organizations engage in proactive communication strategies, designed to modify the organization's environment so it is consistent with the goals and capabilities of the organization, and reactive strategies, which modify the organization so it is consistent with the demands of the environment. Zeitz (1980) labeled this process *interorganizational dialectics* and suggested a mutual ongoing exchange and influence, a dialogue between the organization and the larger suprasystems. Shareholder perspectives of organizational ethics take a similar approach. They emphasize that organizations should take into account the needs and interests of the various groups with a stake in the organization. This includes shareholders, employees, consumers, members of the community, suppliers, and the like. Communication, from this perspective, is particularly important as a mechanism for this organizational–environmental interaction and influence.

Values are also manifest in this process of mutual organizational–environmental influence. Organizations, for example, seek to influence general social judgments of right–wrong, good–bad, desirable–undesirable in ways that benefit the organization. For example, organizations often seek to persuade consumers that their products are environmentally responsible. Individual stakeholders often have very specific issues and values that they pressure organizations to address. Community groups may lobby an organization to modify their building plans in ways that respect historic landmarks. Organizations also have their own value systems, which are influenced not only by general social norms, values, and stakeholder perspectives, but also by the values and ideas of the individuals who make up the organization. An organization, for example, may view itself as a high-tech firm, composed of skilled employees and serving customers with cutting edge technology. The individual employees, managers, and decision makers who are part of the organization are also influenced by the general social context. Each employee, however, has his or her own personal value system. Each has also been indoctrinated into a set of organizational values and norms. In addition, employees are part of particular stakeholder groups with related values and interests. Individual managers and employees must also function within the larger environmental context and are subject to these pressures, influences, and concerns. This dynamic and multidirectional interaction of organizational value systems, social, organizational, stakeholder, and individual values is presented in Figure 2.2.

This mutual and multidirectional influence of various groups and contexts on values, is consistent with the general nature of values. Values and value systems are diverse, dynamic, context specific, and subject to rival interpretations (Beyer & Lutze, 1993). As a consequence, ethical judgments are often radically different and conflicting. The same act often creates entirely divergent ethical judgments from the perspective of different value systems. Weick (1969, 1979) developed a system-based theory of organizing that focuses specifically on the way in which various interpretations such as these are sorted out.

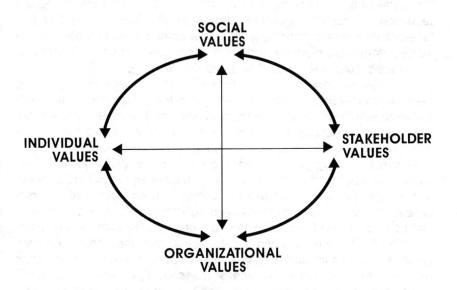

Figure 2.2. Interaction of organizational value systems

WEICK'S THEORY OF ENVIRONMENTAL ENACTMENT

The ongoing process of evolving in relation to the larger environmental context is the fundamental problem of organizing and is the basis of Weick's (1969, 1979, 1995) model of enactment. Organizing, according to Weick, requires the reduction of equivocality of information regarding the organization's environment. Equivocality concerns the variety of possible interpretations and resulting meanings that exist for an informational input. Organizing is a messy, hectic, chaotic, and often disorganized process whereby various interpretations are considered and meanings sorted out (Weick, 1979).

According to Weick, organizations do not exist but are in a continual process of existing as they respond to complex, dynamic, changing, uncertain, and equivocal environments. Weick (1979) suggested that "externalities" or "puzzling surroundings" of organizations only become "environments" when then they are attended to, taken into account, or enacted by members (p. 132). This ongoing organizing process of enactment is grounded in the interactions of members and their efforts to make sense of their activities, experiences, and environments and reduce or clarify the various possible meanings that surround them. Weick viewed this equivocality of possible interpretations as the fundamental input to the process of organizing. "Organizations have developed as social systems for resolving equivocality and increasing the certainty of life" (Kreps, 1990, p. 103). This basic process of ongoing reduction of equivocality occurs through communication. Kreps argued "Weick's theory of organizing is, in fact, a communication theory, representing communication interactions and collective information processing as the primary elements of organization" (p. 121).

The patterns of sense-making that emerge in organizing become standardized in various ways giving the organization a relatively stable repertoire of sense-making processes and devices. These structures, rules, processes, procedures, and devices are called the *residue* of sense-making. An organization, for example, may find that it must deal with a new type of customer request. Initially, this request can be interpreted in a number of different ways (highly equivocal): as a threat, a misunderstanding, a distraction, a problem, an opportunity, a nuisance, and so on. After examining various interpretations and responses that have been used, members find that one interpretation is particularly successful. This interpretation and response may then become institutionalized as a policy and used in all future cases where the organization must process that particular type of message (i.e., when a customer makes request A, a referral form is used to send them to another department equipped to fulfill the request). The interactions which allow for this sense making and the reduction of equivocality are communicative inter-actions between members. The particular process Weick (1979) described is retrospective, illustrated by his grammar of sense-making "How can I know what I think until I hear what I say" (p. 134). When faced with equivocal situations (subject to multiple interpretations; having a number of possible meanings) humans communicate and act, and then observe their actions retrospectively. Those actions, communications, or interpretations that are, in retrospect, successful in reducing equivocality are retained and used in the future when other, similarly equivocal situations are faced. By "talking over and over to themselves to find out what they are thinking," the organization talks, interprets, and remembers (pp. 133–134). This talking over and over is a central process of organizing.

In Weick's model, two elements make up this process of talking over and over: rules or assembly rules, and cycles. Rules are procedures, instructions, or guides that serve to assemble the interactions of members and function in two ways. First, rules are used to assess the relative level of equivocality in an informational input. Second, rules are used in scanning the available repertoire of existing interpretations and responses to select the ones most appropriate. Rules often exist for processing informational inputs with low equivocality. Routine, predictable requests, for example, may be answered with a similarly routine, predictable response (Kreps, 1990). In the event of high equivocality or complexity in inputs, rules may not exist or may not be appropriate for the reduction of equivocality. In these cases, cycles are used. Cycles are essentially the communicative interactions, the double interacts, which allow members to create new interpretations and responses to reduce equivocality. An employee may ask a superior about how to deal with a nonroutine request. The superior may respond with a suggestion, and the employee adjusts his or her actions accordingly. The higher the level of equivocality, the more members must interact to hear what is said in order to select appropriate interpretations.

Another important influence on enactment is the concept of requisite variety. Requisite variety may be described by the notion that it takes equivocality to remove equivocality. Organizations must have sufficient variety (order or disorder) to match the variety in the informational input (Kreps, 1990). They must maintain sufficient internal diversity to sense accurately the variety present in ecological changes in the environment (Weick, 1979). If insufficient variety exists, then only a small proportion of the equivocality will be removed from the informational inputs. The remaining proportion of equivocality will continue to present puzzles for members.

The specific processes of organizing are labeled by Weick *enactment* (acting toward an equivocal situation), *selection* (selecting from among the pool of possible interpretations), and *retention* (retaining those interpretations that proved useful in reducing equivocality). Enactment is a process of socially constructing the organizations informational environment by acting toward that environment (Everett, 1994). An organization, for example, may bracket some aspect of the external environment for closer attention. By so doing so, it creates an informational environment that is then a source of equivocality. Kreps (1990) observed that during enactment, "the organization is made aware of changes in its information environment, the level of equivocality in information inputs is determined, and appropriate rules and cycles are called on to process the informational inputs" (p. 113). Selection involves assessing the affect of the rules and cycles on the equivocality in the information and choosing a sensible interpretation of the inputs. Weick (1979) suggested that organizations build up "cause maps" out of past experiences. "Those maps that are helpful tend to be selected, and those that aren't helpful tend to be eliminated" (p. 131). Retention, the third step, is the process of "storage of the products of successful sensemaking" (p. 131). Through retention, the organization develops a "repertoire of rules . . . to be used as a form of organizational intelligence to guide organizational actions" (Kreps, 1990, p. 114).

Weick's model of organizing is presented in Figure 2.3.

ENACTMENT AND ORGANIZATIONAL ETHICS

Weick's framework is a powerful set of concepts for describing organizational life (Bantz 1989; Bantz & Smith, 1977; Everett, 1994; Kreps, 1990; Putnam & Sorenson, 1982; Weick, 1988, 1989). They emphasize the nonrational, symbolic elements of organizing and the ways in which members reduce various forms of equivocality through symbolic interpretations. Weick's concepts are particularly well-suited for the examination of ethics in organizing and in organizational communication. Ethical issues create their own forms of equivocality or various possible meanings and interpretations. Corporate whistleblowing, for example, can be

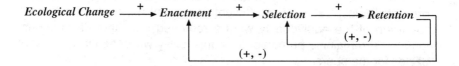

Figure 2.3. A model of organizing (from Weick, 1969, p. 87)

interpreted as a courageous act of self-sacrifice by a moral dissenter or as the act of a disloyal turncoat. Ethical judgments of organizational activities, as with other aspects of organizational sense-making, are retrospective. In observing how decisions unfold, what consequences occur, and what outcomes accrue, ethical judgments are made.

The notion of *equivocality* is particularly useful in discussions of values, ethics, and organizing. As Figure 2.2 indicates, values and the ethical judgments that rely upon them, are particularly dynamic, chaotic, and interactive. The specific interpretation of any question of value is also highly dependent on the perspective that is taken (Johannesen, 1990). Moreover, ethical issues have become more important in society, they have created higher levels of equivocality for organizations. The problem of requisite variety also becomes particularly acute with organizational values. Because organizational members are not usually trained to deal with the complexities of ethical questions and dilemmas, they may not have the capacity to reduce the equivocality of these issues. In many ways, ethical questions are the antithesis of the quantitative, material, and bottom-line issues organizations are most familiar with. Values and ethics are the very sort of confusing, muddy, chaotic, and highly equivocal issues that organizations may find most difficult to deal with. The concepts of equivocality and enactment then point to four reasons why organizations face particular problems with ethics; failure to perceive, failure of rules and cycles, powerlessness, and stunted enactment.

When members or an organization encounter or act toward an ethical issue, a form of ethical uncertainty or equivocality develops. This form of equivocality is associated with the various possible ethical judgments or interpretations that could be made of the situation. This equivocality is usually very high due to the hierarchical and dynamic nature of values. Ethics and values represent arenas that are often outside the familiar production-oriented, empirical world of most managers. The likelihood that a question of values will be perceived as equivocal to a practicing, manager is also quite high. Ethical issues may be interpreted from a variety of different ethical perspectives, values systems, or stakeholder views. Value questions have no clearly right or wrong answer. Organizations often simply choose to ignore issues of ethics. In this case, the organization fails to enact the ethical dimensions of its environment, and fails to reduce the associated equivocality.

A second failure in enactment concerns the available rules and cycles for reducing equivocality. In some instances, organizations may act toward an ethical issue or question, choose to notice the issue, but lack the retained responses, in the form of rules or structures, for interpreting and resolving this equivocality. This represents a failure of available rules and cycles for interpreting ethically equivocal informational input. Weick (1979) suggested that in many cases, a critical mechanism for resolving

high equivocality is communication. Ethical issues, however, are often difficult to discuss. Even in those instances where a member chooses to
notice and bring up a question of ethics, others may be reluctant to
engage in the communicative cycles necessary for resolving equivocality.
Without organizational members talking over and over to themselves to
find out what they are thinking, the enactment of the organizations environment including its ethical environment remains incomplete.

Perhaps this process of failing to notice what is awkward to perceive, difficult to discuss, and painful, if not impossible, to resolve helps
account for the common belief that organizations are simply amoral.
Weick (1988) made a similar point about organizations enacting the
potential for a crisis. "If people think they can do lots of things, then they
can afford to pay attention to a wide variety of inputs because whatever
they see, they will have some way to cope with it" (p. 311). In those
instances where organizational members feel powerless to address
some fundamental ethical dilemma, they may simply fail to pay attention
to those ethical questions. This powerlessness, then, represents a third
limitation on the organization's ability to reduce ethical equivocality. The
fact that organizations so often operate in ways that are fundamentally
inconsistent with the basic standards of ethical conduct may be a function of managers inability to enact what they feel powerless to change.

A fourth constraint on enactment outlined by Weick (1979)
involves stunted enactment through an unwitting collusion among organizational participants. Weick argued that members watch others avoid
certain procedures, objectives, activities, issues, statements, and pas-
times and conclude that some real elements in the organizations environment account for this avoidance. The unstated consensus is that
some areas or activities are avoided for very good, although unstated,
reasons. The result is a form of "stunted enactment." Among the things
many practicing mangers have learned to avoid is any discussion of
complex, chaotic, and sensitive ethical questions.

This concept of ethical equivocality, and these four limitations of
enactment are presented in Table 2.1.

Organizations fail to reduce the ethical equivocality associated
with environmental variations at several points. Some equivocality may
be removed from the informational environment, but that equivocality
associated with ethics and values often remains as a puzzle to the organization.

Using these principles of organizing and the factors that are
associated with the failure of organizations to organize in ways that
attend to ethical issues, it is also possible to suggest some ways to facilitate greater attention to values and ethics in organizations. First, factors
that facilitate members acting toward the ethical and value dimensions of
their informational environments will enhance the ability of organizations

Table 2.1. Four Limitations on the Reduction of Ethical Equivocality

1. Failure to perceive:	Members do not have the background to perceive the value questions inherent in an informational input.
2. Failure of rules/cycles:	Organization does not have the retained rules and structures to process ethically equivocal informational inputs.
3. Powerlessness:	Members fail to perceive ethical issues because they are powerless to address fundamental ethical dilemmas.
4. Stunted Enactment:	An unwitting collusion between organizational members where they learn to avoid ethical issues.

to enact ethical structures. Enhancing capacity to perceive ethical issues, for example, would allow members to enact the value dimensions of their informational environment. Capacity would likely increase requisite variety and further facilitate the reduction of ethical equivocality. Most often, organizations choose to ignore these issues in part due to the complex and dynamic nature of values.

Second, efforts to facilitate discussions of values and ethics enhance the opportunities for members to hear what is said and subsequently know what they think. Making ethics part of the agenda is a difficult task. Without such discussions of values and the ethical responsibilities of members and of the organization, the ability to act toward ethical issues is significantly reduced.

Finally, retained responses or interpretive schemes for dealing with ethical issues, structures, such as corporate codes, mission statements, and ethics committees will enhance the ability of organizations to reduce ethical equivocality. These documents may function both as rules for assessing the level of equivocality and determining responses, and as a reservoirs of retained sensemaking from previous encounters with ethical issues.

SUMMARY

One of the widely used paradigms for examining organizations is systems theory. Systems theory calls attention to the relationship between the organization and its larger environment or suprasystem and focuses on the dynamic interactions between various organizational components or subsystems. Organizational ethics, from a systems perspective, are the product of a synergistic interaction involving the values and norms of society in general, of stakeholders, the organization's own values, and the values and norms of individual members.

One particularly useful and innovative systems approach has been articulated by Weick (1969, 1979). His theory of enactment views organizing as an ongoing process that reduces the equivocality of informational inputs. Informational inputs with value dimensions and ethical implications may also be interpreted in a variety of different and often competing ways. Because organizational members most often choose to ignore issues of ethics, the ethical dimensions of organizational life are often left unattended to. Several processes may help organizational members attend to ethical issues and reduce ethical equivocality. Opportunities to communicate about ethics, for example, allow members to hear what is said. Retained structures such as codes and mission statements may also be useful in reducing ethical equivocality.

CASE: 1994 GENERAL MOTORS ANNUAL REPORT— JOHN F. SMITH JR.'S LETTER TO STOCKHOLDERS

Each year, publicly held corporations are required by law to produce an annual report. These documents have largely been statements of financial conditions including earnings, assets and liabilities, and have been directed toward stockholders and investors. Recently, these documents have taken on a broader public relations and communication mission and are directed toward larger stakeholder audiences. The letter from the CEO is particularly important in setting out the organization's interpretation of the past year and its vision for the future. It is also important in articulating values.

Reprinted here is a letter to stockholders and friends from General Motors' (GM) CEO John F. Smith, Jr. which appeared in GM's 1994 annual report.

Discussion Questions

1. What values or sets of values are manifest in this letter?
2. Which are repeated most often or are emphasized most strongly?
3. How might organizational members or stakeholders use this letter to reduce equivocality?

Geneneral Motors is stepping confidently from the automobile industry shadows into the daylight of stronger profitability and worldwide customer enthusiasm for our products. By strengthening the balance sheet, offering quality products that exceed customer expectations, and plain old working harder, our management, employee, dealer, and supplier teams around the globe have driven this corporation toward financial respectability once again.

Totally regaining that respectability won't be easy, but it is within our long-term reach. We've said our vision is for GM to be the world leader in transportation products and services. There's still a lot of work to do to get there, but our 1994 financial results show that our customers are responding favorably to our efforts to fulfill that vision. Record worldwide earnings were up 99 percent from last year — $4.9 billion on sales of $155.0 billion.

While our earnings have improved, our net profit margin of 3.5 percent remains below what we need to maintain financial strength throughout the industry's business cycle. Our goal is average annual net profit margins of at least five percent. On a more positive note, we strengthened our balance sheet significantly in 1994. Our unfunded pension liability fell to $12.6 billion at the end of 1994 from $22.3 billion at the end of 1993. We plan to make further contributions to our pension plans in 1995, including a major contribution of GM Class E stock held by GM, which will signifi-

cantly reduce the underfunded position. Our cash position at the end of 1994 stood at $11.0 billion, an improvement from $10.5 billion at year-end 1993. During the year, cash flow was very strong, allowing us to contribute $7.7 billion into our U.S. pension plans.

A look behind the hard numbers shows our success is spread across our business sectors and global operations. Our North American Operations (NAO) earned profits. In Europe, we were again the most profitable volume auto manufacturer. In 1994, we introduced all-new cars and trucks around the globe, including Opel Omega and Tigra; Oldsmobile Aurora; Buick Riviera; Chevrolet Lumina, Monte Carlo, Cavalier, and Blazer; Geo Metro; Pontiac Sunfire; and GMC Truck's Jimmy. I am happy to report that every one of these products is a solid marketplace success.

Our other business sectors also turned in solid results. Delphi Automotive Systems is now an independent sector. Renamed from Automotive Components Group Worldwide to more accurately reflect its global customer focus, it's now a strategic partner to our global vehicle operations and growing as a supplier to most of the world's automakers. GMAC expanded its business, notably in international markets. EDS and GM Hughes Electronics reported record earnings; they also strengthened their positions in the fast-moving technologies of information management and telecommunications. GMHE's launch of DIRECTV was the most successful product introduction in consumer electronics history.

These milestones represent, in large part, all our customers' response to our new cars, trucks, locomotives, and services worldwide. We listened to what they wanted and acted on what they said. Good things happen when you pay attention to the boss. The dollars, marks, and yen usually follow.

Every one of our car and truck divisions in North America increased its sales over the previous year, and our truck sales set an all-time record. In Western Europe, our Opel/Vauxhall cars won first place in the market for the third straight year. In Latin America, we set an all-time vehicle delivery record, and in Japan and other Asian markets, we made significant progress.

Yet our struggles are not all behind us — not by a long shot. It's no secret that quick change in a company like GM that has traditionally resisted it causes some internal hassles. But significant steps are taken every day. We're implementing specific plans to cut our cost structure, commonize our processes for product development and lean manufacturing, and craft a culture of continuing change as a way of doing business within General Motors.

Our third quarter financial results, after several quarters of steady financial progress, showed that the road back has bumps and curves. The fourth quarter showed we can nevertheless stay on the road and keep driving ahead. Also, in our relationships with our labor unions around the world, we often agree to disagree on how business changes will affect our represented workers. But new economic order and global

> *"We listened to what (our customers) wanted and acted on what they said. Good things happen when you pay attention to the boss."*

competition are forcing all of us to find new ways to approach these issues together for our long-term vitality. In the U.S., although we encountered some local strike actions in 1994, we have kept our focus on our long-term business goals and the competitive need to improve our productivity. We are working diligently with the United Automobile Workers to reconcile differences, and we both agree on the common objective of making NAO successful and profitable.

In moving ahead with definitive strategies to achieve our vision, General Motors intends to be the company that sets the standards and pace — the one that defines the basis of competition for the industry. We have to compose the music. It just isn't good enough to sing in the choir.

Organizationally, we have what it takes — talented people, high technology, financial strength, and global reach. Our challenge is to blend these essentials as a system that can function as effectively in Detroit as it does in Zurich, Rüesselsheim, Sao Paulo, or Singapore. Through our Global Strategy Board, comprised of internationally focused senior GM executives, we are coordinating vehicle operations, products, and resources to our greatest advantage. A "not-invented-here" attitude has nowhere to hide.

When we can offer similar vehicles in multiple markets, we are bringing together international teams of managers, planners, engineers, and designers to create them. This approach keeps us responsive to local customer needs and tastes while we put our global resources and technology to work. Coming up, it is producing a new Cadillac model based on our top-of-the-line Opel Omega and an Opel van derived from our upcoming new North American minivan.

Such efforts help focus our plans and resources on creating precisely targeted cars and trucks — products that customers want to buy and competitors try to emulate — for the various markets where we compete around the world. We can better:

· Apply highly evolved market research to understand customers' needs and values.
· Use advanced technology and standardization processes to design new vehicles systematically, efficiently, and rapidly.
· Install common processes of lean, agile manufacturing to produce them at world-class cost and quality.

Looking ahead, we plan to further coordinate some of our North American and International vehicle platforms — the common structural systems which are the basis of our cars and trucks. With shared platforms, we can foresee lines of cars with volumes of more than a million units. With common engineering and manufacturing processes, we can build them in several variations and several countries. Right now, for example, we have teams working on several global programs, including new small cars, engines, and transmissions.

By leveraging our global resources, we'll get new products to our markets faster and more efficiently. We'll gain quality, cost savings, and flexible production in our manufacturing operations. We've already gained a lot of experience from running our purchasing activities on a global basis and integrating the engineering and manufacturing operations of our International Operations. We are building on existing relationships where we have them and creating new ones where we need them. Our GM management team already includes men and women educated and experienced in many parts of the world. We're putting a lot of effort into placing globally oriented leaders in all our operations.

As we establish product leadership, I strongly believe that our goal of superior market and financial success becomes achievable. That's how we intend to build our worldwide leadership. GM is changing its ways and will continue changing. The shadow is always over our shoulder. Daylight helps us focus our vision.

John F. Smith, Jr.
Chief Executive Officer and President
January 31, 1995

3

Communication, Responsibility and Accountability

One defining characteristic of large, complex organizations is that many individuals work together to produce outcomes, including goods, services, and the organization's reputation (Jackall, 1988; D. Thompson, 1987). Those individuals who work together to create outcomes must then somehow share or apportion responsibility and/or blame for the outcomes. Because organizations are such complex social structures, this responsibility often becomes diffused and confused to the point that it is not possible to identify any single responsible person. When responsibility is diffused in this way, individuals become disconnected from the consequences of their personal actions and the ethical climate of the organization generally decays.

Because precise and distinct lines of responsibility in organizations are almost never clear, determining responsibility involves communication (Benoit, 1995). As Petress and King (1990) noted, "The question (Who caused what) becomes a matter of rival interpretation" (p. 19). Through communication, rival interpretations about responsibility are considered, and those that are most successful in reducing equivocality are retained. The way in which responsibility is enacted in organizations in turn influences the climate of trust, quality of working relationships, and the level of innovation. This chapter examines the concepts of *responsibility* and *accountability* and how they function in organizational contexts. Understanding organizational responsibility requires understanding how individuals depict themselves as more or less responsible for creating outcomes (Seeger, 1993). Organizational members offer accounts of responsibility based on three levels of organizational involvement and control: individual, organizational, and environmental levels. This chapter also examines recent changes in how responsibility is apportioned in organizations. The quality movement and team approaches to work advocate creating organizational structures where individuals accept personal responsibility for outcomes.

RESPONSIBILITY AND ACCOUNTABILITY

A number of social critics have suggested that the concept of *personal responsibility* is decaying in our modern society. They point to a disturbing tendency for individuals to blame others, their families, environment, or society for outcomes rather than accepting personal responsibility. Noted defense attorney Alan Dershowitz (1994) identified 53 types of excuses used by defendants to alleviate them from legal responsibility for their actions. Some of the more common excuses are "battered women syndrome," "abused child syndrome," "rape trauma syndrome," and the "urban survival syndrome" (p. 3). Some of the more exotic include the "Twinkie defense," used in a murder case where the defendant claimed he was mentally incapacitated from eating too much junk food, and "the meek-mate syndrome" where defendants claim their actions are caused by psychological emasculation (p. 329).

Dershowitz also pointed out that responsibility is the fundamental connection that exists between individual action and the consequences of those actions. This personal connection is a critical component in ensuring that individuals adhere to ethical standards or bear the consequences of failing to adhere to these standards. On the most basic level, the connection between individual action and the consequences of the action is a requirement for the functioning of any social structure, including legal and social codes. Personal responsibility is also necessary for a democratic society to function. Because responsibility means that individuals bear the consequences of their behaviors, it also requires that individuals have freedom of choice about their behaviors (Johannesen, 1990). Freedom and responsibility, then, are very closely connected concepts. Most philosophers agree that personal responsibility is a prerequisite for a society to be both free and ethical (Lucas, 1993; Schlossberger, 1951). The literal meaning of responsibility, then, is the ability to respond, that is, the personal freedom to choose a particular response to a set of circumstances.

Responsibility has three additional meanings (Freund, 1960). First, responsibility as personal accountability means that a person is the sole or primary agent in control of his or her actions and may be called on to explain and bear the consequences of those actions. Mental illness, insanity, or other factors that limit direct personal control reduce responsibility (Pritchard, 1991). Second, responsibility concerns the acknowledgment of a sense of personal obligation to others. Parents are responsible for the actions of small children (Buttny, 1993) and managers are responsible for their employees. Finally, responsibility relates to a consideration of the consequences of one's personal actions (Freund, 1960). According to Johannesen (1990), "responsibility refers to the elements of fulfilling obligations and duties, of being accountable to other individuals and groups and of being accountable as evaluated by agreed upon standards" (p. 227). Kohlberg (1984) suggested that as a personal attribute, "responsibility denotes, first a concern for and acceptance of one's actions. Second, it refers to consistency between what one says one should do and what one actually does" (p. 519).

In his analysis of political accountability, Crable (1978) observed that "The history of questions of accountability is a study of the ways in which people-as-political constituencies argue the existence of impropriety and the ways in which politicians-as-people argue the propriety of their conduct" (pp. 24–45). In offering accounts, individuals who are "responsible" for some outcomes or activities develop arguments and explanations about the propriety of their actions in response to charges that their conduct was somehow improper. Responsibility, as a fundamental human ethic, derives from a person's location within a larger community. Individuals who are prominent members of a particular community, such as designated or elected leaders, are responsible to that community. This form of responsibility to the community entails taking the needs, interests, concerns, and values of the community into consideration in making decisions that may affect the community (Lucas, 1993, p. 186). If the leader fails to operate in a manner judged by the community as responsible, based on agreed on standards or basic norms, the community may call for an account of the behavior. In this sense, individuals, groups, or organizations can serve as responsible agents who are accountable for the consequences of their actions. Leaders of organizations, for example, frequently provide explanations and account for the actions and outcomes of their organizations. The CEO's annual meeting with shareholders involves a detailed accounting of the last year's activities (Ragsdale, 1993).

RESPONSIBILITY IN ORGANIZATIONS

The earliest organizational theorists recognized that responsibility and accountability are both critical and problematic in institutional contexts. Fayol, a management theorist writing in the early 1900s, was among the first to recognize that responsibility was a critical component of organizing. He argued that authority "is the right to give orders and the power to exact obedience" (Fayol, 1949, p. 21). Responsibility in organizations includes the concept of accountability and is a corollary of a person's authority. Those who have authority, managers or supervisors, are responsible for the outcomes within their areas and may be held accountable for those outcomes. Fayol's view became the basis for the organizing principle regarding unity of authority and responsibility (Altman, Valenzi, & Hodgetts, 1985). Authority and responsibility must be unified and delegated in relatively equal amounts. This "unity of authority and responsibility" was necessary to create clear order, rationality and hierarchy in organizations. This view of organizational authority and responsibility has not changed significantly in organizational theory (Altman et al., 1985; Filly, House, & Kern, 1979; Mescon, Albrect, & Khedouri, 1985).

Authority and responsibility are also related to the organization's division of labor, design, and hierarchy. Individual units of the organization are delegated authority and responsibility within specific functions, geographic regions, or product areas. Individuals within these units are then responsible for the activities of those units and are accountable for the associated outcomes. As one moves up the organizational hierarchy, there is increasingly more authority and responsibility. In this way, authority and responsibility are basic elements of the organization's structural design.

ACCOUNTABILITY AS COMMUNICATION

In the literal sense, accountability refers to the ability and obligation to provide an explanation—to furnish a reckoning or an account of one's behavior. The classical concept of accountability can be traced to the close-knit, traditional agrarian societies where transactions were always face to face and where direct causal relations could be drawn between individual actions and outcomes (Petress & King, 1990). Because individuals existed within these well defined communities and regularly interacted face to face, they could be held personally accountable for the outcomes they created. Accountability, in this classical sense, relates to one's association with a community and to communicating justifications and explanations of personal activities and outcomes. Accountability follows from responsibility such that those who are responsible may be called on to provide these "explanations of a predicament-creating event designed to minimize the apparent severity of the predicament" (Schlenker, 1980, p. 136). Buttny (1993) argued ". . . a central feature of human speech [is to] change, mitigate, or modify others' assessments" (p. 1).

Accounts are generally not offered for routine behaviors but only for those instances where some perceived offense or ethical wrongdoing occurs (Benoit, 1995; Buttny, 1993; Scott & Lyman, 1968). Accounts as communication explanations concern circumstances and outcomes that are novel or inconsistent with some generally accepted standard or value. Accounts follow some wrongdoing, unanticipated occurrence, or unexpected outcome. They seek to strategically depict individuals as more or less responsible for creating these outcomes and, in so doing, repair or restore the person's image and reputation (Benoit, 1995). "Accounts involve talk designed to recast the pejorative significance of actions or one's responsibility for it and thereby transform other's negative evaluations" (Buttny, 1993, p. 1). In doing so, they most often frame their interpretations around two general criteria for holding individuals responsible for outcomes: (a) their acts or omissions are in some way a cause of the outcome, and (b) their acts or omissions involve personal volition (i.e., they are not done in ignorance or under coercion; D. Thompson, 1987). These criteria, however, are subject to diverse interpretations and do not take into consideration many of the activities that occur in complex and dynamic organizational contexts.

Philosophers, for example, argue that determination of causality is, at best, difficult (Lucas, 1993; Schlick, 1961). Identification of a causal relationship between two factors requires that an agent is the direct and primary factor in creating an outcome. A causal relationship cannot be explained solely by observing the fact that Event B follows Event A. Rather, the process (motivating, inducing, persuading, urging, forcing, etc.) whereby B is the outcome of A must be understood to establish causality. Changes in A, however, are not always accompanied by corresponding changes in B. In many contexts, a variety of factors and individuals in combination are the causes of an outcome. In other instances, events are separated by a long and complex chain of intermediate events, such as decisions in a hierarchy. Selecting one agent from among the entire causal chain involves determining that this agent is the primary agent in the outcome. Or, as Benoit (1995) argued "If several persons jointly committed the act, we might not necessarily hold them all fully responsible, but we may apportion the blame among them" (p. 72). Causality also implies that the outcomes would not have occurred without the involvement of this particular agent. A person may only qualify as the causal agent if the outcome would not have happened without that person's specific actions or omissions (D. Thompson, 1987). Causality is difficult to determine and highly equivocal, particularly in organizational contexts. Organizational outcomes are almost always a consequence of multiple causal agents.

Context further compounds the complexity of determining responsibility. More and more human activity occurs within organizations. Thompson's second criterion suggests that to be responsible an agent must have control and authority. In the modern organization, authority is highly compartmentalized by division of labor and hierarchy. Individuals specialize according to functional expertise, geographic area, or by product. The latitude of their formal authority is limited to the specific area of divisional specialization. A manufacturing manager, for example, does not have authority over marketing activities. The latitude of authority is also limited by the individual's specific position within the hierarchy so that authority is greater as one moves up the hierarchy. Theoretically, those at the very top of the hierarchy, such as the CEO or board of directors, have final authority. In practice, however, those at the top of the hierarchy may have little control over and may not even have information about specific decisions made at lower levels.

Information systems in organizations are also highly fragmented. These systems are designed to select and transmit information to specific locations. Because of the shear volume of information processed by the modern organization, it is simply not possible for all information to flow through a centralized point or for any single individual to have complete knowledge of organizational operations (see Knight & McDaniel, 1979). Information systems, including the organization's communication networks, function to disseminate specific information to specific places at particular times. In many instances, individuals are uninformed about the activities and decisions undertaken by their coworkers and subordinates. Superiors are often entirely unaware of their subordinates activities for which the superior may later be held accountable.

The hierarchical and divisionalized nature of organizations and the resulting difficulties in identification of causality, and segmentation of authority and information, often make responsibility a characteristic of the system as well as an attribute of individuals functioning within that system. However, some organizational ethicists such as Velasquez (1982) argue that responsibility must be an individual concept where managers and officers are held personally accountable for organizational outcomes. If individuals are not held accountable, the primary basis for responsibility—the individual—is removed from society. Similarly, DeGeorge (1986a) argues that "Because a corporation acts only through those who act for it, it is the latter who must assume moral responsibility for the corporation (p. 95). These views are consistent with the widely held belief concerning the importance of the individual in creating outcomes and the need for closure in matters of responsibility (Petress & King, 1990). Society often requires an identifiable individual to hold responsible, particularly when the outcome is dramatic.

Other critics, such as French (1984) and Werhane (1985), tend to reject these noncollective views of responsibility due to the fact that they incorrectly assume that individuals are self-contained and self-subsistent. By definition, organizations involve a variety of individuals interacting in specialized and compartmentalized, yet highly interdependent ways. Organizational systems define responsibility by defining individual activities, parameters for individual activities and how individual activities relate to one another. Corporate actions and outcomes are the result of a rich and complex compilation of these individual actions and coordinated interactions. It would be inappropriate, according to this view, to hold individuals accountable for outcomes that are produced by a corporation. This strain between collective and individual views of responsibility leaves significant latitude for interpretation. In any activity that depends on the coordinated and specialized interaction of several individuals within a system, the final determination of responsibility is a matter of interpretation. These interpretations form the basis for the communication accounts of responsibility offered by organizations and individual members.

ACCOUNTS OF RESPONSIBILITY

Accounts of responsibility have been examined from a number of perspectives (Benoit, 1995; Buttny, 1993). They draw on mitigating circumstances, explanations, denials, expressions of regret, scapegoating, justifications, excuses, motivational statements, narratives, descriptions, apologies, and concessions in order to repair image and explain ethically suspect behavior to others. In organizations, accounts are usually based on the amount of personal control or volition an individual employee, manager, or organization has over outcomes. Three levels of organizational interdependence and constraint can be identified in accounts of responsibility: individual, organizational, and environmental levels (Seeger, 1993). These levels are presented in Table 3.1.

Accounts of responsibility based on the individual level concern the latitude of the individual's personal causality and volition in creating a particular outcome; that is, they refer to the individual's specific and unique position and authority in the organization. These accounts concern the highly divisionalized and hierarchical nature of individual activity in organizations. It is possible to depict individuals in organizations as "not responsible" for specific outcomes, for example, due to their individ-

Table 3.1. Three Levels of Organizational Accounts of Responsibility

Level I: Individual Level	Employee is not free (a) "I was simply following orders from superiors." (b) "I did not have information about what was happening."
Level II: Organizational Level	Employees are not free (a) Policy precludes individual from taking action. (b) Norms preclude individuals from taking some actions.
Level III: Environmental Level	Organization is not free (a) This action is a consequence of economic/competitive conditions beyond the organization's control. (b) This action is a consequence of governmental conditions/ regulations beyond organization's control.

ual access to information about activities and outcomes, and the individual's position in the hierarchy.

Accounts of responsibility based on access to information follow the reasoning that individuals may not be held responsible when they are unaware of activities (D. Thompson, 1987). A manager in an organization, for example, would not be held accountable for illegal actions of his or her subordinates when those actions are hidden from the manager. Individuals who do not have information about activities leading to outcomes generally are unlikely to be seen as direct causes of outcomes. An associated form of causality, however, may sometimes be established if it can be demonstrated that the manager failed to remain informed when it was clearly his or her responsibility to do so. In some instances, managers may be victims of deception. Subordinates may have engaged in unethical activities that were hidden from the superior. Accounts of responsibility based on access to information are further complicated by "official" versus "unofficial" knowledge of activities (Petress & King, 1990). An individual may be aware of an activity through rumor or an informal understanding but may not be aware of the activity through formal messages or job duties. As long as formal information links cannot be established, the manager may still plausibly claim that he or she was not responsible.

The Iran-Contra affair involving the Reagan Administration's shipment of arms to Iran is a vivid example of how divisionalized information systems created "plausible deniability." The Iran-Contra affair involved cooperation of several individuals from at least two agencies of the federal government, the CIA and the National Security Council. Information was tightly controlled so that individuals possessed only that information necessary for them to execute their specialized duties ("Taking the Stand," 1987). "The complex system of information control based on the chain of command and 'need to know' had provided the real actors with plausible deniability" (Petress & King, 1990, p.18). The planned absence of any specific documentation indicating that superiors had been officially informed about the operation allowed those at the top of the hierarchy to avoid accountability. Oliver North testified that "It was always part of the plan that Director Casey [and other Cabinet Members] should not know" (Taking the Stand, 1987, p. 339). This "fall guy" plan sought to shield responsible agents from accountability. By portraying themselves as out of the informational loop, organizational participants may plausible deny responsibility.

Individuals also deny responsibility because of their position within the hierarchy and their level of authority (Jackson & Morgan, 1978). Individuals usually refer nonroutine or problematic matters to their superiors in the hierarchy (Galbraith, 1971). It is possible for organizational members to depict themselves as "not free agents," who were simply following directives from superiors. As long as subordinates are following their superior's orders, they cannot be held responsible for any harmful results (D. Thompson, 1987, p. 42). These accounts about hierarchy and authority are particularly plausible in highly differentiated hierarchies. Theoretically, every hierarchy has a "final authority" that is ultimately accountable (Jackson & Morgan, 1978). Upper levels in the hierarchy, however, are usually concerned with the broad strategic outlines of decisions. Lower levels are concerned with the ways in which decisions are implemented in relation to specific cases. This process of adding detail to upper management's directives as they flow down through every step in a hierarchy further complicates interpretations based on hierarchical position. Subordinates may claim that outcomes are a consequence of directives from superiors. Superiors may claim that directives were implemented inappropriately by subordinates.

In the Iran-Contra affair, North also accounted for his actions by arguing that he was following the orders of superiors in the hierarchy. North unequivocally stated that he "was authorized to do everything I did" ("Taking the Stand," 1987, p. 107). He added that he had "the approval of my superiors for very one of my actions," and that he had not "violated an order in 23 years" ("Taking the Stand," 1987, p. 13). Because of his position as a lower level subordinate within a hierarchy, North claimed he could not be held accountable.

A second level of accountability exists at the organizational level. These accounts are based on the organization's policy, structures, and norms designed to inhibit the volition and control of employees across the entire system. Organizational policies, for example, are designed to "create consistency, stability, uniformity and continuity in the operations of organizations" (Filly et al., 1979, p. 308). Policy also functions to depersonalize decision-making and limit individual discretion (Jackson & Morgan, 1978). It is designed to reduce the personal volition and control of individuals in a way that limits individual variation and enhances normative behavior across the entire organization. Policy encodes the organization's experience, traditions and routines. Because policy usually represents formal, written behavioral guidelines, there is often little latitude for individual choice in matters addressed by policy. Individuals can deny responsibility because they were following policy and were not free to take any other action. Responsibility is deflected to the policy and those who may have created the policy. Informal norms, in contrast, are usually more general guidelines for behavior and allow for greater flexibility of individual action. Outcomes are presented as a function of "the way we operate," "the way we do things around here," "how we get things done," or simply "the system." As long as individuals follow generally acceptable policy and widely shared norms, they are not exercising their personal free will and, therefore, cannot be held accountable for outcomes.

These references of policy and norms are often featured in the accounts of responsibility offered by politicians. Dershowitz (1994) discussed the "everyone does it" defense as a "Claim that focuses in other similarly situated individuals in an effort to excuse the defendant's conduct" (p. 325). Texas Senator Kay Bailey Hutchinson argued that her misuse of public office was acceptable because her predecessors had similarly misused their offices (Dershowitz, 1994). Similarly, Senator Alan Cranston responded to a strong and severe reprimand by the Senate Ethics Committee for his involvement in the Keating Five scandal by arguing that he "did nothing that other Senators do not do" ("Cranston Lashes Out at Senate," 1991, p. A8). Members of congress involved in the House Banking Scandal argued that they were simply doing what everyone did. In these instances, norms and policy served as the basis for diffusing and denying responsibility.

Organizational spokespersons are also sometimes called on to offer accounts of responsibility for the entire organization. These organizational accounts usually draw on environmental factors that affect entire sets of business, industries, or economies. Frequently, organizational spokespersons depict their actions as a function of broad economic, political, or competitive factors. Organizations exist in a larger environment and are dependent on that environment for resources (Pfeffer & Salancik, 1978). Much of an organization's activities and outcomes may be attributed to environmental factors. Organizations, for example, often say they are not responsible for plant closings because the decision was based on general economic conditions (Garrett et al., 1989). Similarly, organizations may in some instances deflect their accountability by claiming that governmental regulation precludes and/or requires certain actions. This interpretation may also take the form of "I am simply the messenger. Any other person would have taken the same action under these conditions" (D. Thompson, 1987). In either case, responsibility is diffused very broadly to the larger physical, social, economic, technological, or competitive environment in which the organization exists.

In 1988, for example, Lee Iacocca responded to criticism for closing Chrysler's Kenosha Wisconsin Assembly Plant by offering an account based on environmental conditions. Iacocca sought to transcend blame by arguing that larger economic conditions prompted by federal policy and unfair trade practices by the Japanese created conditions under which the Kenosha Plant "cannot compete anymore. [sic] That's the stark, naked reality of the thing. I am just the messenger bringing the bad news" (Iacocca, 1988, p. 3). Any other manufacturer would have made the same decision based on the business conditions. Iacocca proceeded to depict Chrysler as a victim of larger social and economic conditions rather than a villain for closing a major plant and laying off American workers. Although such transcendent strategies may be seen as scapegoating, they allow individuals to deny responsibility based on volition and causality.

ASSESSING ORGANIZATIONAL RESPONSIBILITY

As accounts of responsibility move from the relatively specific level of the individual to the highly abstract level of the environment, it is correspondingly more difficult to identify a single responsible factor or agent who may be held accountable. The accounts deriving from the individual's level in the hierarchy or position in a department incorporate or at least imply, some final authority. A departmental head may be held accountable for outcomes that were clearly a function of his or her department even if he or she was not entirely aware of the activities. Accounts based on the organizational levels of policy and norms diffuse responsibility more broadly to policies or to policy-making groups or individuals. Although it may be possible to identify individuals or groups responsible for policy, it is also likely that specific policies are embedded in the organization's history and responsible individuals cannot be identified. Finally, at the environmental level, responsibility may be diffused far beyond either the individual or the organization. Outcomes are a function of broad social, economic, political, or other industry- or economy-wide factors. The identification of specific human causal agents acting on their own volition is usually not possible.

The process of diffusing responsibility to increasingly higher and more abstract levels results in increasing difficulty in identifying a single, self-contained accountable agent. Because our traditional views of accountability favor humans as causal agents, it is sometimes possible for the organization as a system as well as individual managers to avoid responsibility in instances where single human agents are not readily identifiable. The failure of the Select Committee on Secret Military Assistance to Iran and the Nicaraguan Opposition to identify final accountability for the Iran-Contra affair may be understood in part on these grounds (Marshall, Scott, & Hunter, 1987). In contrast, organizations sometimes identify a human agent as a scapegoat when accountability should be shouldered by the organization. Exxon's public disclosure of Captain Vincent Hazelwood's drinking problems following the Valdez oil spill was partly an effort to identify a human causal agent as a natural target for blame and accountability. Hazelwood was almost immediately identified as responsible due to his position as captain and his drinking problem. Although these strategies for diffusing responsibility to environmental conditions and scapegoating through identification of a single causal agent both seek to disconnect responsibility from accountability, they do so in different ways. In the first instance, the organization avoids responsibility because no causal human agent can be identified as the sole or primary cause and held accountable. In both instances, the core activities and structures of the organization are depicted as not responsible and buffered from accountability.

The central question about these and other accounts of responsibility and accountability concerns the validity of messages that seek to deny accountability based on individual, organizational, and environmental levels. Often, individuals as responsible agents, can be identified and held accountable for outcomes. In instances where it is clear that the individual is not the causal agent, where does final accountability reside? Although our legal and ethical codes focus on the responsibility and accountability of the individual, there are instances where the organization—its policy, structure, design, and norms of operation—is the agent failing in its obligation of responsibility. In other instances, where it is clear that neither the individual nor the organization is the causal agent, where does final accountability reside? There are some instances where neither the individual nor the organization is the appropriate causal agent and the larger community must accept responsibility and accountability.

REESTABLISHING ORGANIZATIONAL ACCOUNTABILITY

Recent changes in the ways many companies organize their activities have dramatically changed the way in which responsibility is conceptualized, discussed, and allocated in organizations. The influential work in organizational quality by W. Edwards Deming and Philip Crosby, the resulting quality movement, and team- and group-based approaches to work have resulted in a fundamental rethinking of responsibility in organizations. These and other writers have argued that a well-developed sense of personal responsibility is critical to maintaining high quality in goods and services and in organizational effectiveness.

Deming was instrumental in the development of Japanese approaches to management and quality including the development of the Quality Control Circle (QCC; Macdonald & Piggott, 1993). The QCC involves a small group of usually lower level employees meeting together regularly to discuss and solve problems of quality. QCCs were a radical change for many traditional American organizations, because they assigned responsibility for maintaining quality to lower level production workers. Traditionally, these employees were responsible only for the production of very specific parts of processes. Quality was the responsibility of a separate supervisor who regularly checked a small sample of the parts produced. Under the QCC system, assembly-line workers, who spent their work hours in the simple and repetitive tasks of drilling holes in axles, bolting parts to frames, or sealing gaskets to parts, were given the responsibility for solving complex quality problems. As part of the process, these groups were often given much broader responsibility. The resulting continuous quality improvement and customer orientation has translated into flatter organizations with fewer levels in the hierarchy, a greater sensitivity to the needs of customers, and a stronger sense of personal responsibility and accountability.

A second related trend has been the movement toward creating cross functional work teams. One of Deming's (1982) famous 14 points was "Break down barriers between staff areas" (p. 62). Breaking down barriers allows for the free flow of information between areas and for individuals to take responsibility beyond their narrow, functional specializations. Both Ford Motor Company and the Chrysler Corporation, for example, have turned to teams composed of individuals from the various traditional functional areas of the organization, to design vehicles. In traditional organizations, a group of engineers might be responsible for designing headlight components, but gave little thought to the way in which these components might be manufactured to fit with the rest of the car. Cross-functional teams, composed of employees from marketing, finance, manufacturing, design, engineering, and human resources, have integrated responsibility for the design of the entire vehicle. Under this system, decision-making responsibility is pushed from higher levels in the hierarchy to lower levels. These systems also reconnect the organization's various divisions and departments.

This reunification of responsibility in organizations is the opposite of traditional approaches to organizational design that break up responsibility into increasingly narrow and specialized areas (Hiam, 1992). The QCC and the cross-functional teams also help reconnect the activities, individuals, and groups in the organization with the consequences of these activities. Working in cross functional teams makes it more difficult to shift blame to another department or division or to claim that the issue is simply "their problem." The result is not only higher quality products, but a clearer sense that individual activities are contributing to outcomes and that they are responsible for those outcomes.

SUMMARY

Questions about responsibility and accountability are increasingly problematic in a complex and increasingly interconnected society. They are also endemic to organizations where many individuals working in cooperation produce outcomes. Because it is increasingly difficult to clearly identify individuals who are the primary responsible agents, we must depend on interpretations of responsibility manifest in communicative accounts. These accounts take the form of messages that seek to persuade others that individuals are more or less responsible for some predicament. Accounts at the individual, organization, and environmental levels present interpretations of individual and organizational responsibility based on the level of causality and volition. As accounts move to higher levels, finding a responsible agent is increasingly more difficult.

Recent changes in the way in which work is organized, however, has modified the way in which responsibility functions. Employees with very specialized and limited areas or responsibility have been brought together in groups or teams to solve problems, make decisions, and design new products. This change in work has resulted in a reunification of responsibility in organizations. Responsibility is fundamental to the efficient and effective functioning of organizations. Because responsibility is the link between behavior and consequences, these changes in the ways in which organizations interpret responsibility promise not only greater efficiency and effectiveness, but also more accountable and ethical organizations.

CASE: QUESTIONS OF RESPONSIBILITY IN THE EXXON, VALDEZ OIL SPILL

On March 24, 1989, one of the most expensive organizational disasters in history unfolded on an obscure stretch of the Prince William Sound, in Alaska. The oil tanker Exxon Valdez ran hard aground on Bligh Reef, and began leaking oil into the pristine waters of Prince William Sound. Eight of the ship's 11 tanks were ruptured and over the next several hours, about 250,000 barrels of North Slope crude oil spilled.

Following the spill, much confusion surfaced over responsibility for the clean-up. Exxon claimed that the clean-up had been delayed by the failure of the State of Alaska and the U.S. Coast Guard to give timely permission for the application of chemical dispersants. Failure to provide permission, Exxon suggested, had allowed the oil slick to become unmanageable. Critics claimed that chemical dispersants only provided cosmetic treatment and failed to remove the oil from the water.

The following letters were exchanged between Exxon CEO Lawrence Rawl and Alaska Governor Steve Cowper portraying competing interpretations of responsibility.

Discussion Questions

1. What interpretation for the failure of the clean up is portrayed by each party?
2. What strategic views of responsibility and accountability does each include?
3. On what basis is each claim about responsibility made?

STEVE COWPER
GOVERNOR

STATE OF ALASKA
OFFICE OF THE GOVENOR
JUNEAU

April 28, 1989

Mr. Lawrence Rawl
Chairman and Chief Executive Officer
Exxon Corporation
1251 Avenue of the Americas
New York, NY 10020

Dear Mr. Rawl,

On a number of occasions since the Prince William Sound
oil spill, Exxon representatives have claimed that the State of
Alaska delayed Exxon's cleanup efforts by refusing to approval
the use of chemical dispersants in a timely manner.

Those statements are demonstrably false. Their continued
repetition suggests a systematic effort to mislead the public.
This letter will set the record straight.

Alaska is one of only a few states that have pre-approved
the use of chemical dispersants in designated areas where significant damage to biological resources is not expected to
result from the use of the chemicals. For several days following
the spill, the slick was largely within the so-called Zone 1, an
area pre-approved for the use of dispersants. Exxon did not need
further State approval before using dispersants there.

The chief problem with the use of dispersants in those
first few days was that they didn't work. I know because the
afternoon of March 24, the day of the spill, I personally
observed a test from the deck of the Exxon Valdez. Waters were
too calm for the dispersant to work effectively and such conditions prevailed for the first days of the spill. These were
ideal conditions for recovery of oil using boom and skimmers.
Exxon and Alyeska Pipeline Service Co. should have made real
progress recovering oil using those methods, but that did not
happen.

The fact is dispersants were used several times during
the early days of the spill, but these attempts simply did not
work very well. When conditions were suitable for the effective
use of dispersants, they were not applied despite approval. For

example, a test drop of 35,000 gallons of dispersants of Day Two was deemed inconclusive by the Coast guard because of calm conditions. On the fourth day of the spill, March 27, the State received a request at 4:30 p.m. for the use of dispersants in Zone 3. Although the State informed the Coast Guard of its approval less than a hour later, at 5:20 p.m., no dispersants were applied.

Your apparent basic assumption—that the State opposes the use of dispersants—is flawed. The State supports the use of chemical dispersants in the right circumstances, but we do not favor the uncontrolled use of those chemicals. Dispersants do not remove the oil from the water; they simply distribute it to greater depths and increase the oil's toxic effects. That's why the State reviews the use of chemical dispersants in the actual conditions present. The arbitrary dumping of hundreds of thousands of gallons of chemicals into Prince William Sound's sensitive environment, as you now suggest would have been warranted, is irresponsible.

It's worth noting that Exxon never had sufficient quantities of dispersant on hand to treat a spill of this size. Based on Exxon's recommended application rate of 20:1, about 500,000 gallons of dispersant would be required. Less than 5,000 gallons were in Valdez the day of the spill and only 110,000 gallons were available six days later—one-fifth the amount necessary for a spill of this magnitude.

The record clearly shows that the State's pre-approval of dispersants in Zone 1 remained in effect during the important early days of the spill. Even in Zone 3—especially sensitive areas of the Sound—the State authorized Exxon's use of dispersants on a case by case basis. Only after Exxon had trouble hitting the target—and instead sprayed the tanker and Coast Guard personnel—did the State decline to approve the use of chemicals in the most sensitive areas.

I urge you to repudiate the inaccurate statements you and other Exxon officials have made regarding the State's actions on dispersant use. If your company decides instead to cling to its story. I think the public is entitled to see some proof.

Sincerely,

Steve Cowper
Governor

L. G. RAWL
Chairman of the Board

April 28, 1989

<u>VIA FACSIMILE</u>

Honorable Steve Cowper
Governor of Alaska
Juneau, Alaska 99811

Dear Governor Cowper:

Unfortunately for all concerned, your letter of April 28 does not set the record straight. In fact, it perpetuates a good many wrong assertions. Repetition of incorrect and misleading statements is helpful to no one.

We have repeatedly said that immediately after the spill Exxon requested approval to use chemical dispersants. We have also said that officials of the State of Alaska and the Coast Guard were in discussions during the first three days on whether dispersants should be sued. We did not receive the go ahead to use dispersants, other than for two tests, until the end of the tree day period, Sunday evening, March 26th. No one has contradicted those statements.

The widely tested and used dispersant worked extremely well during the March 25th test. We have a film showing how effectively it worked during the March 26th test. This film was submitted to the Senate Environmental Protection Subcommittee before whom you testified. If you wish, we will send you the film.

You have repeated once again the incorrect assertion that dispersants increase the oil's toxic effects. There is not a knowledgeable person whom I know of who would support that statement. In fact, if your statements were correct why would California and other jurisdictions have approved the use of Corexit 9527—not to mention the State of Alaska. Even if the dispersant had not worked, there would have been no increase in the toxicity of the crude oil.

Your information regarding the application rate and volume of dispersant on hand is also incorrect. As stated in our application request, an average application retate to treat this type of spill with Corexit 9527 is 5-10 gallons per acre. Satisfactory tests at 5 gallons per acre had been accomplished in other sates previously. One Saturday, March 25th, we estimate that the spill covered about 2500 acres. Our experts on the scene indicate that the 20,000 gallons of dispersants inventory plus the 25,000 gallons that arrived on Sunday would have been adequate to contain the spill and significantly mitigate the impact of the oil on the shoreline. We had another 120,000 gallons in our worldwide inventory, a portion of which was enroute to Alaska, and additional volumes could have been shipped as needed.

It is regrettable that you have chosen to go public on this matter without first discussing these questions directly with us. Your letter asks for proof. It will be provided by Exxon and the various State and Federal Agencies involved when representatives have the opportunity to testify, under oath, in the various hearings scheduled for the next several weeks.

Very truly yours,

4

Privacy and Employee Rights

One of the most popular areas for internal organizational ethics is the concept of *rights*. Rights are micro issues of ethics because they apply primarily to the individuals working inside organizations. The concept of rights, in this context, refers to something that is due to someone by virtue of their position, status, or affiliation (Edwards, 1993). Rights are guaranteed by moral principles, social practice, or legal systems. They also have identifiable ethical dimensions because rights derive from and encode specific value systems. Rights form the moral, correct, or proper ethical position, as in "the right way to behave." Because these guarantees are tangible manifestations of underlying value systems they are useful in making ethical judgments.

Members of an organization have rights because of their contractual, social, or civil affiliations (Lemos, 1986). Some rights are a function of the employee's societal membership. Others are a function of an employee's humanity. Employees may also own stock in the organization and have rights of ownership. Employment contracts also specify rights such as retirement benefits, severance pay, or health and life insurance. Organizations have specific rights as well, including rights of ownership, privacy, autonomy, and self-determination. The right of private organizations to make their own determinations about issues such as products, pricing, and employment, is a central value of capitalistic enterprise. The rights of employees and rights of organizations often come into conflict creating uncertainty about ethics and equivocality about ethical judgments. This conflict is inherent to the concept of rights. Whenever an individual claims a right, he or she does so by constraining the behavior of others. When employees have rights, the organization is precluded from certain activities (Levine, 1980).

The concept of *employee* and *organizational rights* is heavily influenced by social and legal precedents. One such legal concept concerning the employee–employer relationship is *employment at will*. This chapter examines the concept of employment rights including the traditional employment at will approach. This includes discussions of the reactions to employment at will in the form of the employee rights movement. This chapter also reviews issue of privacy as one major communication-based right in organizations and specific forms of intrusion into employee privacy, including testing.

TRADITIONAL APPROACHES TO EMPLOYEE RIGHTS

Historically, employees had only those rights guaranteed under the legal doctrine known as "employment at will," which derived from English common law (Sanders, 1984). Common law is the precedent of common practice handed down through history. Although employment at will is not established in any specific legislation or legal documents, such as the Constitutional provisions for free speech, it is a well established legal precedent that undergirds all employee–employer relationships. In the absence of other contractual relationships or statutory protections, employment at will is the basic legal framework for employer–employee relationships.

Employment at will specifies the fundamental rights of both the employer and the employee. The concept is grounded in the assumption that the employee has rights of ownership over his or her labor. Because employees control their own labor, they may choose to exchange their labor with employers or may choose to withhold their labor. Employers have similar rights of ownership over the job. The employee may work on a job at the will of the employer. An employer may terminate an employee for any reason whatsoever, legitimate or not. Because organizations own the job, they are free to create highly restrictive and specific conditions for the job. If employees fail to meet those conditions, the job may be withdrawn at any time. In essence, the employer has complete control over the conditions of employment. The employee is similarly free to terminate the relationship at any time should he or she find the conditions of work unacceptable. Employment at will assumes a relatively temporary relationship between employer and employee, rather than a relationship characterized by long-term commitment and loyalty.

Historically, employment at will gave employees the right to leave jobs when they chose and gave employers broad latitude to hire whomever they chose (Edwards, 1993; Gorden, Infante, Wilson, & Clarke, 1984; Sanders, 1984). This latitude is basic to the organization's value of autonomy. It was not uncommon during the Industrial Revolution, for example, for employers to require that workers meet a variety of morality and lifestyle tests in order to obtain and retain their job. Henry Ford, in the early days of the Industrial Revolution, even created a Sociology Department at Ford Motor Company to check into the background of workers and ensure that they complied with company lifestyle and morality policies (Seeger, 1987).

Employment at will dominated most organizational approaches to employee rights through the Industrial Revolution and is still very prominent today. With one noted exception, most early organizational theorists simply ignored the idea of employee rights. Max Weber, a prominent organizational theorist interested in broad social processes as well as the functioning of organizations, included the notion of employee rights and responsibilities in his theory of bureaucracy. Weber was interested in the concept of legitimate authority and tried to outline strict parameters for when a supervisor's authority over the worker was legitimate. He argued that the supervisor's authority extended only to the job. When workers were outside the context of the job, either in terms of physical location or in terms of time, the supervisors authority was no longer legitimate. A number of problems arise with this framework when employees have broader job responsibilities that cannot be clearly delineated. Salaried employees, for example, are never off the employer's payroll. Employees frequently leave the organization's premises to call on customers, deliver products, or pick up parts. Many employees work at home using computers and modems. In these cases, clear parameters between job behavior and personal behavior quickly break down. Weber's efforts failed to clearly delineate what behavior is considered "on the job" and under the control of the organization and that which is "off the job" and an issue of employee privacy. His work foreshadowed a number of legislative efforts to clearly delineate employee rights beyond the provisions of the employment at will doctrine.

Federal and state laws subsequently modified the employment at will doctrine indicating that companies may not establish certain types of provisions for jobs. It is unlawful, for example, to establish provisions that specify that only men may fulfill particular jobs. It is also against the law to discriminate against job applicants because of race, ethic background, religion, marital status, or physical disability. In most instances, organizations are precluded from even asking job applicants about these matters. These policies of nondiscrimination are rooted in very strong social values of equality and equal opportunity. These values are sometimes in conflict, however, with the organizational values of autonomy and self-determination. In some instances, other than those previously noted, a private employer is generally free to set limiting restrictions for employment including some aspects of health status, sexual orientation, or lifestyle. The strict legal limits of employee rights are still very narrow. A number of labor activists and business ethicists have advocated social recognition of a much broader set of employee rights.

THE EMPLOYEE RIGHTS MOVEMENT

The concept of employee rights has become increasingly popular as workers have sought to extend the rights that exist in larger society to employees inside organizations. The trade union movement of the middle 1900s gave great impetus to the idea that employees have rights. In 1935, the National Labor Relations Acts guaranteed workers the right to form unions and to bargain collectively (Edwards, 1993). From the mid-1900s through the 1970s collective bargaining was the principle method for protecting worker rights. The employee rights movement was a reaction to the limitations of the employment at will doctrine and increasing employee expectations for ethical treatment on the job. As Osigweh (1987) noted, "workers are making more and more demands that their rights not be protected, but respected as well" (p. 3). The idea of employee rights embraces a view of the employee as a full, long-term participant in the organization. The rights of employees derive from not only the employee's membership in society, but their full member citizenship in the organization.

One of the most active voices in discussing employee rights is business ethicist Patricia Werhane. She proposed a broad set of employee rights based on the proposition that employees are full organizational citizens. Her list of employee rights is summarized in Table 4.1.

The rights Werhane (1985) outlined are supported by three sets of employee affiliations. First, employees are human and have certain rights based on their humanity, such as the right to personal safety and a safe work environment. Second, employees are members of a larger society that grants rights. Free speech and privacy, for example, are Constitutionally guaranteed to all citizens. Werhane extended these rights to the organizational setting. Finally, many of these employee rights assume that employees are full participants in the life in the orga-

Table 4.1. Werhane's List of Employee Rights.

Equal rights to a job and equal opportunity to be considered for a job. Employees cannot be discriminated against because of religion, race, color, economic background, or origin.

Rights to equal pay for equal work.

Rights of job ownership, after a period of probation and assuming adequate job performance.

Rights of due process, including peer review, a full hearing, and outside arbitrations.

Rights of free speech and expression, including rights to object to immoral or illegal acts.

Rights to privacy, including outlawing the polygraph.

Rights to engage in activities of their choice outside the workplace.

Right to a safe work environment.

Rights to as much information as possible about the company, job, hazards, and risks.

Rights to participate in organizational decision making.

Right to strike, to withhold labor when demands for improved workplace are not met.

---

nization. Employees, as organizational citizens, have rights of job ownership, access to information, and rights to participate in organizational decision making.

Werhane's argument that employees are full and equal citizens in the organization suggests that employees also have full rights of communication. Rights of access to information and participation in decision making draw on a view of the organization as a decentralized communication system. Information flows freely between the various organizational levels. Employee free speech, access to information, and participation in decision making also assumes that members of the organization are relatively equal. As full organizational citizens, employees have communication rights regardless of their position in the hierarchy. Privacy, as the right to control access to personal information, also assumes that the employee is partially independent of the organization. The right of privacy is often in conflict with organizational goals regarding control over the conditions of the workplace and over employee behavior.

PRIVACY

The social and legal right of privacy is attributed to two sources. First, social psychologists have argued that the right to control access to self is fundamental to one's sense of self and social experience (Altman, 1976; Westin, 1968). The privacy-related behaviors of controlling territory and withdrawing from social interactions are well documented in primitive societies and among animals (Westin, 1968). This "right to be left alone," was also inferred from the Fourth Amendment of the U.S. Constitution. In particular, the Fourth Amendment protects against illegal searches and seizures and allows for members of a society to withhold information about themselves from public view. Supreme Court Justice Louis D. Brandeis in his dissenting opinion in the 1928 case of Olmstead v. United States succinctly summarized this position. Privacy "is the right to be left alone, the most comprehensive of rights and the right most valued by civilized men" (277 U.S. 438; 478). Westin (1968) suggested that privacy was bolstered in the United States by its close relationship to the concept of American individualism (p. 27). Privacy is well established as a fundamental civil liberty of democratic societies and has also been clearly established as a legal right in such arenas as medical records, educational records, and financial information such as credit history and bank accounts. Employee privacy remains one of the "lest defined, the least understood and the least sanctified by social consensus" (Edwards, 1993, p. 2).

EMPLOYEE PRIVACY

Privacy is an increasing concern in modern organizational settings. Privacy is based on individuals' rights to limit, control, or regulate the access that others have to them or to information about them (Westin, 1968). As a social concept, privacy is related to interpersonal communication and the choice that individuals make to disclose or not disclose personal information to others (Laufer & Wolfe, 1977). Burgoon (1982) identified five factors related to threats to privacy:

1. The degree of control an individual exerts over the release and subsequent use of personal information.
2. The amount of personal information in the hands of others.
3. The number of people with access to personal information.
4. The content of the information.
5. The nature of the relationship with those possessing or having access to the information.

Burgoon argued that the personal choice about disclosing information to another is based primarily on the level of trust that exists in that relationship. When personal choice is not involved or when the levels of trust are inappropriate for the disclosure of information, then privacy is threatened. Privacy may also be threatened when others have access to information. Employee records, for example, may inadvertently be seen by coworkers. It is also important to recognize that some types of information are inherently more personal and sensitive, such as the results of an AIDS test.

Other researchers have suggested that privacy is fundamentally related to a person's sense of self in relation to other persons or groups Altman (1976) suggested that the fundamental tenant of personal autonomy and control is to control access to one's self. Privacy, he argued, is an interpersonal boundary control process whereby relational parameters are established and maintained. These boundaries allow for the development and definition of self in relation to other groups and individuals. A basic right to privacy is fundamental to a person's psychological health and development.

Although privacy is generally accepted as a broad social right, recognized by social critics and inferred by the U.S. Constitution, there is little agreement about its extension to private organizational settings. The social right of privacy has long been recognized by the courts. Private citizens have a legal right to limit access to personal information, such as medical history, financial data, and employment history. The courts have made few extensions of privacy rights in organizational settings. The courts have generally accepted the argument that organizations have a legitimate right to personal information about employees. This information is seen as necessary to protect organizational interests. Employee theft, drug use, noncompliance with company policy, and testing for medical disorders, such as communicable diseases, have been offered as the primary reasons for collecting detailed information about the personal lives of employees (Simms, 1991).

Employee privacy is probably the most divisive issue of employee rights that exists today (Simms, 1991). Three trends have encouraged organizations to collect more detailed personal information than ever before. First, many organizations are facing unprecedented competitive pressures forcing them to be increasingly efficient. Problems such as employee theft or drug and alcohol abuse are significant drains on company resources. Nationally, organizations lose more than $10 billion annually to employee theft. Another $50 billion can be attributed to drug and alcohol abuse. Second, organizations have also faced serious liability problems stemming from employee drug or alcohol abuse. Reports of commercial pilots drinking before flights prompted testing by some airlines. Alcohol abuse may have played a role in the wreck of

Exxon's oil tanker Valdez off the coast of Alaska, resulting in the costliest industrial accident ever. The captain of the tanker, Joseph Hazelwood, had a serious drinking problem. Events such as these have prompted organizations to institute surveillance and testing programs of employees in sensitive positions.

A third reason organizations are collecting more and more detailed information about employees is that the technology of surveillance and testing has become significantly more sophisticated and promises to become even more so. Blood, urine, and hair samples can provide detailed data about an employee's history of drug and alcohol use and related medical data. The advent of genetic testing promises unprecedented insight into an employee's medical condition including susceptibility to various diseases. In 1980, DuPont began testing African-American employees for sickle cell anemia. The company initially defended the tests as a service to employees, but then made the program voluntary (Hoerr, 1988). It is presently possible to determine from blood samples if individuals have a genetic predisposition to a number of diseases including several forms of cancer. It may soon be possible to determine if an individual has a genetic predisposition to psychological problems. Psychological testing, widely used in organizations, already allows for the construction of detailed personality profiles of individuals. Surveillance technology, including remote video cameras and wireless microphones, allow supervisors to observe employees from almost any location, often without employee knowledge (Hoerr, 1988). Many organizations have very extensive networks of remote cameras for security. Vast databases, which can be accessed for a fee, include a variety of personal, employment, and financial information for millions of private citizens. Many states will sell copies of automobile registrations to market research companies, demographers, and in some instances private citizens. Organizations routinely sell information about their customers in the form of mailing lists. Computers and computer-mediated communication have created an entirely new form of employee surveillance. Electronic mail (e-mail) messages are usually stored in some central computer system in files that can be accessed by managers. Several prominent legal cases, including the Iran-Contra investigation, have made use of e-mail messages that the principle parties had assumed were private.

THREE FORMS OF TESTING

This technology of employee testing is disturbing in terms of the depth of intrusion into personal privacy it creates and the speed with which it is being adapted by private organizations. One form of technology that has been applied to organizations for at least 30 years continues to draw the majority of criticism from individuals interested in protecting employee rights to privacy. The polygraph, or lie detector, was developed in the 1920s to assist police investigations (Matusewitch, 1981). It has been widely adapted by private companies to test the honesty of both employees and job applicants, despite the fact that state and federal guidelines limit its use (Hoerr, 1988). It is a very common tool used to combat employee theft and some organizations hold regular polygraph screenings of employees. Many institutions, where employees handle very large sums of money, routinely employ polygraphs and claim that they cut theft by millions (Matusewitch, 1981). The polygraph records physical data, such as heart and breathing rate, blood pressure, perspiration, and electronic conductivity of the skin to assess a subject's level of physiological response to particular questions. Subjects are then asked carefully worded questions. The first set of questions, or control questions, are used to establish a baseline of responses. Those responses that produce physiological responses far outside that baseline are assumed to be producing higher levels of stress. In these instances, the subject's responses are assumed to be less than honest. Although the polygraph is widely use in law enforcement as an investigatory tool, it is not considered to be accurate enough to be admissible in most courts as evidence.

Polygraph them all . . . I don't know anything about polygraphs, and I don't know how accurate they are, but I know they'll scare the hell out of people. (Nixon, July 24, 1971; quoted in Matusewitch, 1981)

To organizational ethicists concerned about employee privacy, the polygraph represents a fundamental intrusion. Werhane (1985) argued "No person has rights to the thoughts and feelings of another person, The polygraph invades a bastion of privacy unique to persons—the self" (p. 120). Polygraphs allow the organization to intrude into the individual's private thoughts, assessing the person's physical and psychological responses to questions. The temptation to use the polygraph to explore unrelated issues is great. Some organizations reportedly use the polygraph annually as a general truth, loyalty, and character test. Additionally, although employees are asked to take the polygraph on a voluntary basis, refusal is often seen as an admission of wrongdoing and the basis for dismissal. The fact that the polygraph has limited accuracy compounds the possibility of abuse. Some studies report that the polygraph has 70% to 90% accuracy under optimum conditions, but a number of celebrated cases have demonstrated the technology's shortcomings. In one case, an Ohio construction worker was wrongly accused of murder when he failed a polygraph (Siegel, 1981). In another, the CIA failed to detect an agent, Aldrich Ames, who had been routinely selling secrets to other countries because he successfully passed the agency's annual polygraph screening. The CIA's failure was due, in part, to its reliance on the polygraph.

A second form of testing that is increasingly popular in organizational settings seeks to determine drug use. The urine test is commonly used to determine if employees have abused drugs or alcohol. Urinalysis for drug use has increased in popularity. Ten percent of Fortune 500 companies reported using such testing in 1982, and 50% in 1989 (Chapman, 1985). As with the polygraph, many organizations conduct regular screenings, often of a random, unannounced nature. In drug testing, urine specimens are screened for the chemical residue of drugs or alcohol. The accuracy of the test is predicated on a number of factors, including the way in which the specimen was collected, the diet of the subject, and the accuracy of the lab. This has, in some instances, promoted very intrusive techniques where employees are carefully supervised as they provide urine samples for analysis. If an employee tests positive for drug use, the organization usually explores a range of possible options, which may include immediate termination, demotion, suspension, retesting, counseling, and rehabilitation. The issue of accuracy, including both false positive and false negative tests, may significantly compound the harm associated with drug testing.

The increasing cost of drug and alcohol abuse through absenteeism, accidents, lost productivity, injuries, morale problems, and legal liability has prompted such testing. A 1984 study estimated that the cost of employee drug abuse is $8.3 billion annually (Bureau of National Affairs, 1987). In addition, many organizations argue that drug testing is part of a larger principled stand against illegal drug abuse. Proponents of testing argue that a slight compromise of employee privacy is a small price to pay to rid the workplace of illegal drugs. Testing sends a very strong message that drug use will not be tolerated (Rothstein, 1989). Finally, the highly publicized governmental "war on drugs" prompted many organizations to become involved in drug testing of employees. In 1983, the Reagan Administration's Commission on Organized Crime recommended drug testing for all private and public sector employees. Although such widespread testing is unlikely, the emphasis given testing by the federal government has tended to legitimize it as an acceptable organizational activity (Simms, 1991).

A third type of testing that is increasingly popular is blood testing usually for medical problems such as AIDS screening (Hoerr, 1988; Simms, 1991). The actual test is designed to detect the presence of HIV and determine if an individual is infected with the viruses that produce AIDS. Although AIDS testing by organizations remains a relatively rare form of employee testing, it has been employed by a number of organizations including the U.S. military, despite the fact that employees with AIDS are protected by laws that preclude discrimination of the handicapped. The military has justified this testing in two ways. First, HIV-infected individuals need early medical attention to slow the progress of the disease. Second, widespread testing may help slow the spread of the disease by reducing incidents of unprotected sex between infected and uninfected partners. Research continues to confirm that AIDS is not transmitted by casual contact. The national Centers for Disease Control (CDC) guides, AIDS in the Workplace, reiterated the fact that AIDS is bloodborn and most often transmitted by unprotected sex or blood to blood contact. Because the disease is not spread by casual contact, routine testing for health service, personal service, and food service workers is not appropriate (CDC, 1985).

The increasing rate of HIV infection and the costs of caring for persons with AIDS has increased the likelihood that HIV testing will become more common. The average cost of treating an AIDS-infected employee could easily exceed $200,000. The total cost nationally is estimated at more than $8.5 billion annually, most of which will eventually be covered by employer health plans (Puckett & Emery, 1988). Employees with HIV could significantly escalate the cost of health insurance. Persons with AIDS are likely to have higher rates of absenteeism, and lower levels of productivity. HIV testing has also been boosted by the general hysteria over this disease. Its character as a sexually transmitted disease, which initially was most common among homosexual males, has fed the hysteria and has given HIV testing a new dimension. AIDS and HIV testing has focused attention on sexuality and provided an additional excuse for job-related discrimination based on sexual orientation. Despite intensive medical research, AIDS also remains a fatal disease. A positive HIV test, then, represents a very serious personal disclosure with direct implications for a persons sense of self, security, relationships.

PROBLEMS WITH TESTING

Organizations have used employee testing to assess the skills of employees at least since the time of the Industrial Revolution and probably long before. Testing an employee's ability to operate machines, such as typewriters, metal lathes, or computers, is necessary to match employees to particular jobs. Job applicants and employees are regularly asked to undergo company medical exams to ensure that their physical condition is appropriate to the job requirements. Such testing does not represent an invasion of privacy because it is not an involuntary disclosure and does not intrude into the employees personal life. Polygraphs, blood testing, and urinalysis represent much more serious and personal invasions of privacy. Intrusion through lie detectors and the collection of bodily fluids allows the organization to probe deeply into the personal life of employees. Specific ethical questions arise under the specter of such testing. Does the organization have a legitimate right to this information? Is there a legitimate purpose for collecting this information? How will the information be used and protected? Are the tests accurate?

Organizations defend testing and the collection of personal information about employees on the grounds that it is necessary to protect efficiency, ensure a safe work environment, and avoid legal liability. Employee theft or drug use compromises organizational efficiency. Drug or alcohol use may compromise safety of workers and in some instances such as air travel, the general public. In these cases, serious legal liability may result. Because it is illegal to discriminate against HIV-infected individuals, blood tests for HIV can only be ethically and legally defended on the grounds that employees need early medical attention.

The way in which test results are used is also important in assessing the ethics of employee testing. Tests results may be used in punitive ways to discriminate against employees, even though federal and state law may preclude such testing. Unsupported inferences can be drawn from test results about an employee's lifestyle. In some contexts, even the refusal to take a polygraph or drug test represents an implicit admission of guilt and grounds for dismissal. Such approaches do not respect the individual's right to privacy or a life outside the context of the organization.

In the cases of drug and alcohol testing, positive results should be coupled with a program of counseling to assist the employee in overcoming his or her problem. In all cases, test results must be kept strictly confidential and only disseminated to those members of the organization with a clear need to know. With drug and alcohol testing, this creates additional dilemmas because value-based choices must be made about who receives information. Should the flight crew of an airline pilot who tests positive for alcohol abuse be informed? Should the coworkers of a heavy machine operator who has tested positive for drug abuse be privy to the test results? Should law enforcement agencies be notified of an employee who tests positive for drug use? Should the family of an employee who tests positive for HIV be informed?

A final set of questions related to the ethics of employee testing concerns accuracy. Even proponents of polygraphs note that this technology may only be 70% accurate. Drug and HIV testing have less than perfect accuracy, although many of the problems concern the specific tests used and the accuracy of the laboratory screening the samples.

The specter of a false positive or false negative HIV test is particularly disturbing, given the magnitude of the potential results. When an organization chooses to tests employees, it has the responsibility of ensuring that the tests and test procedures have reasonable levels of accuracy.

Werhane's view of employee rights suggests that employees are full citizens in the organization. Perhaps the best approach to issues of employee rights is to involve the employee citizen in discussions and decisions about privacy and testing. Specific reasons and justifications for testing should be presented and discussed. Employees should participate in formulating clear and ethically defensible policies for these complex issues.

SUMMARY

There is little consensus about the rights of employees inside private organizations in part because there is disagreement about how to characterize the employer–employee relationship. Some suggest that the relationship is best guided by the doctrine of employment at will. Others have proposed comprehensive rights of full participation for employees. In the latter case, employees also have full rights of communication including access to information, participation in decision making, free speech, and privacy. Privacy is a particularly divisive employee right with important communication dimensions. Privacy concerns the question: To what information can an organization legitimately have access? Because organizing is closely related to information, privacy suggests that there are some areas of employee behavior that should remain outside the parameters of organizing.

Employee privacy has also come under increasing attack from new invasive technologies, such as the polygraph, urine analysis and in some cases, blood tests. Although organizations seek to defend these tests as necessary to provide safe and efficient work environments, the potential for abuse is very great. It is likely that employee testing will continue in its popularity and become even more common. The job application of the future will likely involve much more than filling out the application form, providing references, and participating in an employment interview. Many applicants will be required to pass a polygraph, complete a battery of psychological tests, and provide urine, hair, and blood samples in order to qualify for a job.

Employee–employer rights is a very dynamic area. Case law is continually evolving, offering new legal interpretations. Emerging technologies create unanticipated opportunities for organizations to collect information. The concept of rights remain, however, one the most popular methods to make sense out of the ways general social values, such as free speech and privacy, operate in organizations.

CASE: PRIVACY AND USES OF MEDICAL RECORDS

Nowhere is the right of privacy under more direct attack than in the arena of medical information. Records concerning a person's medical history are some of the most personal, intimate, and potentially damaging information available. Nonetheless, this data is very valuable to organizations seeking to reduce their uncertainty regarding employees and customers. This information has become even more powerful due to two developments; the infection of millions of Americans with HIV and the development of more sophisticated medical testing, including genetic testing.

Organizations often acquire detailed medical information about employees. This information is valuable because it allows the employer to reduce uncertainty about the employee's ability to work and about potential health care costs. Sometimes this information is collected in the form of employment physicals to determine an applicant's medical fitness for a job. In other instances, employers turn to private agencies, insurance data banks, credit bureaus, or investigation firms for employee data. Organizations providing employee health insurance often have access to the medical claims records for employees. Employment applications often contain blanket consent forms that allow employers to collect a variety of information about applicants. In general, there are very few limitations on the sorts of medical information an employer can ask an applicant to provide before offering them a position.

Insurance companies pursue similar lines of inquiry in determining if an applicant for health or life insurance is an acceptable risk. Many insurance companies require a blanket consent that allows for complete disclosure of medical information. In other instances, insurance companies require that applicants over a certain age undergo a physical examination to identify serious medical problems. Applicants with medical problems such as heart disease, diabetes, cancer, or who are infected with HIV, are often denied coverage. Some AIDS activists recommend that individuals wishing to have an HIV test do so at a county health department. These agencies usually assign numbers to patients in order to protect confidentiality and ensure that the results will not become part of their permanent medical record.

Discussion Questions

1. What rights and values do employers and insurance companies use to justify their access to medical data?
2. What are the appropriate purposes to which this information may be put?
3. What limitations, if any, would you suggest be placed on employer and insurance agency access to medical records?

5

Free Speech and Employee Voice

One set of values that is fundamental to democratic societies concerns freedom of speech and expression, and unrestrained dissemination of information. Free speech is both a value and a right and is fundamental to the functioning of democratic institutions and governments. It is a central feature of the U.S. Constitution in the First Amendment and encoded throughout federal, state, and local laws. Free speech and the dissemination of information are also related to rational decision making, free flow of ideas and information, the ability of individuals to make rational choices, a free and unrestrained press, personal expression, and the right of dissent.

Although the principles of free speech are most often associated with legal and political communication, they are also important values in organizational communication. In particular, free speech and free access to information in organizations empowers employees. It is also valuable in ensuring that employees are able to fully express their views concerning organizational activities. This freedom to express ideas, opinions, attitudes, beliefs, and perceptions plays a particularly important role in the successful enactment of the organization's environment. As with other issues of ethics in organizational communication, free speech requires a balance between the needs and concerns of the individual, the organization, and society.

FREEDOM AND RESPONSIBILITY

Freedom, as a latitude of personal choice, is offset with responsibility, or limitations through personal obligations. Modern democratic societies, including the United States, are based on the principle that the individual's rights of personal freedom are protected (Johannesen, 1990). These include freedoms of choice, movement, association, expression, assembly, self-determination, privacy, and speech. These personal freedoms are limited, however, by the fact that individuals have obligations to exercise these freedoms in a responsible manner. The right to drive an automobile, for example, is extended only as long as the individual operates the automobile in a responsible manner. Drunk driving results in the suspension of an individual's driving license. In this case, failure to act responsibly results in the suspension of the right to drive and a reduction in the individual's freedom of movement. A driver has a responsibility or obligation to others to operate a vehicle only when sober. Drunk driving is fundamentally irresponsible because it seriously compromises the freedom, health, and life of other drivers. The freedom to drive is linked to the responsibility of sobriety.

Freedom of speech is similarly constrained by responsibility to others. Society grants individuals significant personal freedoms to communicate to the extent that individuals can say whatever they want with very few prior constraints. Government, for example, is generally precluded from issuing prior restraint or censorship decrees to limit speech. Although individuals are free to express themselves, they may be held responsible or accountable for what they say. Citizens are free to criticize public figures, but may be asked to defend their criticism. When individuals are free to make their own choices, they are expected to accept the consequences of their choices. As discussed in chapter 3, responsibility often becomes confused and diffused in organizations because organizations tend to depersonalize messages.

In addition to this relationship between freedom of speech and responsibility, free speech is also associated with several other democratic values. These include First Amendment guarantees of a free press, rights of protest and dissent, and freedom of political and artistic expression.

FREE SPEECH AND THE FIRST AMENDMENT

Freedom of speech is encoded into the fundamental fabric of U.S. law through the First Amendment of the U.S. Constitution. The framers of the Constitution were concerned that the federal government would eventually seek to censor public criticism and limit freedom of speech through laws restricting content of public messages. Consequently, the free speech of the individual is strongly protected. Free speech as a value and as an ethical standard, therefore, is most often framed as a legal issue. The balance between freedom and responsibility is constantly reexamined and debated in the courts. Because federal constitutional law takes precedent over all other federal, state, and local statutes, both new and existing laws are examined by the courts to determine if they compromise basic free speech guarantees.

Congress shall make no law respecting an establishment of religion, or prohibiting the free exercise thereof; or abridging the freedom of speech, of the press, or of the right of the people to peaceably assemble, and to petition the Government for a redress of grievances.
—Amendment I, U.S. Constitution

The framers of the U.S. Constitution also believed that the rights of dissent and a free and unrestrained press were critical to the functioning of democracy. Democracy rests firmly on a public informed about governmental activities and problems, able to exercise their capacity for logic and reason in choice making, and free from undue influence by any single group or institution (Johannesen, 1990). The free press often calls public attention to social problems and concerns helping to determine the agenda for governmental and social action. A series of newspaper reports on poverty and homelessness, for example, may incite individuals to increase their giving to private relief agencies and force governmental agencies to examine funding for public agencies. A free press guarantees this democratic process. The press, free from censorship and government control, also serves a watchdog function, informing the citizenry about governmental activities, reporting on wrongdoing, and providing the information voters need to make their choices about political leadership. Without a free press, government could conduct activities without public knowledge or scrutiny. Throughout the history of American democracy, the free press has played a critical watchdog role in reporting on governmental activities, including the escalation of the War in Vietnam, the Watergate scandal, and the Iran-Contra affair. Without a free press, these ethically suspect governmental activities might well have remained hidden from the public.

Rights of political expression and dissent are also particularly important to the democratic processes. A citizenry free to express its diverse, and sometimes unpopular political views, ensures a full airing of various political positions. Dissent and protest are in the best interests of society as a whole because they allow for the expression and consideration of alternative perspectives. Pickets, protesters, dissenters, and those who express alternative lifestyles, beliefs, cultures, or political orientations receive broad Constitutional protections. Through political expressions, alternative views and opinions receive attention and are given a full public airing. This airing of alternative political perspectives also serves as a social safety valve. Because minority viewpoints can always be expressed, there is less chance that groups will turn to radical methods to make themselves heard. Protesters and dissenters are even protected when they create unrest. The courts have supported the right of hate groups, such as the Klu Klux Klan to hold rallies on public property despite the fact that such rallies cause significant unrest, spread a doctrine of hate and discrimination, and usually require extra police protection.

The courts, in interpreting the First Amendment, have allowed very few exceptions to the basic guarantees of free speech. Libel, making malicious, reckless, and damaging public statements about a person is very difficulty to prove (Kane, 1983). In the case of public figures, such as celebrities and politicians, there are few if any legal protections against libel. It is possible to severely criticize a political figure in the press, and even make false and misleading statements with disregard for the truth, without facing many legal consequences. Interestingly, the legal protections against libel extended to an organization are sometimes stronger than those afforded politicians. When the television news magazine *Dateline NBC* aired a report on GM's pick-up trucks, the network was forced to retract its story under GM's threat of a lawsuit. *Dateline NBC* had featured a dramatic segment showing a GM pick-up truck bursting into flames when colliding with a car. NBC had led the audience to believe that the explosion was the result of the impact and the supposedly defective GM gas tanks. In reality, the trucks featured in the story had been rigged with explosive devices. GM argued that its reputation and profitability had been severely damaged by false, misleading, and malicious portrayal of its pickups and that NBC had been reckless with the truth.

Strong free speech protections have also been extended by the courts for personal expression, particularly expression that is artistic or political in nature. The violent and sexually explicit lyrics of some popular music, for example, "Gangsta rap," have been defended on the grounds that it is a form of both political and artistic expression. Even "Gangsta rap" lyrics that sometimes glorify violence, such as the murder of police officers, have been afforded free speech protections. These rap artists defend their statements on the grounds that they are simply making artistic expressions of the experience of the poor and politically dispossessed living in the inner city. Limiting this form of self expressions would keep these political and artistic ideas from receiving a full public hearing.

Only in the area of pornography have the courts allowed for strict limitations on freedom of expression (Herbeck, 1984). Pornographic, indecent, or obscene messages that are not seen as having any political, educational, or artistic attributes can generally be regulated by local, state, or federal governments. Unlike speech that expresses alternative views or lifestyles, obscenity has no redeeming value and is beyond constitutional protections. Determining what is and what is not obscene has been particularly difficult. Efforts by the Supreme Court have focused on the application of a "community standard" of obscenity. What is determined to be obscene in Spartenberg, North Carolina, for example may not be obscene in New York City. The development of national media has diluted this community standard and made it more difficult for local governments to enact local controls on obscenity (Cahill & Haskins 1984; Herbeck, 1984). With the narrow exception of obscenity, free speech has a very clear role in the functioning of democracy. Free speech draws its ethical merit from values concerning the unrestrained flow of information and the use of that information in making informed, rational choices.

RATIONAL DECISION MAKING AND SIGNIFICANT CHOICE

In their effort to articulate a universal set of values, philosophers have often sought to identify a body of attributes or characteristics that are unique to humankind. These "essential elements of humanness," according to many ethicists, represent a powerful set of human values useful in making ethical judgments. These elements include the ability to use language, to collect and process information, and to make informed, reasoned choices (Johannesen, 1990). It is this capacity for reasoning and rational choice that supports a value of truthfulness, honesty, and unrestricted flow of information (Jaksa & Pritchard, 1988). Within the public domain, ideas, information, and opinions can be judged, evaluated, and weighed by citizens. Free and unrestrained speech and dissemination of information in the open marketplace of ideas contributes to the discovery of truth.

Capacity for reason and rational decision making is a particularly important feature of humanness because it allows humans to avoid manipulation and subjective, emotional reactions (Johannesen, 1990).

Higher intelligence and the capacity to carefully consider alternatives is unique to humankind. Capacity for rational decision making, of course, requires that individuals have access to the relevant information and that this information is honest and accurate.

Drawing on these ideas and the role of choice making in human nature and democratic systems, Nilsen (1974) proposed a communication-based ethic called *significant choice*. Nilsen emphasized reason as the instrument of individual and social development, the opportunity for individual self-determination, and the realization of individual potential. Communication, in the form of unrestricted exchange of information and viewpoints, discussion, debate, argument, freedom of critique, and inquiry contributes to these values and would be considered ethical. Anything that interferes with discussion, stifles debate, inhibits the free exchange of views, opinions, information and inquiry, and limits choices is considered unethical. This includes withholding information, attacking others to silence them, lying, distorting facts, or appealing only to emotion as opposed to reason and logic. Significant choice is a broad social ethic with application to a number of contexts. It has utility for all types of public messages such as political and product advertising, issue advocacy, and public policy debate. From this perspective, efforts to persuade others using well-reasoned arguments supported by evidence is ethical. Efforts to mislead by knowingly withholding information, providing incomplete or faulty evidence, or diverting attention form real issues is considered unethical. Withholding information about hazardous chemicals on the job would be considered unethical because it denies employees access to information they need to make significant choices about their jobs. Significant choice is a value that operates within any community where rational, reasoned choice is important, such as in organizations (Gorden et al., 1984).

PROBLEMS OF FREE SPEECH IN ORGANIZATIONS

Problems of free speech in organizational contexts are a consequence of the conflicting needs and values of the organization and the individuals who make up the organization. The organization, valuing stability, consistency, and predictability often seeks to limit the freedom of employees to speak about various issues. Public and vocal criticism of management, for example, is inconsistent with the organization's need for stability and order. It is not surprising, then, that organizations limit this form of speech through both formal and informal controls (Gorden et al., 1984). From the perspective of employees, however, the ability to speak out and express their attitudes, ideas, and concerns is an important value. It suggests that employees are full members and citizens of their organization (Gorden & Mermer, 1989). This expression is instrumental for employees seeking to express dissatisfaction, call attention to problems or wrongdoing, or add their insights to important decisions. Free speech as an ethic of organizational communication requires a balance of organizational values of stability, predictability, and order and the individual's values of full participation, involvement, and voice.

First Amendment protections are constitutional provisions regarding the government's ability to limit or control the speech of citizens. As such, they do not apply to private organizations that are not directly affiliated with government (Sanders, 1984). Within the context of private organizations, very few First Amendment guarantees of free speech exist. In considering cases about the free speech rights of private sector employees, the courts have generally sought to balance the organization's right to smooth and efficient operation against the free speech rights of employees (Sanders, 1983). In general, the needs of the private sector organization have taken precedent over the rights of employees. Private sector organizations have been granted very broad legal rights to create rules, policies, and practices that strictly limit the speech of their employees.

In reviewing a number of such cases, the courts have established general principles that guide legal decisions regarding the free speech rights of employees. These include the need for employee discipline; coworker harmony; confidentiality; personal loyalty and confidence; the time, place, and manner of the employee speech; and questions about the good name of the organization (Sanders, 1983). The courts have held, for example, that some employee speech will disrupt employee discipline and compromise the organization's ability to operate efficiently. Personal loyalty and confidence in superiors, for example, may be undermined by employees publicly criticizing or ridiculing managers. The organization may, in these cases, limit such speech. Following the same reasoning, employee speech that promotes disharmony can also be limited. The courts have long held that certain kinds of information, such as formula, computer software, or designs for new products, are trade secrets and have the same status as property. Employees who publicly communicate such information reduce the value of that property. The courts have given broad latitude to organizations seeking to limiting this form of employee speech. For years, tobacco companies were able to avoid reporting what ingredients went into cigarettes because ingredient lists represented "trade secrets." The courts also take into account the time, place, and manner of employee speech. For example, organizations have greater latitude to limit the speech of employees during work hours and on company property than at other times and places. Organizations, for example, may limit certain types of speech to certain locations in a factory. Finally, with regard to the organization's good name, the courts have ruled that statements by employees that might be attributed to the organization may also be limited (Sanders, 1983).

In addition, the formal polices, rules, and procedures that organizations can legally institute to limit employee speech, create another more informal layer of controls exists. The organization's culture, myths, values, and norms also influence what is and is not discussed (Seeger, 1986). New members are socialized into the organizational culture when they join the organization. In addition to learning informal dress codes, language systems, and values, the members are instructed in what can and cannot be discussed. Over time, members often come to identify strongly with their organization and naturally may avoid saying things that might portray the organization in a negative light. Organizational culture represents a form of informal, implicit, and unobtrusive control over employee speech (Tompkins & Cheney, 1985). Because this cultural limitation on free speech operates at an informal, and unobtrusive level, it is a more direct limitation than formal policy or rules (Seeger, 1986). In addition, the limitations on employee speech that are created by cultural identification may be so subtle that even the employees are not consciously aware that their speech is limited. Studies in small group communication focusing on the "groupthink" phenomenon have documented a self-censorship effect where members avoid bringing up negative issues for fear of disrupting the group (Janis, 1972). This form of informal control over employee speech limits the range of topics employees discuss.

FREE SPEECH AND EMPLOYEE VOICE

Another perspective regarding free speech in organizations is called employee voice. This concept is based on the view that employees are full organizational citizens. As Gorden and Mermer (1989) suggested "employees as citizens should not just be compliant, . . . but they also should be influential in role making and shaping the culture of the workplace. They should engage appropriately in the dialectic of managing those institutions that significantly affect their lives" (p. 4). This full participation requires that employees have some freedom of speech and expression within their organization.

The concept of employee voice was initially developed by researchers interested in customer dissatisfaction (Hirschman, 1970). When dissatisfied, customers might simply leave an organization, or they might passively accept their dissatisfaction. In both instances, their dissatisfaction remains unvoiced. In other instances, customers might speak out about or voice their dissatisfaction in ways that resulted in positive organizational change. This positive criticism represents a potentially important form of feedback, if the organization were receptive to customer criticism. Other researchers have adapted this concept of voice to employee responses to dissatisfaction.

Gorden (1988) provided the most comprehensive conceptualization of employee voice. He suggested that employee voice can be classified as active or passive, and as constructive or destructive. Using this framework, it is possible to identify four general types of employee speech:

> *Active/Constructive*: making suggestions, bolstering, argument/dialectic, union bargaining, and principled dissent.
> *Passive/Constructive*: quiet support, attentive listening, unobtrusive compliance, and cooperation.
> *Active/Destructive*: complaining to coworkers, ingratiation, duplicity, bad mouthing, antagonistic exit.
> *Passive/Destructive*: apathy, calculated silence, withdrawal.

From the perspective of the organization, passive and active constructive voice are the most beneficial in calling attention to organizational problems. Allowing employees to fully express their concerns and criticism is also most consistent with human nature values including respect for individuals and their capacity for informed decision making. This fundamental value of respect for the individual is also found in human resources views of organization.

Several researchers have examined the relationship of employee voice to other communicative processes in organizations (Gorden, 1988). Gorden, Infante, and Graham (1988) found that corporate conditions that were receptive to employee voice were most conducive to higher levels of employee satisfaction. Infante and Gorden (1985) found that supervisors were most satisfied with employee voice characterized by affirmation and argumentativeness. Argumentativeness, in this context, is consistent with the values of discussion and debate manifest in significant choice. These studies have generally supported the view that employee voice is important to developing and maintaining employee loyalty. Voice also benefits society's well-being by enhancing the ability of employees to speak about organizational wrongdoing. Freedom of employee speech in the form of employee voice is related not only to important values and ethics, but also seems to create a superior work environment.

Regardless of the potential benefits and ethical superiority of allowing employees to have a constructive voice, a number of impediments exist to free expression by organizational employees. Principal among these are the lack of a supportive and open climates of communication. Climate represents the perceived state of communicative relations between superiors and subordinates and between coworkers in an organization (Redding, 1973; Tompkins, 1984). Organizations characterized by defensive climates, including lack of trust, dogmatism, provisionalism, certainty, lack of concern, and superiority, tend to have lower levels of openness between superiors and subordinates (Gibb, 1961). Employees tend to be less satisfied under these supervisory conditions and there may also be some negative affect on job performance (Daniels & Spiker, 1991) Several researchers have also documented a tendency for employees to distort the messages they communicate upward to their superiors when facing a defensive communication climate (Jablin, 1980). When a fundamental distrust exists between superiors and subordinates, subordinates do not feel free to communicate in an honest, direct, and open manner. This tendency toward information distortion effectively silences the employee's voice, cutting off any honest participation by the employee. It also reduces the likelihood that serious organizational problems will be brought to upper management's attention in a timely manner. In this way, managers may be denied critical information they need to make informed choices. According to the principles of significant choice, this breakdown of superior–subordinate communication is a question of ethics.

FREE SPEECH AND PARTICIPATORY MANAGEMENT

Some useful parallels can be drawn between free speech in organizations and human resources and participative management. A significant body of writing in management theory is founded on the assumption that employees (workers) are valuable resources not only for their physical capacity to do work, but for their problem solving, creativity, and insights concerning their jobs. McGregor (1960) offered the first comprehensive human resources-based theory of management. His Theory X and Theory Y approaches outline two polarized sets of assumptions managers hold about workers. Theory X assumptions, are essentially pessimistic, viewing workers as unmotivated, unworthy of trust, and lacking in creativity or problem-solving capability. Theory Y articulated an optimistic set of assumptions about humankind, including the belief that humans are self-motivated, seek responsibility, and have an inherent capability for creativity and problem solving. McGregor argued that utilizing the problem-solving and decision-making capability of workers is a more efficient use of resources. It is also grounded in the values of human dignity and worth, creative potential, self-determination, and capacity for reason, logic, and rationality.

Because the employee is viewed as a valuable organizational resource, they are encouraged to actively participate in organizational problem solving and decision making. The human resource theorist, Likert (1961) coined the term *participative management* to describe this form of employee involvement. His view of participative management includes open communication, free and frank exchange of ideas and information, flexible channels of communication, and decentralized decision making. Much research in organizational communication treats this participative style of management as the ideal for supervisor–subordinate communication. Not only is participative management consistent with the values of free speech and human capacity for logic and reasoning, but is generally seen as a more effective style of supervision. As with free speech in society, free speech and employee voice in organizations allows for free exchange of information and ideas and the discovery of truth. Gorden et al. (1984) wrote "The argument for the employee's right to speak up, even in critical ways, is based on the notion that an exchange of opinions, even antagonistic opinions, is essential to the marketplace of ideas" (p. 68).

Many recent developments in management have built on the basic assumptions laid down by McGregor and Likert in human resources management. Japanese management, for example, draws heavily on employee participation in decision making and problem solving. The QCC, one outgrowth of Japanese management, encourages active employee participation in solving problems related to product quality. The quality movement has branched out into several areas of employee involvement. The popular team-based approaches to work and management are built on the collaboration and cooperation of individuals from the organization's different functional area, and the free exchange of information, ideas, perspectives, and opinions. This form of unrestricted exchange also benefits the organization's capacity for enactment.

FREE SPEECH AND ENACTMENT

Weick's grammar for sense-making outlines the basic framework for organizing: "How can I know what I think until I hear what I say." This process was discussed in chapter 2 where the relationship between communication and organizing was explored. Weick's view puts a high priority on the ability of organizational members to process information, discuss their perceptions of the informational environment with one another, and communicate competing interpretations. It also follows that those interpretations that are not "said" remain unconsidered. Kreps

(1980) identified some basic recommendations for organizational practitioners that follow from Weick's theory of organizing. His recommendations include

> adequate communication contact among organizational members when processing equivocal information [sic] fostering interactions among organizational members working on difficult organizational tasks, [sic] daily and weekly meetings and problem solving organizational groups. (p. 396)

Weick's model suggests that communicative interactions, including free employee speech and free and unrestricted access to information, facilitate effective organizing. In organizing, those interpretations that cannot be spoken, cannot be considered.

SUMMARY

The free speech tradition is fundamental to the functioning of democracy. Free speech is encoded in the U.S. Constitution and has a prominent place throughout the law. Very few legal protections for free speech exist in organizational communication, however. Private organizations may limit employee speech that is disruptive, that disseminates important information, or that affects the good name of the organization.

Although these limitations on employee speech may seem relatively minor, they do have substantive affects on the organization in two broad ways. First, from the perspective of human resources management, limitations on employee speech means that an important informational resource and problem-solving capacity are lost. Research into the concept of employee voice, for example, has demonstrated that freedom of communication is related to employee loyalty and satisfaction. Climate research has concluded that open and supportive superior–subordinate relationships in organizations may be most effective. Second, from the perspective of organizational enactment, a limitation in the capacity of members to "speak out" reduces the ability of the organization to take various interpretations of its informational environment into account. Free speech contributes to the ability of organizations to effectively enact their information environment by allowing members to express alternative interpretations of their informational environment.

Free speech is a value with both philosophical and instrumental underpinnings. Giving voice to various perspectives, viewpoints, orientations, and concerns is well established as consistent with the ethic of significant choice, respect for the individual, and discovery of the truth. It also creates more effective work relationships and greater problem-solving and information-processing capacity. The ability to communicate and exchange information freely is not only "good" in the sense that it is consistent with important values, but "good" in terms of organizational efficiency and effectiveness.

CASE: COLLEGE SPEECH CODES

In recent years, a number of colleges and universities have been experimenting with so-called *speech codes*. These codes seek to address the fact that some forms of speech, such as racial epithets or demeaning descriptions of women, are oppressive, offensive, and inconsistent with the values of education, free inquiry, and mutual tolerance. Speech codes have been adopted by some universities to discourage demeaning speech and provide a mechanism for dealing with instances of communication that are seen as inappropriate. Critics charge that codes limit free speech and expression. University administrations argue that the free speech is not seriously affected and that the codes are necessary to ensure some groups are not oppresses.

An excerpt from the University of Michigan's Policy on Discrimination and Discriminatory Harassment by Students in the University Environment is reprinted here. This code was struck down by the courts in Doe vs. University of Michigan in 1989.

B
Discrimination and discriminatory harassment in educational and academic centers
Educational and academic centers, such as classroom buildings, libraries, research laboratories, recreation and study centers, etc. are the locus of the University's educational mission. Accordingly, the University as a more compelling interest in assuring an environment in which learning may thrive. At the same time, the University has an equal interest in preserving the widest range of discourse within the classroom. The policy seeks to balance these competing interests. The following types of behavior are discrimination or discriminatory harassment and are subject to discipline if they occur in educational or academic centers.

1. Any behavior, verbal or physical, that stigmatizes or victimizes an individual on the basis of race, ethnicity, religion sex, sexual orientation, creed, national origin, ancestry, age, marital status, handicap or Vietnam-era veteran status, and that:

a. Involves an express or implied threat to an individual's academic efforts, employment, participation in University sponsored extracurricular activities or personal safety; or

b. Has the purpose or reasonably foreseeable effect of interfering with an individual's academic efforts, employment, participation in University sponsored extracurricular activities or personal safety; or

c. Creates an intimidating, hostile or demeaning environment for educational pursuits, employment or participation in University sponsored extracurricular activities.

2. Sexual advances, requests for sexual favors, and verbal or physical conduct that stigmatizes or victimizes an individual on the basis of sex or sexual orientation where such behavior:

a. Involves an express or implied threat to an individual's academic efforts, employment, participation in University sponsored extracurricular activities or personal safety; or

b. Has the purpose or reasonably foreseeable effect of interfering with an individual's academic efforts, employment, participation in University sponsored extracurricular activities or personal safety; or

c. Creates an intimidating, hostile or demeaning environment for educational pursuits, employment or participation in University sponsored extracurricular activities.

D
Sanctions

Certain factors should be considered in fashioning the sanctions, including the intent of the accused, the effect of the conduct on the victim and the University community, the degree of remorse, whether the student has violated the policy in the past, whether sanctions such as education and community service are likely to change the student's attitudes, and the effect of the sanction on the student's standing within the University. The most severe sanctions, suspension from specific courses or activities, suspension from the University and expulsion, should be imposed only when the offending behavior involved violent or dangerous acts, repeated offenses, or willful failure to comply with a lesser sanction.

Discussion Questions

1. What values does this speech code arise from?
2. To what degree, if any, do you believe the code compromises free speech?
3. How would you propose balancing these values?

6

Ethics and Whistleblowing

Perhaps no other issue so completely illustrates the fundamental value conflicts and ethical dilemmas inherent in modern organizations as does *whistleblowing*. This form of organizational communication is characterized by very strong ethical tensions and contradictions rooted in the collective values of organizations and groups and their conflict with the personal values and ethics of individuals (Elliston, Keenan, Lockhart, & Von Schaick, 1990; Jensen, 1987). Whistleblowing is often presented as a personal act of conscience that contributes to the open dissemination of important information. The whistleblower brings episodes of ethically suspect behavior into the light of public scrutiny and debate. It is often framed as the act of a virtuous individual following his or her personal sense of right and wrong. In other instances, however, it is seen as the act of a vindictive turncoat, breaking a confidence and violating the organization's collective values. In these cases, whistleblowing is depicted as an irresponsible form of communication that violates basic principles of loyalty, integrity, and trust. The motives of the whistleblower are usually questioned, while he or she often faces very direct and personal threats and reprisals.

Regardless of how it is framed, whistleblowing is one of the most grassroot methods for calling attention to the serious problems of governmental or corporate impropriety. It is one of the few instances where the ethical conscience of an individual can have a direct impact on a large organization. This chapter reviews whistleblowing and examines the debate about the ethics of whistleblowing. The core questions of whistleblower motives, intent, and credibility are examined. Finally, the legal environment of whistleblowing is reviewed including very recent changes in the law that have modified the way ethical judgments are made about whistleblowing.

A REVIEW OF WHISTLEBLOWING

Whistleblowing has a long history with many celebrated cases, going back at least to the mid-1800s (Kernisky & Kernisky, 1994). In 1973, an anonymous whistleblower code-named "Deep Throat" worked with two reporters to bring the wrongdoing of a democratically elected president to the public's attention. Although Watergate has been described as a low point in the history of democracy, it may also be seen as a victory for democratic principles and the role of public disclosure in combating governmental misconduct. Roger Boisjoly and Allan McDonald, engineers with NASA's contractor Morton Thiokol Corporation, blew the whistle on the flaws in the Challenger space shuttle by testifying before the Roger Commission investigating the Challenger disaster (Goldberg, 1990). Although they were demoted for their actions, they did succeed in bringing fundamental deficiencies to light. Many of the revelations regarding the Hanford Nuclear Weapons facility in Richmond, Washington were brought to light by whistleblowers working with Governmental Accountability Project (GAP), a private whistleblower protection group (Kippen, 1990). Other recent disclosures GAP has supported include "Iraqgate," alleged wrongdoing in the "Starwars" defense program, and questions of impropriety in the National Forest Service (Government Accountability Project, 1991, 1992).

Whistleblowing can be defined "as the attempt of an employee or former employee of an organization to disclose what he or she believes to be wrongdoing in or by the organization" (James, 1990, p. 160). In "blowing a whistle," a person calls wider public attention to what he or she sees as a problematic situation, including sexual harassment, job discrimination, illegal activities, price fixing, issues of public safety, pollution, insider trading, unsafe products, and so on. As Bok (1980) noted "Whistleblowers sound an alarm from within the very organizations in which they work, aiming to spotlight neglect or abuses that threaten the public interest" (p.

10). In calling attention, particularly media attention, to problematic and ethically suspect issues, whistleblowers ensure close public scrutiny and the application of a community-wide ethic. Whistleblowers make effective use of the watchdog function of a free press in a democratic society. Blowing the whistle has "illuminated dark corners of our society, saved lives, prevented injuries, and disease, stopped corruption, economic waste and materials exploitation" (Nader, 1990, p.156).

Whistleblowing is seen as the last option for individuals facing work-related situations they perceive as having serious moral and ethical implications. Murphy (1993) suggested that four characteristics influence whistleblowing behaviors. First, the employee's personal characteristics including high status and high levels of education, encourage whistle-blowing. Second, specific job duties that bring individuals into contact with wrongdoing are more likely to result in whistleblowing. Third, organi-zational characteristics, including strong norms against dissent, tend to discourage whistleblowing. Finally, organizational characteristics, such as climate and structure, influence whistleblowing (Murphy, 1993). Usually, whistleblowers have exhausted the internal, routine channels of complaint and are forced to take their message to outside parties. Whistleblowers are often subjected to serious consequences for their actions including reprisals, threats, intimidation, and termination. In one of the most celebrated cases, whistleblower Karen Silkwood was killed after blowing the whistle on wrongdoings in the nuclear industry.

GAP reported that most whistleblowers almost inevitably suffer severe emotional trauma and personal and economic loss as a conse-quence of speaking out. Not only do they lose their job, but they are often blacklisted. Their former friends and coworkers shun them. They are sometimes accused of fictitious wrongdoing, alcoholism, drug use, psychological problems, or incompetence to destroy their credibility and justify their termination. Retaliation and the fear of retaliation are com-mon experiences for the whistleblower (Near & Miceli, 1986; Parmerlee, Near, & Jensen, 1982). Research shows that for public sector employ-ees, who generally enjoy much more protection than private sector employees, several factors are related to retaliation. First are the levels of managerial and supervisory support for the whistleblower. High levels of support may help shield the whistleblower from retaliation. Second, the seriousness of the wrongdoing is related to retaliation. Accusations that result in legal action, for example, have a greater chance of prompt-ing retaliation. Retaliation is also associated with a choice of external channels. When the whistleblower takes accusations outside the organi-zation, the probability of serious retaliation is enhanced. Parmerlee et al. (1982) also found that organizations were more likely to retaliate against whistleblowers who were more highly valued by the organization and against those whistleblowers whose charges lacked external support.

Based on the experiences of several whistleblower cases, GAP has provided a number of insights into the general process of whistleblowing (Devine & Aplin, 1988). In particular, two general trends emerge in whistleblowing cases. First, organizations often seek to neutralize the message of the whistleblower. This may involve making the messenger rather than the message the focus of scrutiny. Organizations often release details from an employee's personnel file to destroy credibility. This may not only reduce the credibility of the whistleblower, but may create a general chilling effect on any subsequent disclosures. Often, organizations give the whistleblower the impossible job of solving the problems or investigating the abuse. When the whistleblower inevitably fails, his or her credibility again is reduced. This may also provide a convenient excuse to terminate the whistleblower. A second set of techniques involves silencing the whistleblower. Transfers to relatively isolated locations with overwhelming duties are common for whistleblowers. Failure to perform the new duties may again result in termination. Sometimes, the whistleblower is simply ostracized from the group.

GAP has also developed a set of strategies designed to protect whistleblowers and maximize the chances that their messages will be heard (Devine & Aplin, 1988). GAP recommends that employees carefully consider the consequences of whistleblowing and discuss the decision to go public with their families. Second, GAP recommends that whistleblowers work through existing internal channels of dissent before taking their concern to an outside agency. This strategy enhances the credibility of the whistleblower and establishes that he or she is loyal to the organization. Once a decision has been made to contact external agencies, the whistleblower should carefully determine if others share these concerns. In so doing, the whistleblower may discover an informal base of support. GAP points out that when many employees speak out, the credibility of the message is enhanced and the chance that the message can be stopped by muzzling any one employee is reduced. Employees are also encouraged to maintain a clear and clean employment record to minimize the chance that excuses will be used to terminate the employee. Careful records, documents, and supporting materials should be assembled to provide documentation of the charges. Once the charges are made public, the employee's access to such materials is usually strictly limited. Finally, careful selection of supportive journalists and legal advisors is critical to providing support and appropriate channels for communicating the wrongdoing. It is the press that ultimately gives the whistleblower a larger audience.

ETHICAL TENSIONS

The ethical character of whistleblowing and its ethical merits are characterized by two interrelated yet fundamentally conflicting value tensions (Jensen, 1987). The first tension is a function of ethical individualism (i.e., the individual employee following his or her personal value system). Whistleblowers often note that they have a loyalty to a higher community or social ethic or standard and that their organizational loyalty is not blind. "Whistleblowers challenge the notion that what is good for the organization is good for the larger public" (Jensen, 1987, p. 285). Further, in breaking their confidence with the group, they reject the paternalistic assumption that the group, organization, or governmental agency can decide what is in the public's best interest. The whistleblower breaks the confidence of the group based on loyalty to the larger community and the belief that the community should make decisions based on accurate and truthful information. The whistleblower may, therefore, be depicted as a virtuous person, with a well-developed personal ethic, a willingness to stand up for ethics in the face of potential hardships and reprisals, and a sense of selflessness in service of a greater good.

The second tension concerns whistleblowing as violation of a fundamental group trust, loyalty, and confidentiality in light of the value system of the group and the organization (Elliston, Keenan, Lockhart, & Von Schaick 1990; Jensen, 1987). Organizations depend on the strength of employee identification, loyalty, and commitment as a fundamental mechanism for controlling the boundaries of the organization. This internalization of collective values and beliefs serves as a form of unobtrusive control over employee activities (Cheney & Tompkins, 1987). Loyalty and identification serve as mechanisms to promote communication that is consistent with larger organizational goals. Messages that might rock the boat or disrupt the common good are avoided. Those employees who strongly identify with the organization can be expected to communicate positive information about the organization. They can also be expected to avoid disseminating information which may damage the reputation of the organization (see Seeger, 1986).

Whistleblowing concerns the whistleblower's association with, and ultimately separation from the group (Jensen, 1987). As with any form of dissent, whistleblowing can be understood as involving the conflicting loyalties arising from membership in two or more groups (Elliston et al., 1990). The whistleblower is a member of an organization to which he or she has some obligation. The whistleblower is also a member of a larger society that also carries obligations. The employee who blows the whistle on his or her company chooses to break the confidence and loyalty of the organizational association.

Corporate whistleblowers and those who support them are often criticized on the grounds that they undermine the basic principles of loyalty necessary for organizations to function. Drucker (1982), for example, wrote that "Whistleblowing is simply another word for informing" (p. 234). He argued that encouraging whistleblowing inevitably results in the breakdown of trust and a reduction of ethics. Any group, institution, or agency, whatever its cause, must create and maintain some level of loyalty in order to exist. Jensen (1987) argued that this idea of loyalty often involves confidentiality. For a person to spread inside information to an outside audience is a direct violation of the contractual understandings. The whistleblower is often depicted by critics as a "traitor" who shifts his or her loyalty to some other group.

The tension inherent to whistleblowing is a consequence of two competing sets of values. These competing sets of values create ethical dilemmas in whistleblowing. When faced with knowledge about an organizational wrongdoing, an employee must balance the values of organizational loyalty against the values associated with the free dissemination of information. Resolving the dilemma and making ethical judgments about whistleblowing requires that one set of values takes precedent over another.

MOTIVATIONAL QUESTIONS

A primary concern regarding the ethics of whistleblowing involves the motivation of the person disclosing information. Whistleblowing is usually differentiated from self-serving, trivial, or malicious disclosure on the basis of the person's motives. The fact that the whistleblower usually takes a large personal risk to disclose a wrongdoing is often used as evidence of selflessness and credibility. As such, whistleblowing is typically seen as personal risk or sacrifice for the good of the larger community.

In contrast, the "tattletale," "rat fink," "squealer," or "stool pigeon" is a person who divulges information for personal gain or simply to make mischief. Such behavior is generally considered ethically suspect in that it compromises fundamental levels of trust between people and may even constitute breaking an explicit promise. The stool pigeon or turncoat breaks a confidence related to some strong loyalty—professional, family or group—and usually does so because of a personal reward. The stool pigeon is a Judas who sells out the group. In this sense, the whistleblower as turncoat trades what he or she knows or has learned from a personal trust or relationship for some personal gain or to avoid some impending punishment.

The whistleblower, in contrast, is held up as a moral champion, a hero, a person who follows his or her own sense of ethics even in the face of severe personal costs. Those who support whistleblowers use terms such as "'truth tellers' and 'ethical resistors' because [whistleblowers] 'commit truth' . . . " (Clark, 1992, p. 10). He or she places issues of right and wrong above such concerns as "livelihood, friendships, professional relationships, and opportunity for promotion and advancement" (Elliston et al., 1990, p. 99). Whistleblowers are often described as courageous, brave, responsible, ethical dissenters, selfless, and as having a strong sense of personal and professional integrity. Their motives are pure in the sense that no personal gain is involved. It is this strong sense of personal integrity and morality that guides the whistleblower and sets them apart from the squealer, tattletale, or stool pigeon. The former divulges information for reasons of personal morality, the latter does so for personal gain.

This motivational definition of the whistleblower is fundamental to answering ethical questions and provides the basis for the larger arguments surrounding whistleblowers. If a person calling attention to a perceived wrongdoing is labeled whistleblower as moral champion, then his or her charges have more credibility and are more likely to be taken seriously and acted on. In contrast, if a person is labeled whistleblower as disloyal or stool pigeon, then the whistleblower's credibility is lessened and the charges are suspect. Because the whistleblower seeks to make use of the mass media to shed light on wrongdoing, issues of credibility are critical to garnering necessary attention. Moreover, the whistleblower often uses the media attention as a form of protection from reprisal. A whistleblower who is not perceived as credible, therefore, is more likely to be punished or harmed for his or her actions. The strain between these contradictory positions, whistleblower as stool pigeon motivated by base drives of personal gain or revenge, versus whistleblower as moral champion seeking to right a wrong for higher motives of morality, is a central feature of discussions and debates about whistleblowing and its merits (Elliston et al., 1990; Jensen, 1987).

WHISTLEBLOWING AS COMMUNICATION

Although whistleblowing is inherently an issue of personal versus community loyalty, it is important to recognize that it is also an issue of communication. The whistleblower seeks to "speak out" in a vocal and visible way about what he or she sees as misconduct. Elliston et al. (1990) argued that this "raising of one's voice" (p. 17) is a three-stage process of blowing a whistle, making a noise, and being heard. Issues of free speech and employee voice are inherent to such speaking out. First Amendment provisions, for example, give limited latitude to governmental employees to speak out on matters of personal conscience even when disclosures may harm an employer (Sanders, 1983). Private sector employees have not traditionally enjoyed these rights. Private organizations have been free to terminate employees for speaking out (Seeger, 1986). The common law doctrine of employment at will generally allows organizations to terminate employees for almost any reason, including the breach of a confidentiality (Elliston, Keenan, Lockhart, & Von Schaick, 1985; Seeger, 1986). Until very recently, whistleblowers in the private sector, even in those cases where the employer was a contractor for the federal government, had very few protections.

One of the fundamental values of a democratic society, however, is free dissemination of information, particularly information that may influence critical decisions. Nilsen's (1974) ethic of significant choice, for example argued that individuals must have access to information in order to make reasoned and informed choices. Nilsen suggested that "the good is served by communications [sic] that provide adequate information, diversity of views, and knowledge of alternative choices and their possible consequences" (p. 45). Debate, discussion, and free dissemination of information are critical to the functioning of a democracy. Whistleblowing, then, serves "the good" by enriching the available information about critical issues. In many instances, whistleblowing brings to light facts that would not otherwise be known. This free flow of critical information also enhances the individual's ability to make rational decisions about which products to buy and which politicians to support (Johannesen, 1990).

The mass media also play a critical role in disseminating the whistleblower's message. In a democratic society, a free and uncensored press serves a watchdog function, informing the general public about the activities of government and organizations. Since the earliest days of the press in Colonial America to the muckrakers of the 20th century and the persistent probing of Woodward and Bernstein, the role of the press in publicizing and helping correct corporate and governmental wrongdoing has been widely recognized. The whistleblower uses the power of the press and its watchdog function to reach a larger public audience with accusations of wrongdoing. This special role of the press provides an invaluable channel for the whistleblower and the larger publicity generated by the press often helps shield the whistleblower from retaliation.

WHISTLEBLOWING AS A LEGAL ISSUE

Whistleblowing has been the focus of much analysis as a legal issue. Traditionally, very little legal protection existed for employees who chose to speak out about some perceived wrongdoing. The legal doctrine of employment at will made employee confidentiality and loyalty important attributes to retaining a job. Whistleblowers were routinely subjected to ridicule, character assassination, demotions, firing, and blacklisting and had few legal recourses. A complex patchwork of state and federal legislation, however, has been developed to protect whistleblowers from reprisals as a consequence of their actions (Elliston et al., 1985). This includes provisions for free speech in the workplace, wrongful discharge, antidiscrimination statutes, and due process provisions (Barnett, 1992; Kippen, 1990; Sanders, 1983). The courts have generally been moving toward more protection for whistleblowers, particularly when the information is in the interest of society or when the whistleblower's accusations are part of a legal investigation. Most states have also passed legislation to protect both public and private sector whistleblowers. "The intended objective is to provide protection against adverse employment action for employees who, for reasons considered to be in the public interest, disclose violation of law or threats to health and public safety" (Parliman, 1987, p. 26). Although state law varies widely, there is a general recognition that those individuals who speak out need some legal protection against at least the most blatant forms of organizational retaliation.

Federal legislation has also significantly strengthened whistleblower protections. This includes the Whistleblower Protection Act of 1989, the Corporate Whistleblower Protection Act of 1992, and recent changes in the Federal False Claims Act. These changes in the legal environment of whistleblowing have modified both the ethical basis of whistleblowing and the way whistleblowing is perceived.

The legislative environment of whistleblowing has followed a pattern of development that has increasingly protected and even encouraged whistleblowing. Initially, governmental whistleblowers were protected and encouraged as part of a general interest in controlling government waste and reducing cases of gross negligence, waste, or similar wrongdoing. This form of whistleblowing has broad appeal, reaching across political ideologies and functioning as an augment to the general watchdog function of the press. The Whistleblowers Protection Act of 1989 codified at the federal level a series of protections which essentially reduced the threat of reprisals federal whistleblowers faced. The Whistleblower Act of 1992 significantly strengthened these protections and expanded whistleblower protections to much of the private sector. State, case, and these two federal protections now provide a significant body of protections for whistleblowers in both private and governmental organizations (Pearlstein, 1992).

Other changes in federal law and reinterpretation of existing law has taken whistleblowing further. The application of the Federal False Claims Act, in particular, has significantly changed the environment of whistleblowing. The False Claims Act was originally enacted during the Civil War as a way to curb war profiteering. The law allowed individuals who reported war profiteering to share in the economic recovery. In 1986, the law was amended and updated and has since served as the basis for a number of larger economic settlements, with a 15% to 25% "bounty" fee going to the whistleblower (Pearlstein, 1992). Observers have noted that under the False Claims Act, the emphasis of many whistleblower agencies and public interest lawyers has shifted from ferreting out wrongdoing to producing large cash settlements. Currently, whistleblowing is a growth industry representing the potential for huge financial gains for those individuals willing and able to report large scale corporate wrongdoing. Where once whistleblowers could be framed as moral dissenters, virtuous people motivated by their personal sense of right and wrong, they are now more likely to be portrayed as profit seekers, motivated by economic reward.

In 1994, for example, a record number of whistleblower cases were reported resulting in record whistleblower fines. One whistleblower case included a $112.5 million settlement against Teledyne for fraudulent cost accounting. In another, $82.2 million was recovered from Litton Systems for overcharges on computer services (Sniffen, 1994). Another episode involved CAE-Link Corporation's regular practice of overbilling the federal government for flight simulators. The federal government eventually recovered $55.9 million, while the 35-year-old auditor who uncovered the overbilling received a $7.5 million whistleblower bounty (Sniffen, 1994).

These figures suggest two important features of recent whistleblowing cases. First, whistleblowing often results in very large financial rewards for both the whistleblower and the federal government. This represents a radical shift from earlier environments of whistleblowing where the person blowing the whistle could be assured of loss of job, professional ostracism, and financial ruin. Second, whistleblowing episodes are on the increase (Jensen, 1987). Blowing the whistle has lost much of its stigma and the press is increasingly active in seeking out stories of organizational wrongdoing. As a consequence, employees who are aware of some wrongdoing are more likely to call public attention to that wrongdoing. This is not to say that whistleblowers no longer face the likelihood of personal and professional reprisals. The possibility of financial reward, however, may offset these threats and contribute to the increasing number of whistleblowing episodes.

In one of the most celebrated recent cases, for example, Douglas D. Keeth, a senior corporate finance vice president for United Technologies, blew the whistle on billing practices for a Pentagon aircraft contract. In a settlement, United Technologies agreed to pay the federal government $150 million. Keeth, under federal whistleblowing legislation, received 15% of the settlement or roughly $22.5 million for his role in bringing the fraudulent overbilling to light. A number of similar cases have also been reported since 1986 contributing to the estimated $738 million recovered by the federal government from whistleblower disclosures (Holusha, 1994). In most instances, highly placed engineers, account managers, or senior executives of firms with multimillion dollar government contracts report wrongdoing and actively collaborate with investigations to prove their charges. When settlements are eventually made, the whistleblower often receives between 15% and 25% of the judgment.

This addition of a significant economic incentive has added a complex new dimension to whistleblowing. On one hand, whistleblowers may be encouraged by the chance of significant economic reward. Organizations may be much more cautious about wrongdoing knowing that employees could profit by disclosing them to the public. Whistleblowing might become more and more of an economic issue, and less a case of an individual following his or her personal sense of right and wrong.

SUMMARY

Whistleblowers have always occupied a special place in the moral fabric of a democratic society contributing to the open and honest functioning of democracy. Whistleblowing, however, has a schizophrenic character. On one hand, the whistleblower is a moral champion, an ethical dissenter who takes huge personal risks in bringing wrongdoing into the light of day. On the other hand, the whistleblower may be portrayed as disloyal turncoat, willing to sell out the group. These conflicting characterizations rest largely on the perceived motivation of the whistleblower.

Whistleblowing has two other important dimensions. First, it is inherently a communication issue, with implications for the employee's rights of free speech and the role of communication in a free and democratic society. Second, it is a legal issue that relates to the organization's right to privacy and to protect proprietary information. Recent legislative shifts, including the Whistleblower Protection Act and the False Claims Act, have changed the legal environment of whistleblowing. These changes have modified the motivational premise of whistleblowing by creating economic rewards for some types of whistleblowing. Under these circumstances, the moral and ethical dimensions of whistleblower might someday be reduced.

CASE: WHISTLEBLOWERS TELL THEIR STORIES

Reprinted here are two short narratives by whistleblowers who worked with GAP. These narratives are short but powerful personal descriptions of the whistleblowing process.

Felix Smith: Defending the Public Trust
I spent thirty-four plus years with the U.S. Fish and Wildlife Service. It's a good outfit, really. There are some problems running it at times but really it's a good outfit.

I'm also one of those crazy guys who believes in the public trust. The public trust simply means that those resources belong to all the people . . . today and for future generations. The should get a fair shake when you roll the dice in the management of forests, trees, fish, water—whatever it is that belongs to the people. But that is frowned upon in agencies. Agency spokesmen will get on your case if you start talking this way. Now what the hell are these political appointees afraid of? Are they afraid of the truth? Good science in this country depends on the freedom of speech, clear and simple.

In 1983, I was on a research team looking at waste water issues in the Central Valley of California. We had an idea that drainage water coming from the irrigation of these lands was causing some severe problems [with selenium deposits] that we didn't fully understand. In high levels [the mineral selenium] becomes toxic to fish and wildlife. We had hundreds of thousands of mosquito fish but no frogs, no crawfish, no black bass, no blue gill, no crappie. We went to the marsh and, instead of the marsh being a deafening sound of birds and frogs and wildlife making all kinds of noise, it was deathly quiet. Selenium had started to take its toll.

By speaking out on this issue, talking to people such as the National Wildlife Federation, Audubon Society and Congress about what was going on, one gets on the bad side of your administrators. It was difficult speaking up in 1983. It's very easy for me to talk out now.

Sonja Anderson: Environmental Sacrifice Zones.
I used to work for Westinghouse on the Hanford [nuclear weapons facility]. The current mission in Hanford is environmental restoration. Their mission is restoration and cleanup. This year at least 1.7 billion dollars of the taxpayer's money will go into Hanford for environmental restoration.

When I was there, my job was that of Senior Scientist with the environmental compliance unit. I went in and looked at the discharge stack that discharged over 100 cubic feet per minute to the environment. I realized there was no capability to sample, monitor, control, or report discharge of radioactive and toxic materials to the environment.

I started looking at other facilities in the same manner and they just don't measure—because if they did, the would have to report the information about the radioactive and toxic materials that have covered hundreds of square miles since the early 1940s. I documented this in my reports and audits.

In essence, I lost my job for this. Most of the people don't talk. I told. I told and I continue to tell. I brought directly, to the congressional level, four or five major instances where the Department of Energy (DOE) and Westinghouse corporation knowingly violated federal [environmental and safety] laws.

But in all these cases, still, Westinghouse and DOE tend to thumb their nose at the EPA and regulating agencies. Maybe with enough interaction on our part, and support, maybe we will see some change.

Discussion Questions

1. What reasons (values, goals, norms) do the two narratives suggest were behind the decisions to blow the whistle?

2. What personal consequences for whistleblowing were reported in these narratives?

3. According to these narratives, what larger social values does whistleblowing serve?

7

Communication and Organizational Legitimacy

Organizations are sometimes portrayed as self-contained units, insulated from the larger environment. From a social systems perspective, however, organizations are closely connected to and dependent on their environments. A constant exchange of resources between the organization and the environment is necessary for continued operation. This organizational dependency on an uninterrupted supply of critical resources is the basis for a set of ethical and value judgments known as organizational legitimacy. Legitimacy is a macroscopic and generalized value based assessment of the organization made by groups and individuals outside the organization (Parsons, 1956; Pfeffer & Salancik, 1978). Legitimacy concerns the normative and social value of the organization's goods, services, processes, and outcomes—both intended and unintended—and how the organization presents itself to its constituencies and the larger environment.

This chapter examines the concept of *organizational legitimacy* focusing specifically on the ways in which organizations communicate about their value. This includes a discussion of the general expectations society has for communication that seeks to create legitimacy and the ways in which these expectations change. From this perspective, organi-

zations must continually communicate the basis for their social legitimacy. The particular problems organizations face in creating and maintaining legitimacy for multiple audiences and constituencies are also examined. Although legitimacy is potentially problematic for organizations, it
also represents a source of important support for the organization in the
form of a reservoir of good will. Organizations draw on this reservoir
when they face criticism or attack.

DEFINING LEGITIMACY

The idea that organizations have social value beyond their immediate
ability to produce goods, provide services, and make profits has always
been featured in discussions about organizations. The classical organizational theorist Max Weber was among the first to offer a detailed discussion of this larger organizational justification for organizations. Weber
believed that it was not enough for an organization to be profitable; rather
some larger social purpose or value was required. This might take the
form of a legal mandate, social consensus, or a logical and rational base
for an organization's operation. Weber's legitimacy represented a larger
social justification for an organization. Weber also saw this broad consensus as a stabilizing force in society by clarifying accepted power relationships among institutions. Talcott Parson expanded this view by arguing
that in social systems, the output of one part of the system is consumed
by other parts. This output must be desired, useful, and legitimate.
    With private, profit-making companies in capitalistic economies,
the primary justification for organizations as systems is to increase the
wealth of the owners. They do so by processing inputs (raw materials,
information, parts) into outputs. Dowling and Pfeffer (1975), however,
argued that organizations rely on a supply of finite resource inputs provided by the larger environment to maintain profitability. That is to say,
raw materials, energy, and human resources are limited resources and
organizations must compete with one another for these resources. If
these scarce resources are used in inappropriate or "illegitimate" ways,
society may decide to withhold or withdraw the resources. Legitimacy is
necessary for the organization's long-term survival. To maintain legitimacy, organizations must continually argue that they are functioning in a
manner that is consistent with larger, socially defined norms of appropriate conduct. As Dowling and Pfeffer (1975) noted, "Organizations seek
to establish congruence between social values associated with or
implied by their activities and norms of acceptable behavior in the larger
social system of which they are part" (p. 112). This congruence, which
helps ensure social support, is established in part through communica-

tion. "Legitimacy is the process whereby an organization justifies to a peer or superordinate system its right to exist, that is, to continue to import, transform, and export energy, material, or information" (Mauer, 1971, p. 361).

Other organizational theorists, working with the basic notions of legitimacy, have taken these ideas further in exploring how organizations establish and maintain this congruence (Mauer, 1971; Meyer & Scott, 1992; Parsons, 1956; Pfeffer & Salancik, 1978). They have suggested three general sets of legitimizing processes: normative legitimacy, legitimacy through secondary outcomes, and legitimizing linkages. These processes are outlined in Table 7.1.

Organizations create normative legitimacy in several ways: through economic viability, rational operation, operating norms, and through self-created norms. Organizations must initially establish that they are functioning in an economically viable manner. Although this

Table 7.1. Legitimization Processes.

Norms

Profitability: The organization is economically viable; using resources in an efficient and effective

Rationality: The organization is operating in a manner consistent with basic standards

Operating norms: The organization is operating in a manner consistent with various social norms: environmentalism, fair treatment of employees, etc.

Self-inflicted norms/expectation: Specific standards and norms develop from the organization's communication about products, procedures, outcomes, etc.

Secondary Outcomes

Jobs: The organization provides jobs to its employees

Tax base: The organization supports the community through taxes

Family/community stability: The organization contributes to social stability

Philanthropy: The organization supports various "good causes"

Linkages:

Community linkages: Advisory boards, community relations panels

Board of directors: Board members provide linkages to specific stakeholder groups

General social values: Image advertising

---

does not mean that organizations must always be profitable, it does mean that they must be good stewards of limited economic resources (Pfeffer & Salancik, 1978). This economic norm of legitimacy is probably the most basic justification for an organization because it concerns the system's efficient use of limited resources. Capitalistic economies are designed so that resources, raw materials, finances, labor, and so on, accrue to the most efficient systems. Second, organizations must also demonstrate that they generally operate in rational and logical ways according to basic norms for organizational design and management. Organizations, for example, are expected to act rationally and logically in solving problems and making decisions (Ladd, 1979; Meyer & Scott, 1992). Those organizational activities that are erratic or outside the norms of established organizational conduct are seen as illegitimate. A third group of norms concerns the organization's specific operations and outputs. These include environmental responsibility, fair and equal treatment of employees, production of safe and appropriate products, and open and honest exchange with stockholder groups. Specific operating norms develop in society to reflect particular social values and needs and are often encoded in laws and regulations. Although laws do not correspond directly to legitimacy, the two are highly correlated (Pfeffer & Salancik, 1978). Organizations also create a fourth form of normative legitimacy through their own communication. Expectations for outcomes arise when organizations communicate with their constituencies. These "self-inflicted" norms and expectations develop from the organization's self-descriptions, plans, promises, and public goal statements. An organization may gain legitimacy by keeping its promises and meeting its goals or may lose legitimacy if these expectations go unmet.

Although legitimacy derives in part from the organization's effective and efficient use of scarce resources and normative operation, it also concerns the specific value organizations hold for stakeholders. These values are often the secondary outcomes of profitable and efficient operation. Organizations, for example, provide jobs for employees, enhance the tax base for communities, buy products and services produced by other organizations, and engage in philanthropy (Pfeffer & Salancik, 1978). By so doing, they create instrumental resource and outcome dependencies with the larger society. Over time, communities come to depend on the organization for jobs and taxes. Charities rely on organizations for donations. Consumers expect the organization to provide important goods and services. Communities depend on organizations for taxes. These secondary outcomes have very specific and tangible value for the various constituencies. In many instances, these dependencies are related to other important social values such as stable communities and viable local economies. In this way, organizational legitimacy itself becomes a resource that the organization may use to build further support (Reich & Donahue, 1985). When the Chrysler Corporation faced near bankruptcy in the 1980s, the company turned to its stakeholders for support. Dealers, state and local governments, unions, suppliers, creditors, and a wide variety of community groups lobbied Congress to pass the federal loan guarantee package that eventually saved the company (Moritz & Seaman, 1984). Banks deferred loan payments, suppliers extended the company credit, and workers took pay concessions. Even though Chrysler was, for all intents and purposes, bankrupt, it was able to draw on its extensive set of resource dependencies and reservoir of good will to support its efforts to generate much needed financial resources (Reich & Donahue, 1985).

Organizations also seek to develop these stakeholder connections into linkages. Linkages serve a variety of strategic goals for the organization, including exchanging information, helping to obtain commitment and support, and building and maintaining legitimacy (Pfeffer & Salancik, 1978). Boards of directors and community advisory boards usually include members of important constituencies (Pfeffer, 1972). Prestigious and important persons or organizations represented on a board or advisory group symbolically demonstrates that the organization has value (Pfeffer & Salancik, 1978). These connections and linkages also serve as channels of communication and help the organization demonstrate its value and communicate important information to various groups. Following the lobbying effort to pass the Chrysler Guarantee Loan Package, the company appointed the President of the United Auto Workers (UAW), Douglas Fraser, to the Chrysler Board of Directors. This appointment created a strategic linkage for the transfer of information and for enhancing legitimacy. It also symbolically demonstrated the value Chrysler held for the UAW.

In addition to the specific instrumental linkages to stakeholder groups, organizations seek to establish linkages to larger social values. Anheuser-Bush Corporation, maker of Budweiser beer, invested millions of dollars to sponsor the 1996 Olympic Games. This sponsorship allows the company to use the well-known Olympic symbol in its product advertising. The company is linked symbolically to the Olympic ideals of athletic competition. Chrysler Corporation was actively involved in raising money for the Statute of Liberty/Ellis Island renovation. Chrysler featured the Statue of Liberty in many of its commercials as it emphasized themes of patriotism. Because Chrysler was competing with many foreign car campaigns, the implicit "buy American" appeal was particularly important. This linkage of the organization to universally positive symbols is a common and effective legitimizing strategy.

As Dowling and Pfeffer (1975) noted, legitimacy is not solely based on economic issues. Organizations may be legitimate, for example, but may not use resources in an efficient way. Society is often willing to invest millions of dollars to research relatively rare diseases with hopes of saving proportionally very few lives. Using these resources to combat disease and hunger in developing countries would be much more efficient in terms of the numbers of lives saved. Organizations may also be illegitimate, yet enormously profitable. The successful trade in illegal drugs such as heroin and cocaine is an example of illegitimate and illegal activities that capture billions of dollars in profits. Cigarettes cause cancer, emphysema, and heart disease among smokers, yet the tobacco industry, from grower to manufacturer, continues to function as a profitable billion dollar enterprise (Perrow, 1970). Moreover, the industry is subsidized at several points by federal tax dollars. In this case, an industry that most would agree has very limited legitimacy, continues to flourish. This inconsistency between legitimacy and profitability is a function of an organization's specific value for various stakeholders versus the organization's generalized social value. Tobacco companies have very specific and important utility for particular stakeholder groups. Tobacco farmers have, for generations, derived important profits from this cash crop. Many rural communities depend heavily on tobacco to support their local economy.

Legitimacy, then, is a generalized perception and evaluation based on the organization's many diverse outputs. The legitimacy lost due to a controversial product may be offset somewhat by a record of philanthropy, good jobs, and corporate profitability. The fact that legitimacy represents a generalized and broad-based evaluation of the organization by various groups and stakeholders precludes any precise and universal determination of when an organization is or is not legitimate. Consequently, judgments of legitimacy are matters of interpretation and are in part a function of the public statements made about organizations and their activities. As Pfeffer and Salancik (1978) argued, "Organizations may themselves seek to establish their status in society by generating statements of their goals which in the current environment would be found to be acceptable by the relevant publics" (p. 194).

CHARACTERISTICS OF LEGITIMACY

Legitimacy is a complex value-based outcome of the organizing process. Several points help clarify the way in which legitimacy functions in making judgments about organizations. These include legitimacy as a retrospective judgment of the organization, legitimacy as a conferred status, legitimacy as reputation, the role of information in judgments of legitimacy, and the role of communication in assessments of legitimacy.

Legitimacy, by definition, is a retrospective judgment made concerning the organization's past activities (Pfeffer & Salancik, 1978). Past activities, products, procedures, general conduct, and communication are evaluated by the public. The public, then, makes some assessment as to how these activities relate to the general standards and norms of appropriate organizational conduct. An organization's reputation as a good, responsible, honest, responsive company is based on judgments about previous activities and outcomes. Similarly, an organization's reputation as dishonest, irresponsible, or inappropriate arises from judgments of its previous (past) activities. Legitimacy, in this sense, is an inevitable byproduct of the organization's past and the efforts to retrospectively make sense of that past. Observers of organizations use rules, in the form of norms and standards, and communication, to retrospectively interpret an organization's informational outputs and make judgments about legitimacy.

Legitimacy is also a conferred status (Pfeffer & Salancik, 1978). External groups, shareholders, and the general public determine which organization is or is not legitimate. This assessment is "precarious" and may change very quickly (Boulding, 1978). Ben and Jerry's, a company that produces gourmet desert products, is widely cited as an example of a responsible, socially conscious organization. This organization has been featured in news stories and in academic publications for its exceptionally fair treatment of employees. Its status as a legitimate company has been conferred by external groups. The status of legitimacy may also be withheld if an organization is somehow seen as operating in a manner which is inconsistent with social norms. When an organization's activities are seen as illegitimate, comments and attacks will inevitably follow (Pfeffer & Salancik, 1978). Because legitimacy is conferred by external groups, organizations are forced to communicate with these groups to create, maintain, and defend their legitimacy.

In addition, the knowledge that stakeholders, critics, and the general public have of the organization and its activities is almost always imperfect. Stakeholders may be vaguely aware that an organization's products have been criticized, but may not know the specific details. Information about organizational products and processes is often considered a proprietary trade secret, and not accessible to the general public. Tobacco companies succeeded in keeping secret the ingredients that go into cigarettes for years by arguing they were trade secrets. In cases where companies are sued for product liability or negligence, it is not uncommon for the organization to require that plaintiffs not publicly disclose information about the case. Because available information about organizations is imperfect, the resulting judgments of legitimacy are similarly based on incomplete information.

Organizations also actively communicate about their activities in ways strategically designed to build and/or defend their legitimacy. Organizations, for example, may emphasize their social value in creating jobs or engaging in philanthropy. When criticized, organizations often respond by defending, justifying, and explaining their activities in elaborate and sophisticated ways. The defense mounted by GM when NBC attacked the safety of its pickups was a carefully thought out and persuasive argument justifying the company's activities and defending its products. Their argument included detailed information about how the trucks had been rigged to explode following a "simulated" side impact and statistics supporting the truck's safety record. Exxon mounted an extensive public relations campaign to defend its legitimacy in the wake of the Valdez oil spill. This campaign not only presented details about Exxon's extensive clean-up efforts, but also portrayed the clean-up as contributing to the development of the local economy. In other instances, organizations mount more long-term media campaigns designed to bolster their image and enhance their legitimacy. These campaigns often seek to associate the organization with positive images of responsibility, profitability, and patriotism. The tobacco company, R.J.R. Nabisco, for example, sponsored many events celebrating the 200th anniversary of the U.S. Constitution. The campaign associated the company name and logo with the concept of personal freedom, choice, and democracy. These, and other corporate activities, are strategic efforts to bolster the organization's image and legitimacy.

Finally, the norms, standards, and judgments that members of the public or stakeholder groups use to make judgments of the organization are not universal but vary from group to group and change over time. Some members of the public may be more concerned about the organization's economic profitability, others concerned about jobs, and still others about the organization's record of social justice. Although most definitions of legitimacy focus on the idea that organizations must operate in a manner consistent with general social norms, there is little consensus regarding what constitutes appropriate organizational conduct. Moreover, these norms are in a constant state of flux. Many of the most basic norms of appropriate organizational conduct accepted today are relatively recent developments. Environmentalism, equal treatment of women and minorities, and basic concepts of fair treatment of employees are relatively new norms for organizations. Although it is difficult to predict the changing character of such social values, the general trends are to expect more and more from organizations. Organizations today are expected to be profitable, efficient, technologically sophisticated, provide meaningful work, good wages, and maintain a good social and environmental record. Some critics, such as the noted neo-Marxist theorist Jurgen Habermas, have suggested that capitalist society cannot continue to indefinitely meet these ever expanding expectations. Consequently, some argue that capitalist society and its for-profit companies, are inevitably moving toward a crisis in legitimacy (Epstein & Votaw, 1978). This crisis, according to Habermas, will be characterized by a fundamental questioning of the value of capitalist institutions and a break down of social support (Fransiconi, 1986; Habermas, 1975).

These characteristics support a view of legitimacy and legitimizing processes as highly equivocal, dynamic, and subject to multiple interpretations. Observers seek to make sense, retrospectively, of the organization's activities in a way that allows for judgments of legitimacy. Organizations seek to portray their past activities in favorable light and strategically disclose or withhold information. This equivocality also allows the organization to argue that it is operating in a manner that is just and worthy of recognition as legitimate (Dowling & Pfeffer, 1975). Or, as communication theorists have suggested, determinations of legitimacy are, at least in part, rhetorical, where communicators seek to persuade others concerning the legitimacy of various acts and processes (Burelson & Kline, 1979; Fransiconi, 1986; Seeger & Szwapa, 1989).

LEGITIMACY AND COMMUNICATION

Communication researchers have focused on the function of rhetoric in the creation and maintenance of legitimacy. They argue that legitimacy is created and maintained through the organization's public communication. Specifically, organizations communicate about their social value, seeking to persuade stakeholders and the general public that their activities are consistent with appropriate social norms and values. These persuasive appeals are featured in the organization's advertisements, both product and issue, in the public statements of organizational spokespersons, in the organization's publications, such as annual reports, press releases, house organs, and specialized brochures, and in other symbolic behavior.

These persuasive appeals are grounded in the four legitimizing processes presented in Table 7.1. Organizations, for example, make appeals to legitimacy based on profitability in their annual reports. Those organizations that are profitable are able to argue that they are "good stewards" of scarce resources and are operating in a manner consistent with the basic norms of free enterprise and capitalism (Sethi, 1975; Smith, 1993). In some ways, the norm of economic viability or profitability is the most fundamental issue of legitimacy because it relates to the efficient use of scarce resources (Meyer, 1992). Even not-for-profit organizations, such as religious and philanthropic organizations must maintain some basic level of economic responsibility. When it was publicly disclosed that top executives of United Way of America charities received excessive salaries and lavish expense accounts, contributions plummeted. The organization was not perceived as a good steward of philanthropic contributions. Similarly, when the Chrysler Corporation reported record losses three quarters in a row, it was forced to publicly defend and justify its legitimacy as a private, profit-making corporation by communicating about its activities. As Turkel (1982) observed in his analysis of the Chrysler loan guarantee, "Legitimation crisis may result when either the discourse becomes an inadequate basis for the (organization's) justification of and/or institutionalized processes do not fulfill legitimate expectations" (p.167).

In addition to the general norms of profitability, organizations must also communicate that they generally operate in a rational and logical manner (Ladd, 1979). Basic standards and principles of organizational design, operation, and management have developed over time. Organizations must comply with these basic norms of rational operation in order to maintain legitimacy (Meyer, 1992). When it was disclosed that NASA knowingly violated its own safety policies by launching the flawed Challenger, the organization lost legitimacy. This loss was compounded following the crash of the Challenger when NASA reacted to the crash in a seemingly erratic, irrational, and illogical way. This included efforts to impound all news footage of the Challenger explosion and seeking to limit the investigation of the crash (Seeger, 1986). Whenever organizations operate in ways judged as outside of established norms and standards for rational, logical conduct, they risk losing legitimacy.

Through their public communication, organizations create additional expectations regarding specific behavior and outcomes. These norms are self-inflicted because they arise out of the organization's description of itself. When an organization suggests to its stockholders that it will reach a certain level of profitability by a specific date, an expectation is created that may subsequently affect legitimacy. Stockholders may hold management accountable to these expectations. Communicating specific targets for reduction of pollution, hiring of women or minorities, or achieving more equitable wages, creates specific expectations and standards that affect legitimacy. Organizations, therefore, often avoid discussing specific outcomes because they may later be held accountable for those statements (Pfeffer & Salancik, 1978). They also may seek to withhold information that might be judged as negative.

Beyond the norms of profitability, rationality, and specific expectations organizations create for themselves, additional standards for legitimizing communication have also been proposed. Fransiconi (1986) examined Habermas' concept of political and social legitimacy in order to synthesize implications for communication. Justifications that seek to create or maintain legitimacy, he concluded, are largely rhetorical in their character. Four criteria for such legitimizing discourse are evident in Habermas' work: (a) justifications should be consistent with general norms; (b) justifications should be criticizable and capable of being argued rationally; (c) justifications of legitimacy should be in the general or public interest, considered rational; and (d) justifications of legitimacy should involve procedures and presuppositions designed to produce consensus (Fransiconi, 1986). Although Fransiconi offered these criteria primarily for evaluating political communication, they are also useful for examining organizational messages (Kernisky, 1992; Seeger & Szwapa, 1989; Smith, 1993).

By definition, claims and justifications of organizational legitimacy seek to demonstrate that organizations are operating in a manner that is consistent with general social norms. As discussed earlier, however, such norms are equivocal and change over time. Consequently, organizations are free to define and discuss norms in a variety of different ways. They may seek to emphasize some normative aspects over others, link their activities to particular values, or demonstrate that they are operating in a fundamentally ethical manner. When Dow Chemical was criticized for releasing toxic pollutants, the company responded by appealing to general values of economic progress. Critics of the chemical industry, the company charged, were antigrowth, and against innovation, and economic progress (Seeger & Szwapa, 1989). Appeals to such general values as "progress," "economic growth," "patriotism," "free enterprise," and the "American way of life" are often central features of an organization's legitimizing discourse.

A second criteria offered by Fransiconi suggests that justifications should be criticizable and capable of being argued rationally. Efforts to create legitimacy should be grounded in appropriate, open, truthful, and sincere exchanges of messages (Burelson & Kline, 1979). Organizations that withhold important information about their products and processes in order to enhance legitimacy, for example, are violating principles of criticizable and rational discourse because they deny others access to all the facts. Organizations also try to overwhelm criticism with elaborate public relations campaigns, technical arguments, or threats of lawsuits. A common response to criticism of an organization's environmental record is to move the discussion into a technical sphere. Organizations using this strategy may claim that because they hold the technology, they are the only ones capable of making assessments concerning the environmental impact of that technology. Consequently, the general public is essentially excluded from these technological discussions. When environmentalists claimed that DuPont's chlorofloucarbons (CFCs) were depleting the ozone layer, for example, the company initially claimed that no scientific evidence existed to support this claim. Later, DuPont announced its own research program to "find the truth." Exxon used a similar argument in responding to criticism of its effort to clean up Alaska's Prince William Sound following the Valdez oil spill. Assessing the environmental impact, Exxon claimed, would require years of study. The call for "more study" is a common response to claims that organizations are operating in ways inconsistent with basic norms and standards of environmental responsibility. This strategy is designed to suspend the debate and transform discussions into technical debates.

The third criteria synthesized by Fransiconi (1986) concerns the general rationality of legitimizing discourse. He noted, "Justifications of legitimacy should be in the general (or public) interest to be considered rational" (p. 20). Arguments about the legitimacy of an organization's activities should be grounded in the rationality of the general public. That is to say, organizations seeking legitimacy must do so through rational appeals to general or public interest as opposed to narrow or personal interests. Organizations, for example, cannot justify products that endanger the health of the general public on the grounds that they are highly profitable. Such arguments would not, from the standpoint of public interest, be considered rational. Habermas argued that these justifications must be grounded in some relationship to truth.

Finally, Fransiconi (1986) suggested that legitimizing discourse and legitimizing procedures should be designed to produce consensus. Theoretically, legitimizing discourse should provide the opportunity for all interested parties to communicate. The "procedures" of legitimacy should include activities designed to produce general social agreement or "background consensus" through "dialogic process of discourse." This includes the free, honest, and open exchange of ideas, perspectives, opinions, and information. Limitations on discussion, withholding information, cutting off debate, and refusing to disclose important facts, according to Fransiconi, are inappropriate in legitimizing discourse.

The four criteria Fransiconi draws from Habermas point to some of the effects of communication on the legitimizing process. Legitimacy represents a "contestable validity claim" that can be supported or rejected through rational communication. Organizations must continually engage in a dialogue with their stakeholders, and "an ongoing process of reason giving" to establish and maintain their status as legitimate. In those instances where legitimacy is questioned, organizations must respond to specific charges in demonstrating normative operation, desirable secondary outcomes and values, and linkages to stakeholders and to larger social values and ideas. If an organization fails to provide these justifications, it risks losing its fundamental basis of social support.

From the standpoint of ethics and enactment, this ongoing process of legitimacy also has benefits of requiring that organizations publicly communicate their social value. Organizations and their spokespersons must, from time to time consider and discuss the organization's social value. They must "give reasons" for social support. Such communication may facilitate organizational members taking larger social values into account in the ongoing organizing process. This legitimizing discourse may also facilitate stakeholders and members of the general public taking questions of social value into account. Organizations are forced to consider and publicly justify their ethical and social merit. This, in turn, enhances the organizations accountability to society.

SUMMARY

Legitimacy is a complex normative evaluation of the organization, its processes, procedures, products, and personnel and is an inevitable byproduct of organizing. It is a status conferred by an external audience made up of stakeholders and members of the general community who examine organizational behavior, outcomes, processes, and self-descriptions retrospectively. It is also inherently rhetorical, as organizations seek to persuade their external constituencies that they are operating in a manner that is just and worthy of their recognition and support. Legitimation issues create high equivocality for organizations because social values and expectations are complex, shifting, and often contradictory.

Legitimacy also functions as an important regulating mechanism, ensuring that organizations operating far outside the general social norms, standards, and values are forced to change, justify their activities, or suffer potentially damaging loss of support. These justifications often provide the basis for managers and spokespersons to more fully take into account questions about the organization's larger social value. They also provide stakeholders and the general public with specific expectations that may subsequently be used to hold the organization accountable. Legitimacy, as the application of social norms to organizational conduct, is a powerful process ensuring some basic level of ethics. Legitimacy will become increasingly important as information about organizational conduct is more widely available, as expectations for organizations rise, and as organizational observers and critics become more vocal.

CASE: NASA, LEGITIMACY, AND THE CHALLENGER DISASTER

One of the most celebrated cases of organizational crisis is the Challenger space shuttle disaster. On January 28, 1986, millions of Americans watched in horror as 73 seconds into the flight Challenger's booster rocket exploded, killing all seven passengers aboard. The explosion and the public investigation that followed seriously compromised the legitimacy of NASA.

NASA was created by President Eisenhower in 1958, in direct response to the Soviet Union's successful Sputnik satellite program. For the first several years of its operation, NASA took much of its justification from the race with the Soviet Union to control space. This justification was largely based on the fear that if the Soviet Union controlled space, they might orbit weapons of mass destruction over the United States. Thus, NASA's legitimacy was linked to power values of national security. This justification was expanded when President John F. Kennedy vowed to place an American on the moon. NASA's success became closely associated with America's prestige in the eyes of the world. On July 20, 1969, Apollo 11 landed and Neil Armstrong stepped out onto the surface of the moon. America had achieved one of the greatest accomplishments in the history of humankind at an estimated cost of $24 billion. NASA had also promoted a "can-do" attitude, portraying itself as able to overcome the most daunting of technological challenges. By achieving its goal of landing on the moon, however, NASA had in effect compromised its legitimacy. A clear and compelling consensus about the value of NASA specifically and manned space flight in general no longer existed. Space flight, in many ways, had become routine creating a different set of public expectations for NASA.

Throughout the 1970s, NASA struggled with less clear goals, efforts to cut its budgets, and persistent congressional criticism. The program was often justified on the grounds of its science and technological spin off. Congress and NASA explored elaborate plans for a space station that would enhance scientific inquiry, to be served by a reusable "space truck." It was believed that such a system of space travel would be more cost effective because it was reusable. Eventually, the space station was to serve as a platform for a manned mission to Mars. While the plans for a permanent space station were put on hold, the space shuttle program went forward.

The technological complexity of the space shuttle quickly began taking its toll. The program was plagued with cost overruns, and technical problems that seriously threatened NASA's image as a "can-do" agency. Eventually, NASA built four shuttles: Columbia, Discovery, Atlantis, and Challenger. Even when the shuttle program was successful, its technological problems mounted, sometimes causing long strings of launch delays. NASA tried to reduce criticism by having celebrities join missions. A congressman joined the ranks of shuttle astronauts. Astronauts from other countries were included in shuttle missions to demonstrate the program's diplomatic value. Plans also went forward to put a teacher into space. Christa McAuliffe, a high school teacher, was selected and scheduled on the January 1986 flight of Challenger. Promotions were designed to encourage schools around the country to tune in as she taught classes from space.

Before the flight of January 28, Challenger had experienced several launch delays. One well-known television commentator quipped "Once again, a flawless launch proves too much of a challenge for Challenger." When the shuttle was finally launched on the cold morning of January 28, the o-ring seals on the booster rockets failed to seal properly and Challenger disappeared in a ball of fire.

Discussion Questions

1. How did NASA justify itself through linkages to general social values and how did these values change over time?
2. How did NASA's spectacular Challenger failure compromise its legitimacy?
3. What general social value does NASA have now?

8

Communication and Organizational Responsibility

Closely associated with organizational legitimacy is the concept of *organizational responsibility*. This responsibility entails a set of organizational obligations to specific communities and to society in general. Legitimacy suggests that organizations draw resources from their environment and are responsible for the appropriate use of those resources. Organizational responsibility argues more generally that organizations are members of society and such membership carries an additional set of obligations. As Buchholz (1990) argued, organizations are more than economic institutions. They relate to society in ways other than through the simple exchange of goods and services. Organizations are also members of society.

Responsibility concerns the organization's role in supporting important social goals and values and in helping to solve social problems that affect both society and the organization. As the primary means for producing goods and services, organizations are powerful forces in society. Consequently, they have a particularly important role in supporting good social consequences. Many organizational ethicists have focused on organizational responsibility as the primary framework for organizational ethics. In fact, the idea that corporations have broad social responsibilities beyond making profits is a primary basis for the rapid growth in organizational and business ethics (Buchholz, 1990; Madsen & Shafritz, 1990; Steidlmeier, 1987).

This chapter provides a definition of organizational responsibility and reviews the development of specific forms of responsibility. The history and debate about the organization's role in society is also examined. Several of the specific responsibilities associated with private organizations, including philanthropic, environmental, employee, and product responsibilities are presented and evaluated. This includes discussion of the specific ethical parameters associated with each. In addition, the organization's responsibilities concerning communication are discussed within the framework of corporate social reporting.

DEFINING ORGANIZATIONAL RESPONSIBILITY

Organizational responsibility, like so many questions of value, is subject to different interpretations. In the traditional sense, organizational responsibility suggests that corporations comply with and promote various moral positions and outcomes. This view of responsibility is usually grounded in the personal value system of the owner/manager. At the time of the industrial revolution, successful entrepreneurs often promoted causes and issues related to their personal values and sense of morality (Buchholz, 1990). Henry Ford I, for example, promoted education and health care by founding a college and a major medical center. Andrew J. Carnegie promoted reading and helped create many community libraries throughout the country. W.K. Kellogg promoted health food and nutrition. These traditional views of corporate responsibility are characterized by three general assumptions (Bowen, 1953). First, the commitment of the organization, managers, or owner to these social causes is purely voluntary. The organization, manager, and/or owner decides on both the level and specific area of social involvement. In this way, the organization's autonomy regarding its own decisions about involvement is retained. Second, the motivation for involvement in social causes is to improve general social conditions rather than to increase organizational profits. The specific areas of interest, however, are often somehow related to the organization's interests. Henry Ford promoted education in part due to the need to educate the largely immigrant workforce he employed in his factories. Third, the larger social domain in which organizations support good causes is complex and dynamic with many diverse interests. Corporations represent only one effort among many to address these social concerns, and cannot be expected to provide the sole or primary means of social support. Efforts by profit-making organizations to create good consequences, for example, should not replace the efforts of government, religious institutions, or social service agencies.

Because the area of social responsibility is so complex and dynamic, determining appropriate moral positions is always difficult. Often, when trying to determine what constitutes "good consequences," discussions of responsibility have digressed into debates among competing moral positions and motivates (Buono & Nichols, 1995). In some cases, managers have been accused of promoting self-serving agendas in the name of social responsibility. Critics also charge that the corporate responsibility is used as a mechanism to further a particular moral agenda. Often, they suggest, this agenda is centered around middle-class, capitalistic values that support the goals of profit-making organizations. For this reason, many organizational ethicists have abandoned the concept of *responsibility* in favor of a concept of *organizational responsiveness*.

Responsiveness, in this sense, refers to the ability and willingness of the organization to respond to social pressures (Buono & Nichols, 1995; Sethi, 1987). An organization is responsible when it takes account of particular social problems, pressures, and concerns. Responsiveness is more of a morally neutral term than responsibility because it emphasizes the technical capacity and willingness of corporations to adjust to society as reflected in the behavior of the organization. The question of specific moral motives is not as relevant. From the perspective of systems theory, responsiveness concerns the relative permeability of the organization's boundaries and its ability to anticipate and adjust to society's changing character in relation to the organization (Sethi, 1987). It is a function of organizational design, the background and skill of management, and how the organization views its relationship to the environment. Responsiveness allows the organization to focus on more specific issues and questions of social needs and problems rather than on broad philosophical questions of particular competing moralities.

Responsiveness and responsibility most often follow from one another. Sethi (1987), for example, suggested that the concepts of social obligation, social responsibility, and social responsiveness are stages in an organization's response to social concerns. Social obligation involves mere compliance with legal or market forces. Responsibility refers to meeting social expectations before they become part of the organization's legal or regulatory framework. Responsiveness refers to anticipatory and preventative efforts on the part of the organization. These efforts allow the organization to adapt to social values and problems in a dynamic fashion and work to resolve them at an early stage, before they become widespread. An organization may choose to install a waste recovery system as it builds new plants in anticipation of the potential problems of toxic emissions (Sethi, 1987). The ability to address social problems in a timely fashion is important to their effective resolution. As social problems become larger and more widespread, resolving them is correspondingly more difficult. Probably the best example of this relationship is the spread of HIV and AIDS. Initially, the disease was very limited. Failure to address the problem in a timely fashion allowed it to spread to epidemic proportions with massive social and economic costs.

THE ORGANIZATIONAL RESPONSIBILITY ARGUMENT

The debate concerning social responsibility has been intense partly because this issue focuses on the fundamental r*asion d' etre* of private organizations. From one perspective, the argument for organizational responsibility is very compelling. Organizations are part of society and have obligations to support the general development and health of society. Widely accepted social values, such as fairness, honesty, and equal treatment of individuals, is in the best interest of society. Organizations, because they are part of society, have an obligation to uphold basic principles of fairness and honesty. Beyond the fact that fairness and honesty benefit all of society, including organizations, many organizational ethicists argue that honesty and fairness are simply the "right" way to behave. A "good corporate citizen" is involved in the community and works to improve the community. This would include maintaining basic principles of honesty and fairness.

Similarly, organizations often support social values and interests because they are part of the community and are directly affected by these problems. Organizations often adhere to principles of environmental responsibility because of a general recognition that environmentalism is, in the long run, in the interest of the nation, society, and of the organization. Organizations may decide to become involved in the renewal of neighborhoods because the value of their property is threatened by urban decay. An organization may choose to support local arts organizations because of the economic impact of the arts on local economies. Providing summer jobs for youth may provide inexpensive labor and help in the training of future employees.

From another perspective, however, organizational critics have suggested that organizations have no obligation or even right to pursue so-called "good" consequences. As discussed in chapter 1, some critics have suggested that profit-making organizations only have an obligation to make a profit for their owners. Issues of right and wrong, moral and immoral, good and bad, should be set down in the legal and regulatory codes that all organizations must follow. Business leaders, some claim, do not have the experience or background to solve social problems and expecting them to do so compromises their legal and ethical obligation to make a profit. Social responsibility gets in the way of profit-making, reduces competitiveness, and may cloud a manager's sense of objectivity (Madsen & Shafritz, 1990). Compelling social problems should be addressed by government using the taxes paid by organizations. Organizational resources are limited and social needs are endless. The problems of homelessness, for example, could easily soak up the profits of several successful companies. Furthermore, managers might lose sight of economic goals in pursuing good ends and compromise sound business operations.

History shows that organizations are willing to accept at least some sense of obligation and responsibility to society and are generally willing to support the common good, particularly when they have a stake in the outcome. During times of war, for example, profit-making organizations have generally been very willing to make significant sacrifices to support the national war effort. Although it might be argued that long-term organizational profitability was significantly enhanced by these efforts, the initial justification was based on national security.

Probably one of the best examples of organizations responding to social needs is the general "community chest" movement of the early 19th century. This movement reflected a widespread recognition of the importance of social responsibility and the fact that profit-making organizations sometimes cause social ills. Organizations began banding together to provide a stable funding base for community organizations in the early 1900s. In 1918, the American Association for Community Organization was formed to provide coordination and standardization of community-based philanthropy. The community chest movement is often identified as a model of organizational responsibility because it promotes a sense of good corporate citizenship at several levels. First, the larger community benefits from the economic support of organizations. Private support is more flexible, and often more immediate than other forms of support. Second, the business person benefits from the connections and visibility associated with philanthropic involvement. This mutual benefit, then, is a two-way street, whereby the exchange between organizations and community is enhanced and the connections strengthened (Heald, 1970). Third, these connections help legitimize the organization by demonstrating its broader social value and creating broad-based constituencies of support beyond the organization's immediate markets (Pfeffer & Salancik, 1978). Finally, the extended networks precipitated by this social involvement have instrumental value in promoting organizational goals. The relationships formed in working on social issues and causes are often called on when seeking to enhance organizational profitability. In 1970, the community chest association became the United Way of America. The United Way continues the tradition of organizational philanthropy by sponsoring fundraising for charitable organizations in the workplace. Despite recent set backs from charges of mismanagement, the United Way remains a highly successfully manifestation of corporate philanthropy.

One common criticism of such philanthropic involvement is that it constitutes mere public relations in its most base form. Philanthropy allows the organization to provide the minimum level of support for social causes while ignoring all the negative consequences of profit-making enterprises. The organization is able to hide behind these trivial acts of philanthropy. The clearest and most famous example of such base philanthropy concerns John D. Rockefeller. This multimillionaire of the oil industry had developed a negative public image during the 1920s due largely to ruthless competition. His publicity agents began publicizing his good works including teaching Sunday school and handing out dimes to children (Josephson, 1934). These efforts at image management provided critics ample evidence to claim that Rockefeller's form of philanthropy was concerned with image more so than with substance. The modern image of the business executive handing a check to the local United Way Committee sometimes suffers the same criticism.

FORMS OF RESPONSIBILITY

One of the strengths of the organizational responsibility model of ethics is that it takes a variety of different forms in relation to many social needs, values, interests, problems, and concerns. Although these domains of social responsibility are potentially endless, most activities cluster in specific areas. These include responsibilities associated with philanthropy, products and services, workers, and the environment. In addition, specific communication responsibilities for organizations have recently emerged.

PHILANTHROPIC RESPONSIBILITY

The first, and one of the most widespread, forms of organizational responsibility concerns philanthropy. American profit-making organizations generally have an exceptional record of supporting worthwhile causes in a wide variety of areas including charities, education, programs for the poor and homeless, and the arts. This general willingness to support what are seen as worthwhile causes is due in part to the enhanced image that develops as a consequence. News footage of managers from Chrysler distributing free books to first-grade students in inner-city schools or of Dow chemical workers helping build homes on Indian reservations clearly makes good public relations. In many instances, it also assists in creating and maintaining legitimacy. These activities are often featured in public image campaigns as organizations seek to bolster their public persona. In other instances, however, these activities are done without the benefit of widespread publicity.

The widespread philanthropic activities of organizations first began as efforts to address the fundamental social ills of poverty, hunger, and disease. During the development of the Industrial Revolution, the consequences of widespread shifts from an agrarian, rural culture to a manufacturing, urban culture were profound. As society struggled to adjust, disease, hunger, and poverty were widespread and profit-making organizations often provided money and resources to help with these problems. The Great Depression created another round of poverty, hunger, and disease, and private organizations again provided support. This form of support eventually developed into the community chest movement discussed earlier. It also helped solidify a notion that organizations are responsible for helping to offset some of the social hardships they might create.

The concept of philanthropy, although initially seen as relating primarily to hunger, poverty, and disease, has broadened significantly to include many more activities. Social service organizations, arts groups, cultural societies, education, environmental groups, amateur sports, medical and community health organizations, and a broad range of groups and causes fitting under the general category of nonprofit, now classify as philanthropy. This has broadened the opportunity and diversity of organizational responsibility. This broadened definition of philanthropy has also meant that philanthropic causes and organizations compete with one another for a limited pool of organizational support. Organizations have also used their association with good causes in their product and issue advertising. Those organizations that support the U.S. Olympic teams often feature this association in ads. When organizations donate money to their arts, they are often recognized with public notices, plaques, and advertisements. This desire to link organizations to highly visible causes has meant that well-known causes and agencies have a greater likelihood of garnering philanthropy. Less well-known agencies and causes are less likely to benefit.

PRODUCT RESPONSIBILITY

A second form of responsibility concerns the nature of the product and service the organization produces. Product and service responsibility concerns the organization's market relationship to society. This market-place relationship represents one of the most prominent and important connections for organizations because the organization's product or service is one of its most visible outcomes. In addition, products and services are at the core of the organization's identity.

A responsible product or service may be defined as one that offers value and that is consistent with other social values. More specifically, however, a responsible product or service is one that does not pose a reasonable chance of harming the consumer. This last issue has received a great deal of attention from organizational ethicists because harmful products and services may create very costly legal liabilities. It is also a very dynamic arena as product liability and case law is continually changing. Liability concerns tort law, or laws related to civil wrongs, wrongs done by one person, or an organization, to another (Baron, 1993). Issues of liability arise from negligence, breach of warranty, strict liability, or due to proscriptions from specific laws, such as the Consumer Protection Act of 1972.

Negligence relates to an organization's failure to exercise reasonable care in providing goods or services that cause harm to consumers. An organization may be negligent and legally liable, for example, if it manufactures a product that is defective and causes injury to the consumers using the product. Sometimes organizations may be liable even if the product is used in a way other than is recommended.

Issues concerning warranty concern the claims, explicitly or implicitly, made about a product or service. These claims are the information on which a consumer chooses to purchase a product or service. The consumer has a reasonable expectation that the product or service will be consistent with these claims. When the product is inconsistent with the warranty, thereby causing an injury, the organization may be held liable. For example, cigarette manufacturers have been sued for smokers' deaths due to cancer because some of the early advertisements for cigarettes claimed that the product did not cause physical harm. In this instance, the advertisements created an express or implied warranty about the product. The principle of express and implied warranty may also sometimes create conditions where organizations are reluctant to communicate detailed information about their products for fear of creating a legal liability.

Strict liability concerns the general character of a product or service. This form of liability arises when a manufacturer places a product on the market that is, in some way, defective. Strict liability differs from negligence in that carelessness is not required. Moreover, the question of the manufacturer's fault is not considered. The courts do not consider issues of the manufacturer's fault, but rather are only concerned about whether the product or service is associated with the harm (Baron, 1993).

Tort law and the probability of serious legal consequences have made the issue of responsible products and service, at least from the standpoint of safety, an immediate concern of most profit-making organizations. Organizations often go to great lengths to construct products that are safe. They issue elaborate and detailed warnings and disclaimers about how their products and services should be used. Bright labels are attached in conspicuous places to further alert consumers of dangers. In several instances, organizations have stopped making products because the risk of liability was simply too high. In some instances, potentially lifesaving drugs have been removed from the market because of liabilities created by side effects. In such cases, society may be deprived of a valuable product or service because of the legal risks. Many observers have suggested that the legal liabilities associated with profit-making organizations are simply too great. To expect that products and services will have no risk of harm is simply unrealistic. These critics have pushed for significant changes in tort law to reduce organizational liability.

ENVIRONMENTAL RESPONSIBILITY

The idea that organizations have a fundamental responsibility to the environment has taken hold as a major organizational ethic since the 1970s and has captured the imagination of a number of groups, agencies, and organizations. Initially manifest primarily as a program of governmental regulation, concern for the environment has moved from the level of social obligation to social responsiveness. Many organizations are proactive in establishing their environmental ethic and even feature their records as "green organizations" in advertising (Makower, 1993). Product labels often emphasize the use of recycled contents, recyclability, use of nonpolluting manufacturing techniques, and general aspects of "environmental friendliness." Corporate image ads often suggest that an organization respects the environment and takes steps to ensure that the environment is not harmed by organizational activities.

Although environmentalism and conservation were common at the turn of the century, issues of the organization's responsibility to the environment first took hold as a general social concern in the late 1960s and early 1970s. Society was increasingly being made aware of the fact that many organizations produced significant amounts of pollutants as byproducts of their operations. Without any governmental regulation regarding how these byproducts were to be disposed of, organizations generally released them into the waters or air, or simply piled them up on company property. In many cases, the result was serious pollution. In several cases, the pollution created by manufacturing created serious health risks, birth defects, cancers, lung diseases, and a number of other health problems. Often, as with the pesticide DDT, the product itself caused environmental harm. The general decay of the environment, loss of species, and the harm to people became a powerful social issue in the late 1960s and early 1970s, probably as a consequence of the general enhanced social awareness.

In addition, several well-publicized industrial accidents dramatically illustrated both environmental and human vulnerability. News coverage of the Exxon oil spill in Prince William Sound featured pictures of sea birds and otters floundering in the huge oil slick. Economically important fishing areas were closed causing loss of jobs and general economic hardship (McGill, 1994). The explosion of the Union Carbide facility in Bhopal, India caused thousands of deaths. Many survivors suffered from nerve damage, blindness, respiratory damage, and birth defects. One of the most costly and deadly industrial accidents ever, the Chernobyl nuclear plant explosion, had the added feature of a radioactive threat (Makower, 1993). Those regions down wind of the Chernobyl plant dealt with radioactive fallout while those in the immediate vicinity faced radiation sickness, increased rates of cancers, and birth defects. These dramatic events added fuel to the environmental movement and established environmentalism as a primary ethical issue for organizations in the 1990s. They also solidified the link between environmentalism and human health. A number of environmental groups such as Earth First!, Green Peace, and the Sierra Club adopted strategies ranging from lobbying, protests, and issue management to *ecotauge* to pressure governments and organizations to adopt environmentally responsive practices and policies. These groups have been very successful in pushing the environmental agenda and raising public consciousness.

In the United States, the Environmental Protection Agency (EPA), the primary federal body responsible for setting and enforcing environmental policy, was formed by President Richard Nixon in 1970 by executive order. Several federal laws were also enacted at about the same time including the Clean Air Act (1963), the Solid Waste Disposal Acts (1965), the Water Quality Improvement Act (1970), the Safe Drinking Water Act (1974), the Resource Conservation and Recovery Act (1976), and several others (Baron, 1993). These and similar laws and regulations created a specific set of social obligations that organizations were legally bound to meet. Some companies claimed that such regulations, and the federal bureaucracy created to implement them, were overly restrictive and not rational. Critics pointed out that humankind had always exploited natural resources and polluted the environment. Most companies, however, have accepted some environmental responsibility and ceased at least the most obvious and dangerous forms of pollution. In other instances, organizations have adopted a very progressive social responsiveness model, seeking to proactively address environmental concerns.

Environmental social responsiveness goes beyond merely reducing pollutants. Many organizations are actively involved in extensive recycling and recovery programs. This usually involves not only identifying ways in which waste can be reduced, but using recycled materials in production and ensuring that products are labeled for future recycling. In many cases, companies have found that these actions create significant savings. Reducing waste often means streamlining packaging and reducing costs. Using recycled materials may also reduce costs. Processing outputs so that they may be used again in manufacturing reduces raw material costs and also eliminates the expense of disposal. The area of resource recovery and processing hazardous wastes has itself become a lucrative business creating an entirely new industry. Some observers see organizational waste as a new natural resource that can be exploited for its potential as a raw material.

Many observers point to the improving environmental record of organizations as the best evidence of a new environmentalism (Makower, 1993). This form of environmental ethics is characterized by strong public concern for environmental issues, the growth of green marketing and consumerism, broad diffusion and social acceptance of environment values, and increased governmental regulation concerning environmental issues. Makower pointed out that in a fundamental way, environmental ethics are universal and the environmental movement has been institutionalized. This does not suggest, however, that environmentalism is no longer an issue of organizational social responsibility. As long as organizations consume resources and produce waste, the questions of social responsibility to the environment will be present. The standards of environmental responsibility will also continue to rise as resources become more scarce. Environmentalism is well established as a central feature of the social responsibility agenda for organizations.

RESPONSIBILITY TO WORKERS

Another important area of social responsibility concerns the organization's relationship to employees. As discussed in chapter 7, the relationship between organizations and employees is very complex. Worker's rights, in particular, have been a contentious issue for many private organizations. Beyond issues concerning the specific rights of workers, organizational responsibility relates to a safe working environment and potential exploitation of workers.

As with environmental responsibility, the responsibility for creating a safe working environment was first manifest at the level of social obligation. The federal government first began regulating the conditions of the workplace in the 1930s. In 1970 the Occupational Safety and Health Administration (OSHA), as part of the Department of Labor, was created under public law 91-596. OSHA was given broad federal protection to create and enforce policies and "To assure safe and healthful working conditions for working men and women . . . to save lives, prevent injuries and protect the health of America's workers." Through the act, OSHA sets standards for safe working environments, enforces those standards, inspects work sites, and works to improve the safety of organizational technology and practice through technical assistance, education, and consultation.

In addition to concerns about worker safety, a more general set of social responsibilities relates to the exploitation of workers. As organizations have become increasingly international, several observers have raised questions about workers employed by companies based in the United States, but operating in developing countries. Many countries, such as India, China, and Bangladesh, have very lax labor laws when compared to those in the United States. Child labor is common in India and Bangladesh. China has been accused of maintaining labor camps where prison inmates are forced to manufacture goods. Many observers suggest that for an organization to participate in these sorts of activities constitutes irresponsible behavior. This issue was particularly salient during the recent debate about the North American Free Trade Agreement with Mexico. Critics charged that Mexico's labor and environmental laws were lax, and wages were low. U.S. companies, it was argued, would flock to Mexico where it was possible to exploit lax regulation and cheap labor. Many reports have surfaced of severe pollution in Mexican border towns. Most large U.S. corporations with manufacturing facilities in Mexico, however, have treated both the environment and workers responsibly.

COMMUNICATION RESPONSIBILITIES

In addition to other forms of social responsibility, organizations are increasingly recognized as having communication responsibilities. These responsibilities concern providing information to various groups, agencies, and constituencies. This information may concern the organization's activities, plans, production of pollution, and general social record. Some of these responsibilities have been encoded into federal law. Others exist as general norms and standards.

One specific communication responsibility is the Hazardous Communication Standard (HCS), supervised by OSHA, which requires employers to disclose certain types of information to workers. The current scope of the HCS is limited to chemical manufacturers, and importers and distributors who sell chemicals. Manufacturers are required to communicate safety data for all hazardous chemicals used in their workplaces to which employees may be exposed. The HCS provides workers exposed to chemicals with the "right to know" the chemicals' hazards and associated protective measures. This is accomplished through implementation of a hazard communication program in each workplace where employees are exposed to hazardous chemicals. Employers are required to ensure that hazardous chemicals are labeled with chemical identity, appropriate hazard warnings, and the name and address of the manufacturer (Occupational Health and Safety Administration, 1986).

A second specific communication responsibility arises from the Community Emergency Planning and Community Right to Know (EPCRA) Act of 1986. This act requires certain organizations to report the amount of hazardous substances they release into the environment (Makower, 1993). The current reporting requirements apply to facilities in the manufacturing sector that have 10 or more full-time employees, and that manufacture chemicals. The act is based on the premise that members of a community have a right to know what chemicals have been released into their immediate environment (EPA, 1993). The purpose of this requirement is to inform the public and government officials about chemical management practices of specified toxic chemicals. This critical information is necessary for them to make informed choices. Moreover, this information has been very useful to agencies and environmental groups interested in monitoring the environmental record of organizations

The EPA then uses this information to build its Toxic Release Inventory (TRI)—a database that provides information to the public about release of toxic chemicals from manufacturing facilities into the environment. The TRI is available to the media and the general public. Reports on annual releases and heavy polluters are increasingly common in the media and generate a great deal of attention and publicity. Community and environmental groups often use this information to pressure organizations to reduce their toxic emissions. These reports also call attention to environmental issues and the negative publicity they generate encourages organizations to continue to reduce emissions.

More generally, a recent development in the communication responsibilities of organizations has taken the form of corporate social reporting. "Social reporting is the process of communicating the social and environmental effects of organization's economic actions to particular interest groups or to society at large" (Gray, Owen, & Maunders, 1987, p. ix). Much as an organization produces an annual report and financial statement, some profit making organizations are now producing a public report of their social record. This report may be part of the actual annual report or may be an entirely separate report. In either case, the goals are to improve public relations, respond to the concerns and interests of specific constituencies, and generally increase managerial awareness and responsiveness (Preston, 1981).

Some traditional accounting firms will undertake the task of provide a "social accounting" of a firm's activities. These reports most often focus on the areas of community involvement, human resources, physical and environmental contributions, and product and service contributions. Community involvement includes philanthropy, housing, hunger programs, and education. Human resources focuses on employment practices, training programs, pay, and employee–employer communication. Physical and environmental issues include air, water, solid waste, recycling, and aesthetics. Product and services relates to product labeling, product quality, and design and research (Riahi-Belkaoui & Pavlik, 1992). In some cases, social corporate accounting has more specific goals. During the 1980s, for example, the accounting firm of Arthur D. Little established criteria to assess the activities of U.S. corporations doing business in South Africa. The subsequent reports generated by Little were designed to assess the degree to which these organizations were operating responsibly in light of the South African apartheid system of government (Sullivan, 1987). Although these reports were sometimes criticized as inaccurate, they did provide an independent assessment of social responsibility.

Social performance reporting is a new field involving a very small proportion of private, profit-making firms. The development of this activity, however, suggests that these activities are important to both organizations and their constituencies. In some ways, corporate social reporting (CSR) is a natural extension of the well established CEO annual letter to the stockholder where important developments and issues including social issues, are discussed. On the other hand, CSR gives further support to the view that organizations are accepting their roles as members of society and should communicate regularly with society.

SUMMARY

Organizations are members of society and have responsibilities to serve as forces for social good. Although there is debate about the organization's specific responsibilities, there is general consensus that organizations have obligations to pursue "good works," and be "good corporate citizens." The specific responsibilities associated with private organizations include philanthropy, environmentalism, treatment of employees, and characteristics of the product or service. In addition, the organization's responsibilities concerning communication include communicating information about the release of toxic chemicals, and about worker exposure to hazardous substances. Many organizations are going further and provide detailed reports of their social activities that are then disseminated to constituent groups.

Although corporate responsibility remains a somewhat controversial idea, it is a specific and useful way of discussing the ethical issues and obligations that organizations face. When managers are able to frame their ethical imperatives as specific responsibilities, and target specific resources for these responsibilities, the complex and equivocal issues of right and wrong are more manageable. This is one reason organizational responsibility remains a widespread and useful framework for organizational ethics.

CASE: SOCIAL RESPONSIBILITY REPORTING AT AT&T

A number of organizations have begun featuring some form of social reporting in their annual report. These reports most often describe the organization's good works including community service, philanthropy, and environmental activism. On the next page is reprinted AT&T's report on social activities entitled "We keep our Word" from its 1994 annual report.

We Keep Our Word

One reason we're confident we can succeed in the global information age is that we know how to set ambitious goals and make good on them. Our financial results are evident on the following pages. Here are some other goals we set for ourselves and how we have performed against them. As a result of our progress against these goals, we begin 1995 in a better position to serve customers and the communities in which we live and work.

Reduce reportable toxic air emmissions 95 percent by year-end 1995.

As 1994 began, our toxic air emissions worldwide were 92 percent lower than when we established our goal in 1987. We also met our commitment to phase out ozone-depleting chlorofluorocarbon (CFC) emissions from manufacturing operations — 19 months ahead of schedule.

Recycle 60 percent of our paper by year-end 1994 and reduce our use of paper 15 percent from 1990 levels.

We exceeded our goal before 1994, recycling 63 percent of our waste paper (48 million pounds) and reducing our use of paper by 28 percent.

Improve the diversity profile of our workforce to better serve the needs of our diverse customer base.

Some 35 percent of management employees hired in 1994 were women, and 28 percent, minorities. The representation of these groups in the officer ranks is also up sharply: 12 percent are now women and nearly 10 percent are minorities.

Increase our purchases from U.S. businesses owned by minorities and women by 10 percent.

We surpassed our goal, increasing such purchases by 34 percent while deriving additional sales and savings benefits from these relationships.

Increase our support of community organizations and projects outside the United states in areas where AT&T has a major presence.

In 1994, the AT&T Foundation increased its grants outside the United States by 66 percent, providing $1.3 million to nonprofit and charitable groups in the areas of education, health and human services, and the arts. Worldwide, the Foundation has awarded some $329 million in grants since its inception in 1984. In addition, the AT&T University Equipment Donation Program has supplied $287 million in AT&T computer equipment to colleges and universities since 1984.

Discussion Questions

1. What social values are evident in this report?
2. What claims are made (implicit and explicit) about organizational operations in relation to these values?
3. What measures of corporate performance are offered?

9

Stakeholder Perspectives

A relatively recent development in the theory of organizational ethics is the stakeholder model. The model is a reconceptualization of the organization, where the corporation is seen as a compilation of the interests of many diverse individuals and groups. These groups each have a vested interest, or stake, in the organization and consequently, their needs, values, interests, and perspectives should be taken into account in setting the organization's goals, directions, and methods. The stakeholder model of the organization is a sharp contrast to the traditional stockholder model that views a private organization as existing for the benefit of the owners—those who own the organization's stock. The stakeholder model has important implications for the control of organizations, representation on boards, committees and management, and for the communication between the organization and its larger environment.

This chapter examines the stakeholder model—its roots in systems theory, its linkages to communication and public relations, and its utility as a framework for examining questions of macro-organizational ethics. The problem of stakeholder identification is explored along with the problem of balancing stakeholder needs and interests. The manager's role as representative of stakeholder interests is also discussed and specific stakeholder forums for soliciting input are explored. In addition, the question of diversity in organizations is examined within the framework of the stakeholder model.

STAKEHOLDERS AND SYSTEMS THEORY

The concept of *organizational stakeholder* derives from two traditions: general systems theory and the concept of the stockholder as the owner of the organization. First, systems theory emphasizes the concept of the organization's suprasystem or environment. Early systems theorists focused on the organization's environment as a primary factor in determining the organization's structure, design, technology, size, physical location, and, ultimately, success (Katz & Kahn, 1966). Not surprisingly, a significant amount of theory and research went into describing organizational environments and their effect on the organization (Pfeffer & Salancik, 1978). Some theorists described the environment in terms of the technological conditions, which determine the appropriate form of technology (Woodward, 1965). Others described the general structure of the environment, suggesting that homogeneous environments were easier to cope with than heterogeneous environments (Dill, 1958). Researchers also turned their attention to the affect the environment has on the organization, particularly on its managers. Duncan (1972) demonstrated that organizational environments created various levels of perceived uncertainty for organizational members. This perceived uncertainty about the environment affected their ability to make effective decisions.

The stakeholder model is a natural outgrowth of this work. In seeking to characterize the specific environment of organizations, theorists concluded that there are constituent groups who interact with or who have an interest in the organization. These groups closely follow the organization's activities; have specific interests in the organization's success; are connected to the organization; and are important sources of resources, information, and support.

Stakeholders are individuals and groups who are, or who are likely to be, "directly affected by the decisions of the corporation or have an explicit contractual relationship with it. Thus, they are said to have a stake, or an interest in the corporation" (Brummer, 1991, p. 144). Freeman (1984), one of the early proponents of the stakeholder approach, argued that stakeholders are not only groups affected by the company, but also represent groups that can affect the organization. These groups, for example, might withhold resources and support, limit the firm's access to new markets, or boycott the organization's products. Understanding stakeholders, therefore, is necessary to understanding the organization's larger strategic context, conducting effective planning, and carrying out strategic management.

A second set of influences on the stakeholder model is derived from the traditional stockholder model of organizations. Traditional perspectives assert that organizations exist for the economic benefit of the owners. Stockholders have special privileges and access to the organization in recognition of their ownership. Profit-making organizations prepare annual reports for stockholders detailing their activities and performance for the past year. Annual meetings allow the stockholder to question managers and to vote on various initiatives. Many organizations even have specific public relations campaigns directed toward stockholders that seek to ensure that relations with this group are strong. Managers, from this perspective, serve as the agents of the owners. They are expected to manage the organization with the best interests of the owners in mind.

The stakeholder model seeks to broaden the definition of organization beyond stockholder interests and economic concerns (Freeman, 1984). The assumptions underlying the stakeholder model, however, go beyond the simple proposition that the organization's environment is composed of groups and individuals who have a stake in the organization. Stakeholder proponents argue that the interests, needs, and concerns of these constituencies should be taken into account in the organization's decision-making and problem-solving process. Although there is a significant level of variance as to how the interests of stakeholders should weigh in relation to stockholders, there is general agreement that their interests should be heard. The task of managers is to "manage stakeholder relations in a way that achieves the purposes of business" (Freeman & Gilbert, 1987, p. 397).

DEFINING STAKEHOLDERS

One of the difficulties the stakeholder model creates concerns what groups constitute the stakeholders for an organization. Some proponents of the stakeholder model have argued that all of society has a stake in the outcomes of organizations and, consequently, define stakeholders quite broadly. Some theorists have even sought to extend stakeholder status to nonhuman groups (Starik, 1995; Stone, 1992). Most, however, reject these views as too broad and focus on a much more limited set of identifiable stakeholders. The primary criteria used to identify stakeholders is that they "are directly affected by corporate conduct" (Brummer, 1991, p. 147). The initial set of decisions that must be addressed in using a stakeholder view is what constitutes direct affect.

Direct affects can occur as a consequence of intentional action of the organization, unintentional action, intentional inaction, or unintentional inaction. In some instances, the affects of an organization's action may even go undiscovered for some time. Most often, direct effect is operationalized as the regular exchange of goods, services, information, resources, and messages between the organization and external groups and individuals.

While the question of who should be included as a stakeholder is complex, most proponents of this model suggest the following groups: stockholders, workers, consumers, suppliers, creditors, competitors, governmental agencies, professional groups, and local communities (Brummer, 1991; Freeman, 1984; Freeman & Gilbert, 1987). These groups and their most prominent interests in the organization are outlined in Table 9.1.

CHARACTERISTICS OF STAKEHOLDERS

Although the notion of stakeholders initially seems simplistic, this model is complex and dynamic. It also has important implications for questions of organizational and communication ethics. These include stakeholders as opportunities and constraints, stakeholders as audiences for organizational messages, stakeholders as complex and multifaceted groups, the manager as a representative of stakeholder interests, and problems in balancing stakeholder interests.

One of the most fundamental features of stakeholders is that they represent both opportunities and constraints on organizational activities (Freeman, 1984). They are sources of critical resources and support, markets for goods, and sources of information that organizations need to operate. At the same time, however, stakeholders constrain organizations by forcing compliance and limiting the organization's activities in some areas. Stockholders, for example, may seek to limit certain risky organizational ventures while at the same time providing the financial capital necessary for expansion. Environmental groups might pressure organizations to use more environmentally friendly technologies while at the same time publicly acknowledge and support environmentally responsible organizations.

A second feature of the concept of *stakeholder* is its similarity to the concept of public from *public* relations. A public constitutes an audience for organizational messages. A public is an identifiable group that has a vested interest in the organization. *Public* and *stakeholder* are based on the same premise, and both emphasize the communication connections between organizations and their environment (L. Grunig,

9.1. Stakeholders and Their Interests.

Stakeholders	Primary Stakeholder Interests
Stockholders	Profitability of firm, dividends, stability of the firm, value of stock. Secondary interests (i.e., specific values: retirement benefits, community involvement, philanthropy, etc.)
Workers	Economic gain, job stability, opportunity for growth and promotions, benefits, working conditions, nature of work, supervisor and employee climate, retirement benefits. Secondary interests (i.e., specific values: community involvement, philanthropy, etc.)
Consumers	Continual supply of goods and services, product value, product support. Secondary interests (i.e., specific values: environmental impact, community involvement, etc.)
Suppliers	Markets and market stability for products and services, market growth, cooperation with organization. Secondary interest: organizational support
Creditors	Return of capital investment, risk-free or low-risk relationship, future lending opportunities, cooperative relationship. Secondary interests (i.e., specific values: environmental impact, community involvement, etc.)
Competitors	Stability, predictability, and limitation of competitive environment, "fair" competition.
Governmental agencies	Compliance of firm with regulations, cooperation with regulatory agency, economic stability. Secondary interests (i.e., specific values: environmental impact, community involvement, etc.)
Professional groups	Clients for continual representation, compliance with professional norms
Local community	Stability of community, tax base, support of other local groups, environmental responsibility, aesthetics of plants and facilities, continued opportunity for growth

Grunig, & Ehling, 1992). With publics, the emphasis is generally placed on a group as the audience or receiver of organizational messages (Newsom, Scott, & Turk, 1989). With stakeholders, the emphasis is usually placed on managers both sending messages to and receiving messages from stakeholders as organizations continually negotiate their relationships with external groups. Some theorists have also argued that publics are more aware and are more active than stakeholders (J. Grunig & Repper, 1992). Freeman and Gilbert (1987) noted "The stakeholder approach spreads the traditional PR role among every manager responsible for formulating strategic programs, where multiple stakeholders must be taken into account" (p. 415). Stakeholder status is not merely a function of those groups that have a vested interest in the organization. It is also constituted around the ongoing exchange of messages. This notion is also consistent with other work examining organizations and their environments. Many theorists view the relationship as a dialectic of mutual communication and influence where the environment and the organization simultaneously act on one another (Dirsmith & Covaleski, 1983; Zeitz, 1980).

A third characteristic of this model relates to the complexity of stakeholders. Most theorists point out that these groups and individuals have complex and often contradictory perspectives, needs, and motivations. Freeman (1984) argued that the organization's external environment is a rich, multistakeholder context, with contradictory interests competing with one another. Employees, for example, are not a homogenous group, but may represent a variety of cultural, ethnic, professional, union, and political interests. They may also hold company stock and consume company products. As discussed in chapter 2, the values and norms of stakeholders are also very dynamic, interacting in complex, unpredictable, and equivocal ways. Organizational critics sometimes buy stock so that they can express their criticism more directly to management. Employees may belong to environmental groups. This rich, multistakeholder context significantly complicates how organizations interact with and manage stakeholder relations. Cheney (1992), for example, pointed out that because organizations face multiple and complex audiences, they must present different faces to different publics. Stockholders are most often interested in the face of profitability, whereas employees are interested in job security. One critical process for an organization involves managing these complex and sometimes contradictory, multiple identities. In so doing, organizations sometimes seek to play one stakeholder interest off against another (Pfeffer & Salancik, 1978). Corporations may argue, for example, that concerns about profitability (stockholder interests) overshadow concerns about job security (employee interests). Interests of retirees for stable benefits may be used to offset the demands of employees for raises. The stakeholder model requires a delicate weighing and balancing of these conflicting needs and interests.

An additional characteristic of the stakeholder model is its emphasis on the role of manager as a representative of stakeholder interests. Managers are expected to serve as the internal representatives of the various stakeholder groups. As such, they are both public relations officers and boundary agents. Managers represent the organization to stakeholder groups, serving as a conduit for important information and messages about the organization. They interpret organizational information and messages for stakeholders, and seek to clarify and strengthen the relationship between stakeholders and the organization. They must also represent stakeholders to the organization. This includes collecting important information from stakeholders, synthesizing and transmitting that information to appropriate organizational divisions and members, and interpreting stakeholder messages for the organization (Aldrich & Herker, 1977).

Freeman (1984) provided several useful propositions in exploring management's role in the stakeholder model. He suggested reorienting "our thinking externally in order to be responsive to stakeholders" (p. 74). The interaction should be voluntary, and based on cooperation, communication, and negotiation. Organizations should communicate and "explicitly negotiate with stakeholders on critical issues and seek voluntary agreements" (p. 78). Freeman pointed out that voluntary processes are not only more consistent with our general social structures but are also much less costly than other approaches such as regulation, boycotts, or litigation. Negotiation and communication, he noted, elicit cooperative relationships between stakeholders and organizations. Investing in cooperative relationships is warranted because these groups ultimately help determine the organization's success. Boundary-spanning communication, public relations, public affairs, and marketing should be incorporated into the strategic formulations of the organization to help ensure cooperative relations. Freeman (1984) also suggested that managers "anticipate stakeholder concerns and try to influence the stakeholder environment" (p. 79).

Freeman and Gilbert (1987) suggested that management needs to be refocused into the role of external affairs manager. This role involves five tasks:

1. Identifying new stakeholders or calling attention to stakeholders whom other managers have overlooked.
2. Beginning the process of explicitly formulating strategies with these stakeholders.
3. Helping to integrate the concerns of multiple stakeholders.
4. Negotiating with key stakeholders on issues of mutual. concern.
5. Searching for new issues and illuminating new concerns for other managers in the firm (pp. 415–416).

A final characteristic of the stakeholder model relates to the inevitable problem of balancing stakeholder interests and concerns. The various stakeholder interests, needs, and values will, inevitably, come into conflict. Weighing these conflicting demands in relations to one another falls on the shoulders of managers. In many instances, managers are forced to make very difficult choices between the needs of various stakeholders. Some critics have suggested that this balancing is where the stakeholder model unravels; that such balancing is simply not possible with complex firms that face diverse and often contradictory stakeholder interests. The model assumes a level of agreement among stakeholders that simply does not exist. Freeman, however, suggested that managers prioritize stakeholders, ranking organizations according to their level of importance in determining the firm's success. Organizational resources should then be allocated accordingly. Others suggest that effective stakeholder management involves cooptation— where members of stakeholder groups are brought into the organization. DeGeorge (1986b), for example, argued that multinational organizations can benefit by hiring managers from the countries within which they operate. This helps ensure that local values, needs, and perspectives are taken into account.

STAKEHOLDERS AND DIVERSITY

The logical extension of the stakeholder model creates implications for diversity in organizations. As society has become more diverse and has created greater opportunities for women, minorities, and people of diverse ethnicity, backgrounds, orientations, and abilities, organizations have been forced to both accommodate new groups of workers and new environmental constituencies. Demographic data indicates the age of the homogeneous workforce is over. The Workforce 2000 study concluded that by the year 2000, over half of the new workers will be women, African Americans, Hispanics, Asian Americans, or immigrants (Johnson & Packer, 1987). The changes in the workforce and in the organization's larger environment has created a great deal of uncertainty and equivocality for organizations. Issues of racial and ethnic diversity are highly complex and sensitive and can be interpreted from a number of divergent perspectives. Stakeholder approaches have been very useful to organizations seeking to sort out these conflicting interpretations.

Management, according to the stakeholder view, should be broadly representative of stockholders and their interests. Management should also be sufficiently diverse to reflect the diversity of stakeholder interests. Those organizations with significant minority stakeholders should, therefore, incorporate managers who are minorities. This diversity and linkage to stakeholder groups can also be accommodated by boards, advisory panels, community meetings, and similar forums. Boards of directors, for example, many be constituted to include diverse stakeholder interests. This may include union, creditor, suppliers, and community representatives, as well as members of ethnic, racial, and other groups. Advisory panels of consumers sometimes are created to advise managers. Community advisory boards are created to assess stakeholder concerns. These and related activities increase the ability of the managers to accurately represent the diversity of stakeholder needs, interests, and values. These linkages to diverse elements of society and inclusions of diversity within the organization increases the ability of the organization to represent and take into account stakeholder needs and interests.

Diversity has also created a new communication-based ethic that embraces differences, values pluralistic perspectives, and seeks to broaden avenues of opportunity. Diversity enriches social contexts where individual contributions and dignity are celebrated and where divergent contributions are encouraged. This ethic is based in part on the lingering social and institutional exclusiveness inherited from decades of systematic racial, gender, and cultural discrimination. It also derives from the larger value of human dignity and the pragmatics of a changing social contexts. The ethic of diversity requires that individuals from various ethnic, racial, and gender backgrounds communicate with one another so that they may come to appreciate each other's views. The ethic of diversity is particularly challenging in this regard because communication between heterogeneous individuals is generally more complex than when individuals are homogeneous. Similarity of communicators is rewarding as an interaction variable and tends to encourage interactions between individuals who are alike (Berscheid & Walster, 1978). The potential pool of information and the value of that information, however, is likely to be much greater when individuals who are diverse interact. Diversity, from this view, has a very pragmatic side in that it allows individuals to understand and function in a multicultural world.

Despite changing demographics, social pressure, and pragmatic arguments, some critics argue that the core of American society is still Eurocentric. The columnist George Will (1989), for example, argued that America should be "Eurocentric" at its most basic. This legacy has resulted in a successful and admirable society that should not be rejected simply because of its Western origins. Proponents of multiculturalism counter by noting that the Eurocentric view is incomplete. While this debate has developed, most organizations have recognized that in a society where markets, employees, investors, and communities are diverse, these diverse stakeholders must be represented in the organization.

STAKEHOLDERS, ENACTMENT, AND ETHICS

Although the complexities and dynamic components of the stakeholder model create some problems, particularly with regard to the role of management, the model has two important strengths. First, the model emphasizes an external orientation. Second, the model is a useful framework for organizational communication ethics. Management is conceptualized as fulfilling a boundary spanning, public relations, and external affairs function. This external orientation, in turn enhances the ability of managers to perceive and take into account larger social definitions and questions of right–wrong, good–bad, desirable–undesirable. The stockholder model enhances the ability of the organization to enact its environment particularly with regard to values and ethics.

The stakeholder model complements the framework of organizational enactment. As discussed in chapter 2, Weick's (1989) model suggests that organizing reduces the equivocality of informational inputs. This is accomplished through enactment (acting toward an equivocal situation), selection (selecting from among a pool of alternative responses and interpretations), and retention (retaining those interpretations useful in reducing equivocality). When organizations systematically identify their stakeholders, the organization also acts toward, or enacts, these groups. Stakeholder processes are also helpful in selection and retention because they potentially increase organization's requisite variety. Weick (1989) observed "It's because of requisite variety that organizations have to be preoccupied with keeping sufficient diversity inside the organization to sense accurately the variety present in ecological changes outside it" (p. 188). When organizations incorporate a variety of stakeholder characteristics, they are better able to the reduce the equivocality of messages from those stakeholder groups.

In addition to its implications for the capacity of enactment, the stakeholder model is useful in examining organizational ethics. Freeman and Gilbert (1987) suggested that organizations by definition must take into account values, and in particular, the values constituted within external stakeholder groups. They suggested that the traditional external, values-based framework, corporate social responsibility, is too general to be of utility. Frameworks for organizational ethics should include "rights and duties, consequences and values all of which refer to specific strategic [stakeholder] actors" (p. 105). Identifying specific and identifiable stakeholder groups allows the organization to operate in a manner consistent with the values of that groups. Freeman (1984) argued that the concept of stakeholder is a natural progression from corporate social responsibility and responsiveness.

The stakeholder model suggests a particular kind of organizational ethic based on communication. Organizations should be open to stakeholder groups, and should actively seek to take the diverse needs, interests, and values of these groups into account. The process whereby such openness occurs involves communication, cooperation, and negotiation. Managers and stakeholders engage in a dialectic exchange of messages, perspectives, and information. Such openness is desirable and ethical because it is inclusive of groups, individuals, and interests who have a stake in the organization. Moreover, stakeholder theorists argue that a stakeholder approach results in more effective strategic management including greater stability and cooperation in external relations. It also requires that the organization operate in conjunction with sets of concerns and needs that go beyond economic interest. This is a particularly important shift that responds to the most common criticism of profit-making organizations. An organization managed according to stakeholder interests is concerned with more than profits.

SUMMARY

The stakeholder model represents a fundamental reconceptualization of the organization that contrasts to the traditional stockholder model. The stakeholder model expands the basic premise of the organization beyond profit-making concerns. Managers are expected to manage the organization with the needs interests, and perspectives of diverse stakeholders in mind. This requires diversity or requisite variety matched to the variety of the organization's environment. The stakeholder model emphasizes the values of openness, plurality of background and perspectives, cooperation, negotiation, and communication
The stakeholder model can be criticized on several grounds. Some observers suggest that it calls for an unrealistic balancing of diverse needs and interest. Others suggest that its creates confusion about who owns the company, conflict, and lack of coherent goals. In an increasingly diverse world where more demands are placed on institutions, the stakeholder model represents a powerful and comparatively concrete way of conceptualizing the organization's macroscopic communication responsibilities.

CASE: STAKEHOLDER PROFILES, VALUES, AND EXPECTATIONS

During the last few years, many colleges and universities have undertaken elaborate strategic planning initiatives. These include systematically examining where the organization is positioned in relation to important stakeholder groups, identifying the ways in which the organization interacts (exchanging information and resources) with stakeholders, and clarifying the expectations and values stakeholders have for the college or university. Often, elaborate stakeholder maps are constructed to help members visualize the relationship between the organization and these groups. Members are often encouraged to meet with stakeholders so that expectations and values can be clarified. These efforts are generally seen as allowing colleges and universities to be more successful in serving stakeholder needs.

Discussion Questions

1. Using your college or university as an example, identify and describe the primary stakeholder groups.
2. How do these stakeholders interact with the university or college? What expectations and values do they have for your school?
3. What sorts of information in what message form do these stakeholders receive?

10

Ethics and Advertising

One form of organizational communication that has generated much ethical debate is advertising. Advertising is the planned effort to communicate and persuade about issues, products, and services. It is not only one of the most common forms of organizational communication, it is also the means whereby most of us come to know about organizations—their products, services, and the issues that affect them. Advertising has also been scrutinized regarding basic ethical standards including accuracy, completeness, honesty, and appropriateness. Concerns about ethics in advertising led to the Federal Trade Commission (FTC) Act that regulates these messages. Despite extensive regulation, advertising still represents an area where ethical questions are common.

This chapter reviews the ethics of issue and product advertising as a macro form of organizational communication. Specifically, this form of communication is viewed as persuasion. Issue and product advertising raise specific questions about honesty, accuracy, completeness, as well as more general questions about appropriateness, undue influence, and the promotion of materialism, and the creation of consumer needs. Because advertisements are widely disseminated public messages, they also have particular importance in organizational enactment.

ADVERTISING

Advertising has a very long history, tracing its roots back to "criers" of the Middle Ages who called out to customers notifying them of the goods available from shops, markets, or street venders. "A vender's cry, somewhere between speech and song, typically remains unchanged for many years and is passed down from generation to generation" (Dixon, 1994, p. 15). Criers framed their messages as songs or poems to increase the appeal and recall of the message. These songs would include much detailed information about the availability, price, and quality of specific goods. The Guilds, which oversaw various trades, often regulated this early form of advertising, specifying how many criers could be employed by any single craftsperson, who can cry, when, and where (Dixon, 1994).

Today, advertising is a complex, multibillion dollar industry encompassing all forms of media outlets including film, video, direct mail, television, newspaper, magazine, newsletters, radio, computer, billboards, flyers, sponsorship of special events, celebrity endorsements, as well as dozens of other, traditional and nontraditional channels of communication. Advertising is typically defined as "paid, non-personal communication forms used with persuasive intent by identified sources through various media" (Sandage, Fryburger, & Rotzoll, 1983, p. 5). As a paid form of communication, advertising seeks to maximize the impact of these messages. Advertising is "nonpersonal" in the sense that it is directed toward large audiences through channels of mass communication. As a form of persuasion, it seeks to change attitudes and behaviors.

PERSUASION AND ETHICS

Ethics and persuasion have been subjects of much discussion, research, and criticism in the communication field (Johannesen, 1990; Nilsen, 1974). *Persuasion* is traditionally defined as "the process whereby one person or group affects, influences, or changes another person or group" (Littlejohn, 1992, p. 133). As discussed in chapter 1, questions of ethics were central features in the classical approaches to persuasion developed by the Greeks and Romans who argued that emotional and logical appeals should be balanced. It is a central feature of social interaction, including convincing others to think or behave in different ways, inducing change or acceptance of new ideas, procedures, and activities, as well as influencing the purchase of goods and services. Persuasion also relates to the general efforts to induce acceptance or support for organizations. This work largely focuses on information processing and cognition and views persuasion as the consequence or outcomes of processing information, appeals, and arguments. Other definitions of persuasion have sought to be more inclusive in examining the concept of *persuasion* and have broadened the focus beyond the speaker/message to emphasize the receiver/context.

The central questions concerning ethics in persuasion relate to both process and motivation. In general, persuasion theorists from classical Greece on have suggested that advocacy, seeking to persuade others to a particular position, can facilitate the discovery of truth. Advocacy contributes to the available pool of information, perspectives, and arguments, to the critical examination of these, and, ultimately to the selection of the best. Persuasion contributes to the functioning of the open marketplace of ideas. Where truth is the value or motivation, persuasion, from this perspective, is generally considered ethical (Johannesen, 1990). Politicians, arguing about funding for particular programs or passage of specific legislation, contribute to the complete examination of proposals and the discovery of truth. Corporations seeking to market products within a competitive environment also contribute to the available pool of information and the discovery of truth. Advertising contributes to the diversity of consumer choices and the available information needed by consumers to make fully informed choices (Collins, 1992). Advocates of advertising often note that it is a form of speech, and as such, enjoys some protection in a free and open society. The courts have accepted this argument and extended some free speech protections with the commercial speech doctrine.

Using these principles, it is possible to generate comparatively specific guidelines for ethics in persuasion. For example, persuasive processes that promote openness, completeness, and truthfulness would serve the goal of discovering truth. Full and rational debate using sound reasoning and argument also contributes to truth. Any communication strategies or procedures that limit complete honesty and openness would not be judged as ethical. This includes withholding information, distorting facts, silencing critics, and limiting or stifling discussion and debate. Providing only incomplete or general information may be judged as deceptive because it may lead to a false conclusion (Johannesen, 1990).

This view of persuasion ethics also emphasizes the ability of individuals to make free choices. Messages that deceive or distort may limit free, informed choice. Similarly, those messages that feature an explicit threat are often judged as coercive. A threat to physical or economic harm or a fear appeal, for example, may limit the ability of persuadees to carefully and rationally consider a message. In these instances, the specific strategies used in the process of persuasion are unethical. This is the basic principle that undergirds the judgment that propaganda is unethical. Cunningham (1992) pointed out that "the propagandist's attitude toward truth is inherently equivocal: He or she will use either truthful information or misinformation depending upon which is most likely to succeed . . ." (p. 237). Truthfulness is not the central consideration in constructing propaganda. Parallels can easily be drawn to some advertising where the question of truthfulness and accuracy are sometimes outweighed by questions about the utility of various persuasive strategies.

ADVERTISING AND ETHICS

Ethics in advertising are frequent topics of discussion by critics, advertisers, regulators, and consumers (Ferrell, 1985; Johannesen, 1990; Laczniak & Murphy, 1981). Issues include the amount of free choice in advertising, the accuracy and completeness of the information, the general content of the messages, and the degree to which advertising creates false needs (Miller, 1992). Critics often point out that advertising messages, considering volume alone, are so overwhelming as to have a profound influence on society. Maintaining some fundamental adherence to ethical principles in advertising, then, is a particularly important goal.

The issue of advertising and control concerns the degree to which the target audience for advertisements are somehow controlled by those messages (Miller, 1992). Subliminal advertising—messages which are designed to appeal to the receiver's subconscious—are often cited as examples of such "controlling" messages (Key, 1973). Because subliminal messages are said to appeal to the subconscious, they exert a more fundamental level of influence on receivers. Although there is little evidence that subliminal ads are actually effective in changing behavior or attitudes, these messages do raise ethical issues about the persuadees' ability to critically evaluate messages (McDaniel, Hart, & McNeal 1983; Moore, 1982). If messages operate below the level of consciousness, the receiver cannot critically evaluate the appeals.

Similar arguments are made about advertising directed to children. Because young children have more limited ability to weigh persuasive arguments, discriminate and evaluate appeals, and make informed choices, they are more susceptible to advertisements (Laczniak & Murphy, 1981). Some types of advertisements may then be judged as inappropriate or even unethical when targeted to children. Television commercials that confuse programming with commercials, for example, are discouraged by the Federal Communications Commission (FCC). Television cartoons sometimes feature characters and accessories that are also marketed as consumer products. Young children may not be able to distinguish between those advertisements designed to be persuasive and programming designed for entertainment. In addition, children have a more limited ability to weigh and evaluate persuasive messages. In one case, "Spiderman Vitamins" associated the strength of the cartoon character Spiderman with the vitamin product. Critics pointed out that young children might be tempted to take more than the recommended dose in hopes of acquiring super powers (Miller, 1992).

Similarly, the Camel cigarette advertising campaign featuring the camel cartoon character "Old Joe" is often criticized on the grounds that it appeals to young children. Cigarettes, of course, should not be marketed to children and the tobacco industry makes explicit claims that they do not engage in such marketing practices. Research has shown, however, that the "Old Joe" campaign has strong appeal to young children. The "Old Joe" character has a higher recognition rate among young children than does the cartoon character "Mickey Mouse" (Fischer, Schwartz, Richards, Goldstein, & Rojas, 1991).

Although most observers reject the notion that advertising exerts any direct control over the receivers of the messages, they point out that our society is dominated by thousands of sophisticated consumer messages. Miller (1992) reported that each person receives about 1,600 advertising messages each day. Given this mass of persuasive messages, it is reasonable to suggest that these messages exert a very profound influence on behavior.

Related to the issue of control is the issue of ethics and deception. Although the 1933 Wheeler Amendment to the FTC limited the most obvious deceptive messages, some advertisers are very adept at creating messages that mislead, distort, confuse, or deceive (Collins, 1992). General appeals, puffery in describing products, and misleading images are common features of much commercial advertising. In the confines of a 30-second commercial, the strict and complete truth is often left on the cutting room floor in favor of flashy images and powerful emotional appeals.

Deception, as it relates to adverting, can be defined in a variety of ways. Lying, for example, is a form of deception that involves a strategic deception that the communicator knows is false. A more common form of deception in advertising occurs when the advertiser causes consumers to have false impressions about the products or service (Miller, 1992). Advertisers may leave out critical details, emphasize some features over others, or provide misleading images. Lending institutions, for example, sometimes promote the idea of "fast and easy money" through home equity loans. Details about exorbitant interest rates and the possibility of foreclosure in the case of default are left out. Health insurers have sometimes promoted their products to the elderly by providing misleading information about the cost of health care and the availability of medicare while leaving out important details about their products. Although these messages often do not meet the strict definition of lying, they are deceptive in the sense that they create false impressions.

A more fundamental issue of ethics and advertising concerns the creation of needs among customers. The economist, John Kenneth Galbraith (1967) has argued convincingly that advertising does not simply satisfy existing consumer needs, but also creates new wants and needs. The marketing of expensive designer clothing, for example, is based on creating a need for social status that the product then fulfills. Each year, a new line of designer clothes is produced and promoted to create demand (Miller, 1992). Tobacco clearly does not fulfill a defined consumer need; rather it creates a need through its addictive properties. Companies marketing sports shoes often promote expensive products to urban youth by featuring celebrity endorsements from well-known sports figures. These ads often exploit the low self-esteem common among economically disadvantaged teenagers to sell expensive, high profit margin products. Galbraith argued that the continual creation of new needs and wants is basic to the uninterrupted growth of an industrial society. Capitalistic society requires the continual expansion of consumer demand (Sandage et al., 1983). Advertising sustains the "propensity to consume" that drives the capitalistic system (J.K. Galbraith, 1967). The result is a society not only based on consumerism, but obsessed with materialism and consumption. Galbraith pointed out that advertising provides "a relentless propaganda on behalf of goods" (p. 209). Wealth and material possessions become the measure of the individual's worth. The popular bumper stickers "Born to shop," "A woman's place is in the mall," "Shop till you drop," and "He who dies with the most toys wins" are reflections of the power of the materialistic values that dominate our consumer-based society (Miller, 1992).

Materialism is highly problematic from an ethical perspective because it supplants other values that have positive social consequences. The idea that an individual's worth is measured by personal possessions, for example, undercuts the fundamental notion that individuals have inherent worth and are equal. Moreover, materialism tends to debase the individual's ability to make informed personal choices and engage in self-determination. "Success, happiness, joy—are all depicted as produced by external consumable things" (Miller, 1992). This promotion of an external view of individual value is inconsistent with a belief that success and satisfaction are determined by personal choices and actions. Individual self-worth and self-image are always inadequate because another material good is always being promoted by the relentless advertising propaganda. This relentless advertising of goods and promotion of materialism also reduces the ability of individuals to look beyond material value. Miller suggested that advertising promotes the idea that our social problems, personal inadequacies, and need for personal meaning are all satisfied by consuming.

Another ethical issue in advertising related to materialism concerns appropriateness and good taste. Issues of taste relate to the specific appeals used to promote products and services, the places the advertisements appear, and the products themselves. Promoting some controversial products, such as condoms, on television might be judged as inappropriate because of the product itself. Public service announcements that promote condom use to prevent AIDS have been criticized on these grounds. Tobacco is banned entirely from television advertising because of the nature of the product. However, advertisements for these products are considered appropriate when appearing in print, billboards, or in sponsorship of special events. Questions about taste and appropriateness are most often associated with the specific appeals and images used in advertising.

Advertisers quickly learned that shock, violence, and sex were particularly effective persuasive appeals. Associations between a product and images of sexuality, for example, have become standard in the promotion of a wide range of goods including cars, beer, clothing, candy, sporting equipment, perfume, toothpaste, eyeglasses, food, music, and a host of others. Concomitant with the change in general social norms about public portrayal of nudity and sexuality, advertisers have continually pushed the prevailing social standards. Much advertising now leaves very little to the imagination as attractive models parade across the television screen to promote underwear, caress each other in passionate embraces to sell perfume, provocatively zip and unzip their designer jeans, and jog across beaches in bathing suits to sell beer. Sex is an effective selling tool for many products through its appeal to basic human drives and sexual fantasy (Laczniak & Murphy, 1981). These images also promote sexuality, prurient interests, and, in general the idea that sex and sexuality are dominant parts of life. Such advertising may be particularly inappropriate for some audiences, such as young children. In one recent case, a designer jeans manufacturer featured partially clothed adolescent youth in its ads. These ads were severely criticized for exploitation, for promoting the sexuality of children, and lead to charges that the ads bordered on child pornography. The ads were voluntarily withdrawn.

Violent images have been used to promote clothing, music, and sports. The clothing company, United Colors of Benneton, received much criticism for its use of violent and shocking images in its advertisements to promote designer clothes. Pictures of an African mercenary holding a human bone, of an AIDS patient at the moment of his death, and of a car bomb explosion that killed an Italian politician were featured on billboards along with the company name and logo. Although

Benneton argued that it was simply seeking to call attention to important social problems, critics suggested that the company was using these sensational and shocking images to promote its products.

Widespread use of sexuality, shock, sensationalism, and violence as primary persuasive appeals in advertising have several implications. First, these messages and other mass media messages, have helped foster a homogeneous community standard regarding appropriateness. At one time, regional communities and audiences might have reacted very differently to controversial ads. Today, most audiences encounter messages tailored to the lowest common national standard of appropriateness. As audiences become accustomed to these standards, the shock value of appeals is lost. Advertisers then feature even more shocking appeals, forcing the accepted standard even lower. Second, critics have reacted to advertising's tendency to objectify, stereotype, and marginalize some groups, particularly women, in their efforts to promote products with sexual appeals. Women are most often portrayed as adornments, objects to be acquired along with a product, or the object of sexual desire and fantasy (Ferrell, 1985). The advertising industry's record of using racial and ethnic stereotypes is also poor including cases such as the "Frito Bandito" and "Aunt Jemmima." These images can be oppressive and inconsistent with values of individual worth and equality. The advertising industry has become more sensitive to these issues, partly as a response to protest and partly in response to the increasing buying power of racial and ethnic groups. The image of "Aunt Jemmima," for example, has been updated and portrayed more positively as a middle-class Black woman.

ADVERTISING AND THE LAW

Many of the basic issues of ethics in advertising have been addressed by laws and federal regulations. Advertising and advertising law is based on the premise that advertisers should have a "reasonable basis" for all objective product claims. Consumers do not have the capability to test whether claims for a product are accurate. Given the inevitable imbalance of knowledge and resources between a business enterprise and its customers, it is more reasonable, and far less costly for society to require manufacturers to confirm advertising claims rather than burden each consumer with testing and investigating the claim (FTC, 1995). Moreover, the nature and diversity of claims are such that most consumers do not realistically have the capacity to determine their accuracy. Rather, the FTC under the FTC Act of 1938, is responsible for monitoring advertisements and enforcing basic standards of accuracy.

The FTC enforces requirements for accuracy and substantiation; that is advertisers and ad agencies have a reasonable basis for their public claims before communicating them. Although FTC guidelines and legal interpretations allow for some flexibility in general claims about products, they do require that "advertisers substantiate express and implied claims, however conveyed, that make objective assertions about the item or service advertised" (FTC, 1995). Objective claims must be backed by a "reasonable basis" for those claims. This legal and ethical standard is based on the assumption that consumers use the information from advertisements to make informed purchase decisions. Consumers would rely less on advertising claims for products and services if they knew the advertiser did not have a reasonable basis for making them. A company's failure to have a reasonable basis for claims, according to the FTC Act, constitutes unfair and deceptive practices (FTC, 1995).

Much debate exists about what constitutes "substantiation of a claim." If explicit claims are made in advertisements such as "tests show," "three out of four doctors recommend," and "scientific studies demonstrate," the FTC (1995) expects the company to have at least the level of support it has advertised. This usually means that the studies referenced must currently exist and support the advertised claim. Generally, the FTC has required that the type and level of substantiation be at least as great as the advertised claims. When an ad does not make an explicit reference to support a claim, the FTC relies on a standard of "reasonable basis." FTC determination of reasonable basis depends on several factors, including "the type of claim, the product, the consequences of a false claim, the benefits of a truthful claim, the cost of developing substantiation for the claim, and the amount of substantiation experts in the field believe is reasonable" (FTC, 1984) .

Although the explicit claims in ads require substantiation, other more generic claims such as "low fat," "environmentally friendly," or "recyclable" are difficult to substantiate and regulate. The FTC has developed guidelines for a number of products and claims including plants, trees, and seeds; luggage; tires; shell homes; shoe composition; pricing; mail order insurance; adhesives; warranties and guarantees; pet products; beauty and barber equipment; home furniture; use of the word *free* in advertising; wigs; feather and down products; vocational school claims; endorsements; fuel economy claims for new automobiles; and many other product categories and claims (FTC, 1992).

With the claim of environmental benefit, for example, two specific guidelines have been offered. First, the claim should distinguish between benefits of product and the package. Environmental marketing claims must be presented in a way that makes clear whether the environmental claim refers to the product, the packaging, or to some part of the product or packaging (FTC, 1992). Second, regarding overstatement of environmental attributes, "Marketers should avoid implications of significant environmental benefits if the benefit is in fact negligible" (FTC, 1992). For example, a trash bag should not be labeled "recyclable" without qualifications because trash bags will ordinarily not be separated out from other trash for recycling. "Even if the bag is technically capable of being recycled, the claim is deceptive since it asserts an environmental benefit where no significant or meaningful benefit exists" (FTC, 1992).

Although the FTC and advertising law, in general, has sought to regulate specific claims in order to ensure basic accuracy, it also recognizes that advertising, by its very nature, employs hyperbole and hype. The FTC allows organizations to employ "puffery" in describing products. The seller has the right to "puff up" the product in advertising generally in expressing opinions about the product or service rather than in representations of "fact." Even with the latitudes granted to advertisers regarding puffery, there is little doubt that the FTC has elevated the ethical level of commercial advertising. Although the warning *caveat emptor*—let the buyer beware—still applies to all advertising messages, the most blatant cases of inaccuracy, distortions, and false claims are at least less common.

ISSUE AND IMAGE ADVERTISING

Product and service advertising is very well established, with a long history of professional association and norms, and a set of clearly articulated values and standards. Issue and image advertising, however, are relatively new forms of macro-organizational communication that go beyond the description and promotion of goods and services. These new forms of advertising create an additional set of ethical questions. These questions concern undue influence, image as deception, and false and misleading information.

Image and issue advertising first came into common usage in the 1960s and 1970s. At that time, organizations began promoting themselves through universal appeals and images and began promoting specific political agendas that might benefit the organization. Although some organizations, such as railroad companies and AT&T used issue and image advertising in the early 1900s, these messages did not become common until the 1960s and 1970s. Heath and Nelson (1986) traced the development of this new form of advertising to changes in the social and political environment. The general questioning of institutional authority, environmentalism, and rejection of middle-class values during the 1960s put organizations on the defensive. In addition, changes in federal campaign laws during the early 1970s prompted fuller corporate involvement in politics (Heath & Nelsen, 1986). These practices had become so widespread and generated so much controversy that in 1978, the Senate Subcommittee on Administrative Practices and Procedures held hearings to examine issue and image advertising. The hearings explored the question of tighter legislative restrictions on these forms of advertising. The FTC regulates advertising, whereas the FCC is also responsible for advocacy advertising, and Internal Revenue Service guidelines specify what forms of advertising are tax deductible and the courts, with the commercial speech doctrine, determine which messages have First Amendment protection (Heath & Nelsen, 1986; Subcommmmittee Hearings on Administrative Practice and Procedure, 1978). The legal environment for issue and image advertising, therefore, is very complex.

Issue or advocacy advertising is an effort by the organization to influence the specific regulatory or legislative environments through public messages. These messages offer the organization's response to some point of controversy or contestable claim about public policy which has the potential to affect the organization (Crable & Vibbert, 1985; Heath & Nelson, 1986). During the Clinton administration's effort to revise the national health care system, for example, insurance companies, the American Medical Association, and hospital associations produced ads supporting or criticizing various parts of the proposed change. These messages had a profound influence on the development of the national debate on health care reform and on its ultimate defeat. One of the most fundamental questions about such issue or advocacy advertising is: Should organizations be involved in discussions of public policy? Traditionally, only individual citizens were involved in these debates. Increasingly, however, public policy debate are controlled by those corporate interests who can afford mass media advertising. Although some observers are concerned by this change, others, such as Jones and Chase (1979), argued that organizations are simply contributing another perspective to a public policy debate. Ultimately, this involvement enhances the pool of available information necessary to make informed decisions.

Another ethical question regarding advocate advertising concerns the specific strategies and tactics used. Sethi (1977) suggested that corporations might use advocacy advertising to mislead the audience and overwhelm public policy debates. He reasoned that private organizations often have significantly greater resources than other groups and might simply flood the public with sophisticated messages supporting their positions. Other critics have taken similar positions, arguing that the deep pockets of corporations will buy undue influence in the public domain (Heath & Nelson, 1986). There are also questions about the appropriateness of examining complex public policy though 30-second television commercials.

The concerns raised about the ethics of image advertising are more general than those surrounding issue advertising. Image advertising seeks to associate the organization with positive themes, social values, and images. The goal of such advertising is to create a strong and positive perception of the organization in the minds of the general public. These messages may seek, for example, to associate the organization with the value of technological sophistication to create the impression that the organization is a technological leader. They may feature sophisticated manufacturing processes, images of space flight, and high technology laboratories. Other advertisements seek to associate organizations with environmental responsibility by placing the company logo or product in a natural settings. One oil company featured otters and seals "applauding" in response to the announcement that the company would feature double hulls on its tankers. Stridsberg (1977) suggested that these efforts are designed to "sell the organization," differentiating it from other organizations, enhancing legal, financial, and governmental support and in general creating a positive identify. Dennison (1978) observed that these messages are designed to appeal to the financial community, prospective employees, lending institutions, suppliers, and consumers as well as regulators and the general public.

It is image advertising that focuses on the organization's record of environmental responsibility that has generated the most criticism. Observers suggest that image advertising promoting the organization's environmental record often has little basis in fact (Dennison, 1978). In these cases, image advertising is used to distort and mislead. The appeals and claims of such advertising are often so general, however, that organizations can avoid charges of intentional deception. Advertisers can argue that these campaigns make no claim about the organization's record but only suggest that the organization has particular values. These appeals also probably enjoy much broader free speech protection than traditional advertising because they do not seek to market specific goods and services.

ADVERTISING AND ENACTMENT

Advertising messages, whether issue, image, or products, have a particularly important role in the organization's ongoing interpretation and enactment of its informational environment. Because advertisements are very public messages, often disseminated in the most diverse and broad channels possible, they create a number of opportunities to hear what the organization is saying. Consumers, critics, stockholders, members of the community, as well as members of the organization receive these messages. For some, these may be the only messages received from the organization and their perceptions of the organization are often based entirely on these messages. Even the perceptions of those groups and individuals with other sources of information are heavily influenced by the frequent and sophisticated advertising messages.

Members of the organization can also be expected to use advertising messages to know what to think and how to interpret the organization's environment. Sophisticated advertising slogans, image appeals, logos, and responses to issues are symbolic representations and interpretations of the organization, its products services, and environment. They are often retained as fundamental interpretations for the organization's equivocal informational environment. Successful promotion themes are often replicated for subsequent campaigns and borrowed for other equivocal situations. "See the USA in a Chevrolet," "Just Do It!," and "Quality is Job One," come to define the ways members of particular organizations make sense of the uncertain and equivocal situations they face. Weick (1979) suggested that when interpretations are communicated publicly, they constitute public commitments to positions that members feel obligated to support and justify, and that they adhere to strongly. Advertising messages, because of their public character, wide dissemination, and sophisticated appeals, often become central organizational interpretations. Advertising messages potentially have important implications for organizational operation, culture, and ethics. Ads that obviously deceive, mislead, and distort may help foster a belief that such hypocrisy and deception is acceptable.

SUMMARY

Advertising is the most prominent and one of the most powerful forms of macro-organizational communication. Corporations produce hundreds of thousands of sophisticated public messages each year to promote goods, services, the company image, or to advocate specific issues. The sheer volume of messages that organizations produce and the weight of their influence makes advertising a critical area for communication ethics. The ethical issues associated with this form of communication are compounded by the fact that advertising is almost always designed to influence attitudes, perceptions, and behaviors.

The ethics of advertising as a form of communication are often defended on the grounds that they contribute to the available pool of information consumers can use to make informed decisions and choices about goods, services, and issues. Advertising enhances competition, leads to better products and services, and enriches the marketplace of ideas. Critics claim that advertising is deceptive, promotes materialism, and often uses inappropriate appeals. Advertising probably does both. Its power and frequency, however, suggest that this form of organizational communication should be held to the highest standards of honesty, accuracy, good taste, and appropriateness.

CASE: ADVERTISING CONDOMS

One recent advertising controversy concerns ads promoting condom use as a way of slowing the sexual transmission of HIV. Proponents of such advertising have argued that the only way to slow the sexual transmission of HIV is to broadly educate the public regarding the use of condoms. This method is consistent with a long tradition in community medicine relying heavily on public education and information dissemination to address public health issues. Advertising regarding cigarette smoking, drug abuse, high blood pressure, alcohol abuse, and other public health issues are common. Widespread dissemination of information about condoms is particularly important because of traditional taboos and misunderstanding surrounding both HIV and sex. This is particularly so with the high school and college age population most at risk for HIV infection. To be effective, ads must be targeted to this young audience.

Opponents have argued that the public advertising of condom use is in poor taste and amounts to publicly advocating extra marital sex. In some cases, the ads may be offensive to the audience. Some conservative religious groups, such as the Catholic Church, also object further to these ads on the grounds that they also promote birth control. Critics point out that television commercials, magazine ads, and billboards are available to very young children. These issues, they claim, are simply inappropriate for such a young group who may not understand the nature of the issue and the purpose of the ads.

Discussion Questions

1. What ethics and value are manifest in the debate about condom advertising?
2. How specifically might the issue of appropriateness be dealt with in such advertising?
3. What limitations, if any, would you suggest be placed on these forms of ads?

11

Ethics, Communication, and Organizational Change

One of the most constant forces in modern organizational life is change. *Change*—alterations in the organization so that people behave differently—is required to accommodate new perspectives, participants, information, and values. It is an ongoing process whereby the organization seeks to continually adjust to new informational inputs and environmental contingencies. Change also has a profound impact on the people inside organizations. Often, they are required to abandon old, familiar attitudes, behaviors, and values in favor of new, untried approaches. As such, change is fundamentally an issue of ethics.

This chapter examines the nature of organizational change, the role of communication in this process, and the values and ethical issues that are inherently part of the change process. Some of the most common approaches to organizational change, including change by decree, participative change, and training and development, are discussed. Strategies for overcoming resistance are examined and the impact of change on individual members is also explored. A set of questions are offered as a way to examine the ethics of organizational change. Downsizing and terminations are discussed as changes with particular ethical significance. Some general ethical guidelines for downsizing are discussed.

THE NATURE OF ORGANIZATIONAL CHANGE

Discussion of organizational change and development are usually grounded in three broad social trends (Cummings & Huse, 1989; French & Bell, 1984). The first involves changing demographics. Organizational development (OD) theorists are fond of pointing out that the population is undergoing dramatic shifts. Americans are living longer. More nontraditional employees are joining the workforce. Single parent and other nontraditional families are increasingly common. Fewer households have only one wage earner and families are smaller. These changes have dramatic impacts on products and markets, the delivery of goods and services, advertising, and who is employed by the organization. A second trend concerns the information revolution and the continued development of the "third wave" information-based economy. The volume of information, the speed and diversity of its dissemination, and the application of information through technology have increased at a mind-boggling pace. New bodies of information make existing, long-established technologies, obsolete. Economies and markets are increasingly global as physical distance offers fewer and fewer impediments to interaction. Computers have revolutionized the speed with which information can be moved and processed. It is difficult to speculate what impact the connection of hundreds of thousands of computers thorough the Internet might eventually have on society and organizations. Virtual communities already exist. Virtual universities are common on the World Wide Web, while profit-making corporations are now exploring the possibilities created by this entirely new format of human interaction. A third trend concerns the continually shrinking pool of natural resources. As populations grow and the finite pool of natural resources is consumed, organizations are forced to be increasingly efficient in their operations. Developing countries, seeking consumer-based economies, put further pressure on finite resources as they seek their share of the economic pie. Americans, they point out, consume a disproportional supply of the world's resources.

Although these trends taken together often constitute an overwhelming set of alterations, it is the accelerating pace of change that is particularly striking. Manufacturing organizations may go through several major changes in technology within a period of a few years. Rapid shifts in the political climate of developing countries may jeopardize the supply of scarce resources. Markets may shift in abrupt and unpredictable ways. New competitive threats often emerge with little warning.

Organizations, of course, must continually adapt and plan their adjustment to these changes (Goodman & Kurke, 1982). From the perspective of systems theory, organizations accept a stream of dynamic inputs from the environment and must adjust their outputs to meet ever shifting environmental expectations. When workers change, organizations must change their employment policies, management systems, and values. The diversity value often discussed in organizations, is a direct response to the changing demographics of the workforce (Fernandez, 1993; Stewart, 1993). Changes such as these are necessary for the organizations to survive. They also allow the organization to more effectively meet the needs of customers and members of the community. The laboratory training movement, survey research traditions, and the work of small group theorist Kurt Lewin has given rise to a body of principles concerning planned organizational change known as OD (French & Bell, 1984). OD focuses on planned, systematic, and strategic processes of organizational change designed to improve efficiency and effectiveness.

Change also has a profound impact on the people inside organizations because they are required to think and behave differently. This impact includes the disruption of established routines, a loss of personal control, and higher levels psychological stress. These factors often translate into strong employee resistance to planned change efforts.

Widespread organizational change by definition disrupts the established routines, procedures, and accepted ways of operating in the organization (Cobb, Wooten, & Folger, 1995). These routines constitute the organization's fundamental ground rules, laid down over time as organization's retain interpretations, cause maps, and responses to equivocal situations. These ground rules provide the basic elements of organizing processes and serve to create familiarity, comfort, and predictability in the system. Employees are invested in the present system because they have taken time to learn the accepted interpretations and cause maps that make up the system. When the organization changes, the value of this investment is reduced or lost. The result is higher levels of personal uncertainty. Members will create new interpretations and cause maps and seek out information about the new ground rules. Because these rules are in the process of being enacted, selected, and retained during change, this communication is "likely to be episodic, inconsistent and vague" (Cobb et al., 1995, p. 159).

Second, change is almost always accompanied by a sense of adversity and personal loss (Cobb et al., 1995). Kotter and Schlesinger (1979) observed "One reason people resist organizational change is that they think they will lose something of value as a result" (p. 107). The loss often concerns a personal investment in the old system. Employees are forced to learn new ways of behaving, interpretations, systems, and procedures. They may also lose personal status, prestige, and power. In addition, employees often feel as if they have lost personal control over their work situations, particularly with change that is initiated from the top. Employees may feel that change is being forced on them and, in many instances, may question whether they have the capacity to adjust to a new system. Ultimately, one of the fundamental yet unspoken questions accompanying major organizational change concerns job security

Concomitant with uncertainty and loss of control, change also produces high levels of stress. Uncertain situations, where future circumstances cannot be predicted and where individuals are unclear as to what might be expected of them, are threatening. These threats in turn produce psychological stress. Such stress consumes valuable energy and resources, and may reduce the employee's capacity to do their job. Sometimes, high levels of stress limit the ability of individuals to respond to changes in systematic and rational ways. These high levels of stress eventually reduce the organization's efficiency and effectiveness.

Disruption of established routines, loss of control, and psychological stress have a number of subsequent affects. Rumors about the causes and consequences of change often develop. Organizational politics often become more active. Trust and morale may decay. Important problems and issues may go unnoticed. Most importantly, however, employees may resist the change. Communication is generally seen as an important process in alleviating some of these negative affects. Communicating about the change may reduce uncertainty, foster a sense of employee involvement in and control over the change, and provide assurances regarding job security.

THE VALUES OF CHANGE

Organizational development, as a domain of theory and practice, is grounded in a relatively specific set of values and associated ethics (Stephens, D'Intino, & Victor, 1995). OD practitioners make choices about what aspects of an organization are good, desirable, right, and worthwhile, and seek to persuade others to accept these choices. French and Bell (1984) pointed out that OD subscribes to values of individualism, humanism, and organizational democracy, in creating and implementing solutions to organizational problems. In addition, Cobb et al. (1995) suggested that OD is fundamentally grounded in the value of justice.

The OD values of humanism and individualism are drawn from the human resources tradition, which emphasizes individual creativity, ingenuity, and commitment. Employees are seen as important resources with creative problem-solving capacity. They have valuable information and insight into organizational problems. Organizations must find ways to unleash this problem-solving capacity and make full use of the human resource. OD often emphasizes processes that facilitate this input such as small group decision making, team approaches, and employee training and development. In addition, OD emphasizes the capacity of individuals for self-determination. Authoritarian systems of supervision and control are inconsistent with the values of individual dignity and enhancing self-worth. Rather, individuals are encouraged to determine for themselves what solutions and changes are required. OD theorists point out that this self-determination facilitates commitment.

Democratic values are manifest in the emphasis placed on rational problem solving, and in employee participation in change. As in democratic political systems, OD argues that access to information facilitates organizational problem solving and rational choice. Participation in management processes ensures that employees have a voice and that all important information and perspectives are represented in making decisions. OD theorists often point out that many systems and structures preclude the full participation of employees in organizational life. Centralized management structures, authoritarian superior–subordinate relationships, and punitive policies and procedures may all create a "dampening and throttling effect" on personal growth and full participation (French & Bell, 1984, p. 46).

A third set of OD values relates to fairness. Cobb et al. (1995) argued that three forms of organizational justice—distributive, procedural, and interaction—are associated with organizational change. Distributive justice, concerning the apportionment of resources, is almost always affected by changes in the organization. Change usually involves a strategic realignment of scarce resources such a personnel, equipment, time, and money. "Whereas distributive justice focuses on the perceived fairness of resource distributions, procedural justice focuses on the fairness of how distributive and other decisions are made (Cobb et al., 1995, p. 257). Procedural justice is grounded in systematic processes that ensure equal representation in decisions and appropriate appeals and recourse when a grievance arises. Procedures that are perceived as fair are particularly important in generating support for systematic modifications of the organization. Finally, interactional justice refers specifically to communication about change: its impetus, ideological foundation, and anticipated affects. Cobb et al. (1995) suggested that organizational leaders have responsibilities to provide communicative accounts about change to those affected. These accounts "provide a common understanding of, and help give coherence to, the change program as well as produce an overall perception of fairness" (p. 273).

APPROACHES AND STRATEGIES OF OD

Organizational development generally focuses on planned organizational change; that change strategically undertaken for the purpose of
improving the organization. This change usually targets the behavior of
employees, the structures of the organization, or a combination of
behavior and structure. OD practitioners are often called on, as either
internal experts or external consultants, to manage planned organizational change. This form of change employs various organizational
approaches, strategies, and targets.

Greiner (1970), for example, identified three general approaches
to organizational change based on the degree to which power and
authority are shared. The first, unilateral action, occurs when power and
authority are centralized at the top of the organization. Change by
decree, for example, is an authoritarian approach where top management simply announces change. Similarly, top management, by replacing individuals or modifying structures, creates change. In the second
general strategy, power sharing, some level of cooperation between top
managers and the employees most affected is used to create the
change. Group decision making, problem solving, joint management–
labor committees, and teams are popular approaches that use cooperation, negotiation, consensus, and agreement to create change. Finally,
delegated authority strategies occur when lower level employees affected by change are given the control over the change process. Some
quality programs, for example, delegate authority over quality issues
directly to the organization's lower levels. Organizational training is often
designed to give employees managerial skills so that they may self-man-
age. Although delegated approaches are more closely aligned with the
values of OD and the ethics of humanism and self-determination, they
are generally much slower in producing change than more direct
approaches. Moreover, managers have a more difficult time ensuring
specific outcomes because they no longer exercise complete control.
Unilateral action, in contrast, generally produces faster results and
allows managers to exert more control over outcomes. It is inconsistent,
however, with many of the values of OD and often produces strong
resistance among employees.

Kotter and Schlesinger (1979) described six strategies that may
overcome resistance to change. The first, education and support, relates
directly to communication about the change. They argued
"Communication of ideas helps people see the need for and the logic of
a change" (p. 109). The second, participation and involvement, makes
use of the fact that "in general, participation leads to commitment, not
mere compliance" (p. 109). Facilitation and support is the third strategy.

This involves a range of activities that recognize and seek to offset the demands of organizational change. Managers may provide training in the new behaviors, flexible responsibilities, time off to accommodate new demands, or simply provide the opportunity for employees to express their frustrations. The fourth strategy, negotiation and agreement, involves bargaining, compromise, and tradeoffs to elicit support for a change. Manipulation and cooptation, the fifth strategy, involves covert efforts to elicit support. The difference between cooptation and participation is that the former only creates the perception of involvement in the change. Finally, explicit and implicit coercion, involves the covert or overt use of threats about such issues as job loss, promotions, transfers, or other similar punishments. Kotter and Schlesinger (1979) pointed out that coercion, like manipulation and cooptation, may create resentment and anger among workers. Implied threats, however, are probably the most common strategies used to induce acceptance of an unpopular organizational change.

ETHICAL ISSUES OF ORGANIZATIONAL CHANGE

The range of strategies and approaches to change and the values associated with OD demonstrate that ethical questions permeate all aspects of the organizational change process. Organizational change has a fundamental impact on the work, personal life, security, and general well-being of members. Ethical issues in change concern the analysis of the present organizational system, techniques employed in the change, control over the change, the degrees to which change is supported by theory and research, and the impact of the change on employees (Seeger, 1984).

Much planned organizational change begins with needs assessment, attitude survey, or audit. These systematic research techniques are used to examine some part of the organization in order to identify weaknesses, problems, needs, and breakdowns as well as strengths and opportunities. As research methods, they raise questions about ownership of data, confidentiality, and intrusiveness of techniques. In addition, organizational change makes implicit assumptions about the members of the organization. Among other things, change may view employees as committed, empowered, and informed, or as powerless, uncommitted, and uninformed. Change also carries with it fundamental questions about the honesty of the change efforts and the right of the organization to unilaterally impose change. Change efforts, particularly training programs, are often criticized on the grounds that they are short-term, one-time fixes. Critics charge that employees are often trained to behave differently and then returned to an organizational system that is not structured to accept the new behaviors.

These concerns raise specific questions that are useful in clarifying many of the ethical issues associated with organizational change (Seeger, 1984). These questions are presented in Table 11.1.

Examining organizational change efforts with these or similar ethical questions in mind is useful for several reasons. First, the effectiveness of organizational change efforts is often reduced because of low credibility. Many employees, having seen a number of change programs wash over their organizations, have learned simply to ride out the change programs and wait for them to fail. Change programs grounded in a specific set of values are more credible and have a greater probability of being accepted and supported by employees. Second, change programs often create cynicism. Top–down programs of change, in particular, are often judged as unfair, window dressing, manipulative, and hypocritical. Programs are often perceived as fads, backed by little forethought, poor information, and minimal planning. Changes grounded in appropriate assumptions about members, which are honest, and long term are less likely to prompt cynical responses on the part of the targets of change. Finally, change efforts often fail because the values associated with the change are incompatible with those of the organization or members. Careful evaluation of the ethical issues of change programs may help clarify these value conflicts earlier in the process when the conflicting values may be discussed and reconciled.

Table 11.1. Questions for Assessing Ethics of Organizational Change.

1. What assumptions are made about employees?

2. To what degree does the evaluation of the organization (survey, audit, needs assessment) respect the integrity of members?

3. To what degree are the principles and practices advocated grounded in and supported by sound theory and research?

4. To what degree does the change program address the larger system within which the new behavior is to be practiced?

5. To what degree is the change long term?

6. To what degree does the organization have a right to void the present system and substitute a new system?

7. To what degree are the purposes and principles of the change program honest?

DOWNSIZING

One form of organizational change that raises particularly powerful ethical issues is downsizing. *Downsizing* is the process of reducing the number of employees, through attrition, retirements, layoffs, and terminations. Although at one point termination of employees was fairly uncommon, increased competitiveness and changing workforce demographics have made termination a common event in the lives of many workers (Sweet, 1989). Corporate giants, such as AT&T, IBM, and GM, once able to offer very high levels of job security have recently cut entire layers of middle managers in order to enhance competitiveness. Such downsizing is often described as radical surgery designed to save a sick company. Critics have also charged that the rush to downsize is an effort to maximize short-term profits on the backs of workers. In several cases, organizations have closed entire production facilities, laying off thousands of employees, devastating community tax bases, and stripping local economies of their basic support. Communities have sometimes responded by suing organizations, seeking compensation for years of tax abatements (McBride, 1993). Downsizing is inevitably a legal issue covered by the common law principles of at-will employment, the specific contractual relationship between the employer and employee, and the 1988 Worker Adjustment and Notification Act. This act requires 60 days notification of termination or layoffs for those organizations employing more than 100 workers.

Downsizing and termination is almost always a negative experience. Employees face loss of income, health insurance, and the esteem and security associated with their jobs. Terminations are associated with increases in mental illness, divorce, suicide, and crime, including domestic violence, alcoholism, and stress related disorders, such as heart disease (Batt, 1983). Most of the workers who are successful in reentering the workforce do so at a lower income level and at a less prestigious job (Kincki, Bracker, Kreitner, Lockwood, & Lemak, 1992). Older employees may have a particularly difficult time finding jobs due to changing demographic patterns. Equally devastating is the fact that these employees may never again be able to trust employers. Even those employees who keep their jobs are often shocked by the realization that they could be downsized in the next efforts to increase competitiveness. Managers, forced to carry out the termination, often find themselves burdened with guilt and self-doubt.

The downsizing process often digresses into serious conflict between those employees leaving the organization and those remaining. Managers may fear the actions of angry employees waiting for their last pay check. It is not uncommon for terminated employees to be supervised as they clean out their personal possessions and then escorted off company property. Managers, fearing loss of productivity and potential retribution, often postpone announcing termination decisions until the last possible moment. The result is less time for employees to plan, prepare, and adjust.

Although downsizing is surrounded with negative emotions, threats, and potential conflict, it is possible to conduct this difficult activity in a responsible manner. Coulson (1981) offered a number of guidelines for employee termination. He argued that the manager's first responsibility is to try to save the worker's job. This may involve seeking transfers, new opportunities, retraining, or even reduction of hours for several workers so that all may keep their job. In some cases, early retirement is an option. Coulson (1981) also suggested that employees should be told why they are being terminated and given the opportunity to discuss the reasons. He proposed, for example, a series of interviews with employees where the termination is explained. Finally, Coulson (1981) argued that termination and downsizing take place with a sense of humanity. This may include providing as much lead time as possible, active assistance in seeking other positions, and emotional support.

Sweet (1989) emphasized the obligations, legal and ethical, that exist in the employee–employer relationship. He argued that in instances of termination, four specific employer obligations exist. First, the employer should provide a "truthful, realistic rationale for what is happening" (p. 14). An explanation reaffirms the value of the employee as a rational person capable of understanding and learning. Second, the employer should manifest "professional respect for the individual" (p. 14). Even in those instances where jobs are lost due to lack of competitiveness, or new technology, the employer should actively recognize the skill and capability of workers. Third, the employer should not procrastinate. Managers should notify workers at the earliest convenience in order to provide as much time to plan and prepare for the termination as possible. Finally, the employer should provide some form of financial support. Sweet reported one survey that showed more than 90% of employers provided severance pay.

Although downsizing and termination are inevitably difficult and painful, it is possible to approach job loss in a manner consistent with the obligations of the employee–employer relationship and with a sense of humanity. Some estimates suggest that one third of middle management positions have been eliminated from American organizations in the last decade and that this trend is continuing (Sweet, 1989). The magnitude of this trend and the potential for severe emotional, economic, and social consequences, make the ethic of humanity and a sense of obligation critical ethical imperatives for organizational downsizing.

SUMMARY

Change requires that employees and stakeholders abandon old, familiar attitudes, behaviors, values, interpretations, and cause maps for organizing. The results often include disruption of established routines, loss of personal control, and higher levels of stress. Communication pays a particularly important role in the change process. It can function to signal the need for change, generate support, reduce resistance, and facilitate input. Change also raises a number of fundamental ethical questions about the right of the organization to impose change on employees, about their levels of control over and input into the change, and about the specific procedures and strategies employed. These issues relate not only to the level of ethics manifest in a change program, but also to the way in which the program is perceived, and, ultimately, to its effectiveness. One context of organizational change that raises serious ethical questions is employee termination and downsizing. The potential for severe emotional, economic, and social consequences is particularly strong. Although downsizing is often undertaken in an expedient manner, some critics have suggested an ethics rooted in a sense of obligation and ethic of humanity.

Change is a constant force in modern organizations. Process views argue that organizing is an ongoing and dynamic activity where change is the only constant (Weick, 1982). Downsizing will continue. Technology and its applications will expand. Demographic shifts will accelerate. The pool of natural resources will continue to shrink. Maintaining a sense of good and bad, right and wrong, desirable and undesirable is particularly challenging under such dynamic conditions.

CASE: COMMUNICATING THE CLOSING—GM AND WILLOW RUN

In the early 1990s GM faced significant operating losses. The company had over capacity, an aging product line, and some of the highest production costs in the industry. At a February 25, 1992 press conference, GM's Chairman Robert Stemple announced the company's plans to close 11 plants and eliminate 16,000 jobs. This included closing the Willow Run Assembly Plant. The decision was announced to GM workers via closed circuit television prior to the public announcement. Willow Run was slated for closure in mid-1993.

Willow Run and its "sister" plant in Arlington, Texas had been under review for some months. It was clear that GM would close one of these plants in response to the $4.5 billion in losses for 1991. Industry observers suggested that GM would close Arlington because it was farther from the major parts suppliers that were located in southeastern Michigan and because Willow Run had slightly better production facilities. The local Arlington United Auto Workers (UAW), however, had offered major contract concessions but few observers believed that these would outweigh the logistic advantages enjoyed by Willow Run. The political establishment in Michigan and the local UAW were shocked, therefore, when GM made its announcement. UAW workers and political leaders reported feeling blindsided. Many politicians from the city of Ypsilanti, where Willow Run was located, were angry, pointing to the numbers of jobs dependent on Willow Run, the impending loss of tax dollars, and the tax abatements GM had accepted over the years.

Critics offered several explanations for why Willow Run was closed. First, the UAW local at Arlington had offered concessions. Some saw GM's decision to save the Arlington plant as a signal to the UAW that the era of intense worker–management cooperation was over. Second, Arlington is located close to Mexico and the North American Free Trade agreement may have prompted more parts suppliers to locate in Mexico. Third, some observers noted that GM was able to expand its base of political support by having plants in more states. Others speculated that then President George Bush may have been involved in lobbying for his home state of Texas. GM responded unequivocally that this was a business decision based on the fact that it had to significantly cut its losses, that the company sincerely regretted any hardship created, and would do whatever was feasible to reduce the impact of the closings.

The backlash about the closing was particularly harsh. Several Michigan politicians called for explanations while the city of Ypsilanti filed suit to halt the closing. The UAW accused GM of "whipsawing," playing one union local off against another to get more contract concessions. Some customers canceled orders for GM cars and critics suggested that this is just one more example of the heartless nature of corporate America.

Discussion Questions

1. What obligations did GM have to communicate about the closing, including justifying the closing of Willow Run?
2. What obligations does an organization have to workers and the community during a plant closing.
3. To what degree did the fact that GM was facing major losses mitigate its obligations and justify the closure?

12

Ethics and Organizational Leadership

It is difficult to overstate the role of leadership in organizations and in the ethics of organizations. Leadership is a necessary process to any goal-directed social system so much so that "the absence of leadership is often seen as the absence of organization" (Smirich & Morgan, 1982, p. 257). Ethics, in the form of virtues and credibility, are central elements in the leadership process. The top leaders in any organization have an instrumental role setting the moral tone and determining what values, processes, and goals will be seen as important by followers and stakeholders (Bennis & Nanus, 1985).

    This chapter reviews the concept of *leadership* including theory and research concerning leader traits, style, contingencies, and symbolic leadership. The leader's role in setting the ethical tone of the organization by signaling what is and is not important is also explored. Credibility and the concept of *virtue ethics* are explored as primary ways of examining ethics in organizational leadership. In addition, the values inherent to the leadership process are discussed.

LEADERSHIP

No single concept in social research has generated as much interdisciplinary theory and research as leadership. In fact, leadership literature is so diverse as to preclude any universal propositions or generalized summaries. Despite the plethora of work in this area, leadership remains poorly understood and highly equivocal. Stogdill (1974) pointed out that researchers even have difficulty agreeing on leadership definitions, offering a variety of views rooted in several research traditions. These definitions include traits, behaviors, interactions, roles, styles, goals, followers, culture, and symbols, among others (Yukl, 1989). Smirich and Morgan's (1982) definition is useful because of its breadth: "Leadership is the process whereby one or more individuals succeeds in attempting to frame and define the reality of others" (p. 258). Framing and defining follower reality is accomplished through communication.

Although leadership theory and research is diverse and complex, several themes can be identified (Shaw, 1981; Stogdill, 1974; Yukl, 1989): traits, styles, contingency views, and symbolic leadership. These four themes follow different initial assumptions about leadership and have different goals. Research into the traits of leadership followed the assumption that leaders have identifiable characteristics such as "tireless energy, penetrating intuition, uncanny foresight, and irresistible persuasive powers" (Yukl, 1989, p. 269). Although these studies generally failed to identify any universal set of leader traits, Shaw (1981) observed that "ten or more studies reported consistent evidence indicating that the average leader exceeds the average group member on sociability, initiative, persistence, knowing how to get things done, self confidence, initiative, confidence, insight cooperativeness, popularity and adaptability" (p. 325).

Styles of leadership, a second research trend, was based on the observation that different leaders manifest different approaches and behaviors. Work in this area began by examining autocratic, democratic, and laissez-faire leadership. Autocratic leadership determines all policy, "dictates techniques and actions" and is "impersonal and aloof." Democratic styles allow "the group to determine policy," provide general direction, and allow members to work with substantial freedom. Laissez-faire, or a style of nonleadership, does not participate, "giving the group complete freedom to make it own decisions . . ." (Shaw, 1981, p. 236). Although the results of style studies are not entirely clear, Stogdill (1974) concluded that leader styles emphasizing structure are somewhat related to higher group productivity. Those leader styles that emphasize consideration are somewhat related to member satisfaction. A number of other situational factors, however, are probably involved in these member outcomes.

The third approach to leadership emphasized these situational variables. These views argue that the effectiveness of various leadership behaviors is contingent on variables of the situation, including such things as the nature of the followers, the leader's power, and group relations. Efforts have focused on identification of situational factors that influence leader behavior, identifying levels of leader discretion, describing leader interpretive processes, and determining moderator variables (Yukl, 1989). This research has demonstrated both the importance of situational variables and the complexity of leadership processes.

The final approach that can be drawn from this broad body of research concerns leadership as symbol and cultural process. Pfeffer (1981) suggested that management can be understood on two levels: substantive, largely determined by situational constraints, and symbolic, where managerial leadership "constructs and maintains belief systems" (p. 1). This area emphasizes the role of the leader in giving meaning to organizational activities, providing a sense of vision, and serving as an important cultural symbol. In addition, the leader's use of language, leadership myths, rituals, and performance are examined (Meindl, Erlich, & Dukerich 1985; Pfeffer, 1981). These views also tend to emphasize the value, normative, and ethical aspects of leadership.

An important question regarding leadership in these research traditions concerns the effect of leadership. Although the question is complex and influenced by a number of divergent variables, leadership does appear to have important symbolic and substantive affects on organizations. Chaganti and Sambharya (1987), for example, argued "Every organization reflects the background of its most powerful top managers; what the organization does and the way it carries out its functions could be explained in part at least by the profile of its upper echelon" (p. 393). The profile of top leaders is also expected to influence the ethical climate of the organization in important ways.

Schein (1985) provided a useful framework for understanding how leaders affect their organizations. He observed that "some of the mechanisms that leaders use to communicate their assumptions are conscious, deliberate actions; others are unconscious and may be unintended" (p. 223). These mechanisms involve articulating visions, signaling priorities, and establishing a philosophy for the organization. Because the leader exists at the top of the organization and controls the organization's formal power, she or he is highly visible to employees and other members of stakeholder groups (Mintzberg, 1973). This visibility ensures that followers will observe and assign meaning to much of the leader's behavior.

Probably the most powerful mechanism leaders have for communicating what they believe in or feel is important is "what they systematically pay attention to" (Schein, 1985, p. 225). This involves those aspects of the organization that are "noticed and commented on," and "measured, controlled, and rewarded" (p. 225). A management system created to measure quality, for example, signals that quality issues are priorities for the organization. Based on this notion, it also holds that those aspects of the organization that do not command systematic attention are unlikely to be seen as priorities. A second mechanism involves leader reactions to critical incidents and organizational crises. Schein reported that leader responses to these critical incidents "create new norms, values, and working procedures and reveal important underlying assumptions" (p. 230). Crisis situations are high uncertainty, high equivocality events that often require new interpretations and responses (Weick, 1988). A crisis involving loss of life, for example, may promote supportive, humane, and timely action by leaders. In contrast, leaders may respond in an expedient manner, seeking scapegoats, and avoiding public comment. In both cases, the leader's assumptions, priorities, and values are clarified resulting in equivocality reducing interpretations for followers. A third mechanism of leadership affect outlined by Schein (1985) was deliberate education through role modeling, teaching, and coaching. Leaders make explicit efforts to communicate what they believe in or feel is important through a variety of explicit channels including speeches, mission statements, policies, goal statements, annual reports, newsletters, and informal interactions. In addition, a very powerful set of priorities are communicated by the leader's own behavior. A leader who meets regularly with lower level employees, for example, may serve as a role model for other executives. A CEO who takes time every day to walk the floor of the plant and chat informally with workers may set a tone for other managers. Criteria for rewards and status, and criteria for recruitment for selection, promotion, retirement, and excommunication are Schein's fifth and six mechanisms. He noted, "if founders or leaders are trying to ensure that their values and assumptions will be learned, they must create a reward, promotion, and status system which is consistent with these assumptions" (p. 235). Finally, values and assumptions are passed down and perpetuated by the recruitment, selection, promotion, retirement, and excommunication processes in organizations. Hiring, promoting, and retaining members who share certain values perpetuates those values and signals to others that rewards are associated with specific values and priorities.

These mechanisms have important implications for how leaders transmit and embed values and ethics. Because leaders have access to the formal channels of communication, stakeholders are more likely to hear what they have to say. Leader messages, in turn, are powerful mechanisms for enactment, allowing stakeholders to know what to think. These messages take on more meaning when supported by leader behavior, enhanced through modeling, coaching, and teaching, backed by reward systems, and perpetuated through hiring and promotions. In the most fundamental sense, the leader's behavior creates a repertoire of interpretations for equivocal information. The leader's behavior also establishes a repertoire of appropriate responses to these situations. Andrews (1989) pointed out that the leader's office amplifies his or her behavior and messages increasing the likelihood that even the most off-handed remark or behavior will be taken into account by followers. Leadership, through explicit and implicit means, sets the ethical agenda and moral tone for the organization and provides interpretations and responses for reducing ethical equivocality.

CREDIBILITY AND VIRTUES

One theme that dominates many discussions of leadership and communication is *ethos*, or credibility (Cronkite & Liska, 1976). A credible source generally enhances the persuasiveness of a message. Credible leaders are more effective because they have greater success in persuading their followers to think and behave in particular ways. Leadership theorists point out that followers always grant leaders the right to lead. Low credibility, then, translates directly into ineffective leadership. Aristotle recognized that credibility is associated with ethics and character. He wrote, "Persuasion is achieved by the speaker's personal character when the speech is so spoken to make us believe him. We believe good men more fully and more readily than others." Although results are not universal, W. Thompson (1975) suggested, "Competence, trustworthiness, good moral character, and dynamism, as a consensus, are the major elements comprising ethos (credibility) in most circumstances" (p. 59). The concepts of *trustworthiness* and *good moral character,* in particular, have utility in understanding leadership and ethics.

Trustworthiness is associated with a communicator's honesty, truthfulness, consistency, reliability, and objectivity. Trustworthiness is a function of past reputation and develops as the leader communicates with a particular audience through his or her demeanor, use of evidence, appeals, and language. As a value, trustworthiness is fundamental to human communication in a variety of contexts (Johannesen, 1990). Credibility is particularly important in contexts of leadership because followers grant leaders the right to lead. In essence, followers put their faith in leaders and are particularly susceptible to manipulation, deception, and the possibility of being led far astray. History has many examples of charismatic leaders, such as Adolph Hitler, Jim Jones, Idi Amin, David Koresh, and Joseph Stalin, who violated, manipulated, and ultimately destroyed their followers. Most often, however, the leadership process itself forces leaders to comply with at least the minimum requirements of trustworthiness. To say it another way, because leader and follower are linked roles, a fundamental breakdown in follower trust may result in a loss of leadership. When this occurs, the leader must maintain his or her position through coercion and force. "Followership" is no longer voluntary.

Good moral character, the second major component of credibility and ethics, is more difficult to define. At its most basic level, we expect leaders to comply with the basic norms for morality in society. This compliance signals something about the leader's internal ethical and moral orientation. Character comes from the Greek word for "engraving," suggesting that character is a stable, internal personality trait (Barber, 1972). Issues of character are important to leadership because they represent a propensity to behave in particular ways inferred from previous behavior. Fisher (1987), in developing his narrative paradigm of communication, argued that the believability of a story rests on the "reliability of the characters, both as narrators and as actors" (p. 47). Character, he argued, is "an organized set of actionable tendencies," and suggests that contradictions, changes, or strange shifts in these tendencies result in the questioning of character (p. 47). If a leader is unable to keep promises regarding fidelity in marital relationships, questions arise about his or her ability to remain faithful in other contexts. If a leader demonstrates a propensity to distort the truth in one context, character judgments would suggest that they may distort the truth in other contexts. These assessments of character are important because they generally are seen as having predictive power. Without leader predictability, "there is no trust, no community, no rational human order" (Fisher, 1987, p. 47). Because character is conceptualized as an internal drive, it is not expected to change from context to context. Followers use these judgments about a leader's character to determine whether or not to place their trust in the leader.

Although character and trustworthiness are important to leader credibility, a more general set of ethical assessments are offered by the study of virtues. Virtue ethics have become increasingly popular as a way of clarifying how ethical principles are operationalized in behavior (Herrick, 1992). In this approach, various habits of behavior that are particularly meritorious or worthy of recognition and praise are examined. Johannesen (1990) suggested that in Western, Judeo-Christian cultures, these virtues include "courage, temperance, wisdom, fairness, generosity, gentleness, patience, truthfulness and trustworthiness" (p. 12). Herrick (1992) identified virtues associated with rhetorical acumen and honesty or what he termed the "goods inherent to rhetoric" (p. 145). These virtues include, "attentiveness to issues, inquisitiveness to investigate questions, discernment of reasoning errors, and articulateness," and "candor and courage" (p. 146).

In leadership, these virtues not only constitute good in terms of ethical standards, but are also related to credibility and leader effectiveness. Virtue is a fundamental standard on which leaders assess followers and grant them leadership. The virtues associated with leadership may also become part of the organization's larger culture serving as models for others and helping to signal priorities and establish a philosophy for the organization. Leaders are visible personifications of the organization and their virtues often become associated with the larger organization.

LEADERSHIP VALUES

Theorists and critics interested in organizational leadership from the perspective of symbols and culture have also begun examining the values manifest in the leadership process. These approaches are broad-based and seek to understand leadership as a set of leader–follower relationships and as a set of processes designed to create consensus about the integration of organizational values and systems around these values. Much of the impetus for these views comes from Peters and Waterman's (1982) work on leadership and corporate culture. Leadership, or "transforming leadership," that "builds on man's need for meaning, leadership that creates institutional purpose" is necessary for strong and effective organizational cultures (p. 82).

In the area known as *values leadership*, emphasis is placed on leader–follower relations. Heller and Van Til (1986) noted, "Leaders and followers, in any context, share a common fate of responsibility for their family, group, organization, or nation. From their joint participation emerges the success or failure of their enterprises" (p. 406). Interpersonal values such as honesty, trust, openness, and commitment are important to the success and quality of the leader–follower relationship. In addition, values leadership emphasizes self-determination and cooperation among various stakeholders. Fairholm (1991) argued that values leadership embraces stakeholder views of organization, the creation of strategic visions, cultures based on values of service and innovation, and the use of interpersonal relationships and teaching roles in leader–follower dyads.

In a more general sense, the effective organizational leader is "primarily an expert in the promotion and protection of values" (Peters & Waterman, 1982, p. 85). The process of creating consensus around a set of core organizational values involves communication. The process, according to Fairholm (1991) "involves the leader in setting and articulating the vitalizing vision of the organization" (p. 123). This process is inherently rhetorical requiring the leader to symbolically position the

organization, its goals, process, and outcomes, in relation to a set of values. This clarifies for followers what the organization "is and can be" (p.
123). Organizational visions crafted by leaders are functional in the
sense that they tell members how to contribute to desired outcomes.
They are also motivational in the sense that followers come to share the
values associated with the vision. Visions may also function as fundamental interpretations that members can use to reduce equivocality. As
noted earlier, the leader's position provides a visible platform for offering
interpretations that followers may then use to know what to think.

Researchers also point out that leadership processes must create systems integration around values, or what is termed *organizational
integrity*. Integrity, "in this sense is an interaction process that involves
the discovery and enactment of ever new forms of dialogue organization
that heighten and sustain the relational life of the whole" (Srivastva &
Cooperrider, 1988, p. 10). In common usage, integrity refers to the unification of a system, emphasizing wholeness, integration, and undivide-
ness. This unification requires open, ongoing communication among the
various subsystems. Integrity also refers to integration of the personal
ethics with organizational values, including the values of productivity and
profitability. When a leader has integrity, his or her behavior is consistent
with a core set of personal values. Wolfe (1988) pointed out that "interdependence is the fundamental character of all human life" (p. 142).
Integrity is the recognition of this condition and the integration of self with
environment and subsystems with a dynamic whole. Integrity, as an
ethic of leadership relates to the stakeholder perspective of organizational ethics and the ability to integrate the diverse needs and values of various stakeholder groups.

Waters (1988) examined the process whereby integrity of values
is created in organizations using the metaphor of a "good conversation"
(p. 189). He suggested that value integration in organizations occurs
through the process of good conversations among various organizational stakeholders and participants. These conversations promote an integrated consensus around values, goals, and solutions to problems.
Although the goal of totally integrative solutions to complex organizational problems is idealistic, the opportunity to be heard, to express one's
views and to be understood are important goals in the service of integrity. The executive's communication, according to Waters, is important in
establishing the central integrative moral position of the organization. He
suggested three characteristics of this communication: a) elimination of
ambiguity regarding the organization's ethical stances, b) initiation of
open discussions about obvious problems, and c) holding good conversations routinely and regularly (Waters, 1988).

Leadership is largely a process of communication among leader
and followers. The communication serves to create effective leader–fol-

lower relationships, consensus around organizational values, integration, and a shared vision concerning the organization's future. A relatively specific set of ethics related to this leader communication can be identified. The first is honest and candid discussions of organizational problems, positions, and issues. Honest and candid communication is necessary to build effective relationships and enhances the leader's credibility. The second is ethical organizational leadership that is open to discussion of issues and accessible to stakeholders and followers. Openness also enhances leader–follower relationships and is necessary to integration. The third is that such leadership has regard for all positions and perspectives manifest in the organization. This regard facilitates the ability of leaders to create consensus around organizational values and also serves the goal of integration. The final ethic is leader communication that is cognizant of the responsibility associated with control of the organization's channels of communication and with the trust followers and stakeholders place in their leaders.

SUMMARY

Leadership plays a dominant role in the strategic processes of organizing and in establishing the overall ethical tone for the organization. Followers attribute great affect to leadership and grant them the right to frame the follower's reality. Leadership has been examined from a number of diverse perspectives including traits, style, and contingency approaches. The concept of symbolic or cultural leadership places particular emphasis on communication, values, and ethics.

Leadership is a process of communication that creates effective leader–follower relationships, consensus around organizational values, integration, and shared vision about the organization. Ethics for leadership include honesty and candor, openness and accessibility, regard for all positions and perspectives manifest in the organization, and a sense of the responsibility associated with control of the organization's channels of communication and trust followers and stakeholders place in their leaders. In a fundamental way, leadership sets the agenda for the rest of the organization. Leaders who regularly discuss organizational values, ethics, and responsibilities can help ensure that others discuss these issues. These conversations about the good enhance the enactment of ethics by giving members and stakeholders a chance to hear what is said in order to know what to think.

CASE: LEADERSHIP AND RESPONSIBLE COMMUNICATION

Leadership is generally recognized as a core process of organizing. Leaders are the most visible manifestation of the organization and often personify the elements that define the organization. Lee Iacocca, formally of the Chrysler Corporation, is one of the most vivid examples of this form of leadership.

Iacocca was fired from the Ford Motor Company in 1978 and hired by the failing Chrysler Corporation. Through extreme cost-cutting measures, aggressive advertising, and through the support of the federal government in the form of $1.2 billion in guaranteed loans, Chrysler was saved and turned into a flourishing and dynamic company. Iacocca received much of the credit. As part of his campaign for federally guaranteed loans, Iacocca had attributed Chrysler's slide to oppressive federal polices and the unfair competition by the Japanese auto companies. Iacocca, as an industry leader, became widely known for speaking out about a number of business-related issues, but the persistent criticism of the Japanese and the trade deficit with Japan would become his most notable cause.

The issue was complex and controversial. Iacocca claimed that U.S. companies were systematically and intentionally kept out of Japanese markets by governmental red tape, manipulation of international monetary policies, a maze of closed distribution channels, and close relationships between the Japanese car companies. At the same time, he claimed, the Japanese were exploiting the American car market, flooding it with cars through illegal "dumping," and driving Americans out of high-paying jobs. Critics countered that these attacks on the Japanese were a smoke screen, designed to hide the incompetence of the U.S. automobile industry. Iacocca was called anti-free trade, an apologist for U.S. industry and, by some, a racist for his attacks on the Japanese.

His most biting speech on the subject occurred in Detroit, after traveling to Japan with then-President George Bush on a mission to break down trade barriers and help stimulate a stagnant American economy. In that speech, Iacocca used images of a war between Japan and the United States and argued "They're winning. They're beating our brains in." The result was "unemployment . . . closed plants. . . lost tax bases. . ." and "insidious Japanese economic and political power within the United States." He described Japanese trade practices as "predatory" and "ugly mercantilism at its worst." In response to the charges that the trade deficit was the fault of uncompetitive American companies, Iacocca charged "That's like blaming our army and Navy for Pearl Harbor." Critics charged that the speech was inappropriate and irresponsible in its level of attack and use of war imagery. Others argued that Iacocca was simply pointing out a serious business problem that had gone unaddressed for much too long.

Discussion Questions

1. What leadership values and responsibilities were evident in Iacocca's discussion of the Japanese trade deficit?
2. Discuss the appropriateness of Iacocca's descriptions of the Japanese.
3. What responsibilities do business leaders have for speaking out about controversial political and social issues?

13

Making Ethics Part of the Organization's Agenda

Weick's (1969, 1979) enactment-based approach to organizing emphasizes the role communication plays in the ongoing process of creating
and recreating organization. Weick argued that organizational members
must hear what is said in order to know what to think. This process allows
members and stakeholders to make sense out of their informational environments. As discussed in chapter 2, the opportunity for organizational
members and stakeholders to honestly and openly discuss questions of
right–wrong, good–bad, desirable–undesirable is frequently stifled in
organizations. Often, issues of ethics are simply not discussed, resulting
in circumstances where members, failing to hear what is said, do not
know what to think. Several factors limit the ability of organizations to
take ethical issues into account. Ethics are difficult to talk about and are
highly equivocal. Managers are usually not trained to discuss ethics.
Members often suffer from perceived powerlessness with regard to ethical issues. Sometimes, an unwitting collusion develops in organizations
resulting in the systematic avoidance of ethical questions. Frequently, the
values associated with the organization's competitiveness and profitability overwhelm all other considerations. In these instances, the equivocality
associated with ethical issues goes unaddressed.

This chapter examines three ways in which ethical questions and issues can be placed on the agenda and become part of the organization's regular ongoing talk. These methods include programs about ethics, ethical audits, and the development of codes of ethics. These methods are proposed as ways to stimulate discussion and debate and allow members the opportunity to hear what is said about values and ethics. These methods create opportunities for feedback, or metacommunication, about how ethical issues are discussed. Ultimately, these discussions can facilitate the creation of interpretations and responses that make sense of the organization's complex, confusing, and equivocal value and ethical environment.

ETHICS PROGRAMS

Ethics programs, symposia, colloquia, lectures, case studies, and other forms of formal discussions about ethics and values are increasingly common in organizations and professional associations. Surveys suggest that about 30%-40% of firms conduct some form of ethics programs (Delaney & Sockell, 1992). Delaney and Sockell found that the public administration industry has the largest percentage of such programs followed by agriculture, mining, construction and finance, and insurance and real estate. They also reported a positive impact of such programs on ethical behavior in organizations in terms of fostering an environment that allows employees to avoid unethical conduct without facing a negative impact on their career.

These programs generally seek to acquaint organizational members with the language of ethics, review for members some of the major ethical issues faced, inculcate organizational and professional values, and describe ways of addressing these issues. Most often, these programs are structured as training workshops often using a case study and discussion format. Codes of ethics are also frequently featured as elements of these programs. These efforts are particularly useful in raising the general awareness of ethical issues and creating opportunities for members to speak out about ethics and hear what the organization and others think. This opportunity to communicate about issues of ethics can be particularly useful in providing equivocality reducing interpretations and responses. As Weick (1995) suggested, meetings have a particularly important role in organizational sense-making. Ethics programs also have the benefit of bringing outside experts and other stakeholders into the discussion of core values and ethical conduct. This involvement may increase the ability of the organization to confront its informational environment by enhancing requisite variety.

One of the first and most widely recognized ethics programs was developed by the General Dynamics Corporation in the early 1980s. After charges of fraud, deception, and graft, General Dynamics instituted widespread organizational change, including creating a comprehensive companywide ethics program (Barker, 1993). The program included naming ethics directors for all divisions, appointing internal ethics trainers, and training all salaried and nonsalaried employees in a set of ethical standards developed by the company (Barker, 1993). Efforts were made to communicate the scope and goals of the program to all employees through newsletters and company publications and to solicit employee involvement and support. The program included a procedure for investigating employee violations of General Dynamics' code of ethics. The entire program is supervised and evaluated by the Committee on Corporate Responsibility of the General Dynamics Board of Directors. In evaluating the program, Barker (1993) reported that General Dynamics has been successful in creating and communicating a clear set of ethical standards. The company has been less successful, however, in creating more humane working conditions for employees. Based on this conclusion, Barker cautioned organizations instituting ethics programs to avoid creating unrealistic expectations for employees.

Another form of organizational program that has become increasingly popular since 1990 are quality initiatives. As discussed in chapter 3, quality initiatives are fundamentally designed to address issues of quality goods and services but do so within a human resources paradigm of employee empowerment and participation in problem solving. Organizational structures are established to create an ongoing process of quality improvement. These programs have been widely adopted by both manufacturing and service organizations including many organizations in the public sector. Employees are encouraged to take responsibility for quality issues regardless of how these issues might fall within the organization's traditional divisions of labor. Quality becomes an integrating organizational value. Quality teams are often created to examine specific problems and redesign processes that are inefficient or ineffective. These teams often meet with customers and other stakeholders. Quality initiatives also emphasize clearly understanding and meeting the expectations of stakeholders, articulating a clear set of goals and values, and creating a supportive team-based environment in which the organization can continually improve. Although quality initiatives do not necessarily address ethical issues in a direct way, they are designed to create more responsive and responsible organizations through the empowerment of employees. The also foster the development of a clear articulation of organizational values.

ETHICS AUDITS

Some organizations have approached the issues of ethics by conducting audits, formal surveys, and analyses of organizational conduct to assess the overall level of ethicality. As described in chapter 8, traditional accounting firms even provide this service as a form of "social accounting" of the organization's activities. Other organizations include several questions about ethics as part of annual employee attitude surveys. Sometimes, it is a charge of ethical misconduct that prompts a systematic review of the organization's activities. In other instances, organizations undertake social accounting as part of strategic planning activities. Audits typically seek to examine the organization's activities, climate, outcomes, and decisions in relation to sets of employee, organizational, professional, stakeholder, and social values. An ethical audit, for example, might examine the impact of a new plant on a local community and on the environment. Audits might examine the affect on cost-cutting initiatives on employees and suppliers. The conclusions of these audits are sometimes featured in the organization's annual report along with more traditional data about financial performance. Although still relatively uncommon, these social audits support several important goals.

First, they signal that ethical issues and questions of responsibility are important (Delaney & Sockell, 1992). Information theorists point out that regularly measuring some aspects of an organization's activities enhances the chances that members will attend to those activities. By regularly measuring the level of ethical conduct, organizations signal that ethics are important and should be attended to. Second, audits are usually systematic in examining potential areas of value conflict. Because values are complex and interactive, and because organizations must take into account the needs and interests of diverse stakeholders, the potential for unforeseen conflicts is very great. Systematic examination of the organization's activities in relation to these diverse values can help identify and resolve unforeseen conflicts. Third, audits enhance the ability of organizations to take value issues into account in organizational decision making. The value dimensions of a decision can then be weighed more fully and systematically. This is particularly useful when stakeholder values are in conflict. Finally, as with ethics programs, ethical audits can help prompt discussion and debate, and create the opportunity for members to hear what others say about ethics. Audits are retrospective in the sense that they look back on the organization's activities and create a material record of ethical issues. In so doing, they create rich opportunities for retrospective sense-making.

ETHICAL CODES

One of the most common approaches used by organizations to deal with issues of ethics involves formal ethical codes (Frankel, 1989). Almost all large organizations now have formally adopted some type of ethical code. Codes are systematic descriptions and articulations of the organization's formal position with regard to values and ethical positions. They have been common documents for organizations and professional associations at least since the early 1900s. Codes range from general statements of principles, goals, and values the organization has formally adopted to specific statements of "oughts" and "shoulds." They may even specify appropriate channels for dealing with ethically suspect behavior. Although there is much variation, codes are usually structured around a series of statements regarding what is valued, what the organization stands for, and what the organization seeks to achieve. Codes usually offer specific guidelines for common ethical dilemmas such as conflict of interest, sexual harassment, or suspicions of managerial wrongdoing. Sometimes ethics committees are created to deal with these issues. Codes are also usually limited to specific topical or issue areas related directly to work or work-related activities. Frankel (1989) suggested that codes are designed to appeal to a variety of interests, and constituencies including clients, media, shareholders, professional associations, the general public, and the government. They often articulate the organization's perception of its responsibilities and obligations to these groups.

Corporate ethicists point out that codes serve several additional purposes (Frankel, 1989). First, they provide clear moral guidelines for members of the organization. As discussed in chapter 1, ethical issues in organizations are often complex, highly politicized, and uncertain. Ethical codes provide some general direction in these uncertain and unfamiliar situations. Codes, and the process whereby the code is created and adopted, represent systematic efforts to create and communicate interpretations of the organization's ethical position. As with ethics programs and audits, they facilitate the enactment, selection, and retention of ethical guidelines.

Second, some critics have suggested that codes are legalistic documents meant primarily to limit and control employee behaviors. They point out that many codes are structured in highly legalistic ways. Some even require that employees sign a formal statement indicating that they have read, understand, and agree to abide by the code. Failure to abide by the code might then translate into specific punishments. These codes often focus on values and ethical issues that are most important in improving the organization's profitability, such as employee theft or drug abuse, maintaining quality products, or serving the customer.

A related function of ethical codes concerns their value in limiting the organization's legal liability. Organizations may use codes of ethics as evidence that they do not condone or accept certain forms of illegal or unethical behavior. Organizations facing sexual harassment suits, for example, might be able to mitigate some of their liability by showing that their code of ethics specifically precludes this behavior. A code may help protect employers from charges of customer fraud or deception. Probably a majority of organizational codes are rule-like in their character in part to help protect the company from the unethical conduct of employees and reduce legal liability (Cressy & Moore, 1983).

A fourth function of ethical codes concerns their use in relating to the organization's larger communities. Several critics have suggested that most codes are designed primarily as public relations devices. Organizations often point to codes as evidence that they take questions of right and wrong seriously. In this way, codes are legitimizing structures allowing the organization to demonstrate that it is operating in a manner that is consistent with general social norms and values (Frankel, 1989; Pfeffer & Salancik, 1978).

Much debate exists regarding the relative effectiveness of codes in creating a higher ethical standard for the organization (see Stevens, 1992). Critics point out that code effectiveness is contingent on effective use by employees and managers. Moreover, most employees are likely to follow their personal or group values, before they adhere to organizational values. Regardless of the various functions codes serve and their relative effectiveness, they have the benefit of stimulating discussions of values and ethical issues. Codes are most often created by committees, usually composed of a variety of organizational constituencies including employees, managers, suppliers, and customers. These committees are charged with systematically sorting through the various issues the organization faces and reaching some consensus about equivocality reducing interpretations. The process of drafting an ethical code is often very demanding as the members are forced to balance competing values and encode ethics in ways that are acceptable to a variety of diverse groups. The resulting code usually outlines a repertoire of equivocality reducing responses for ethical issues. In general, however, the effectiveness of a particular code is likely to be influenced by the degree to which the specific exigencies of the organization and its context are taken into account.

ETHICAL ENACTMENT AND METACOMMUNICATION

Programs, quality initiatives, audits, and codes of ethics facilitate the process of enactment, selection, and retention in part be stimulating metacommunication processes. Metacommunication is a specialized form of feedback concerning communication (Kreps, 1993). Metacommunication is rooted in systems theory and is seen as a fundamental process whereby the system is either reaffirmed or modified (Littlejohn, 1992). Codes of ethics, for example, are organizational messages that may encourage certain forms of reporting when unethical behaviors are identified. Codes may reaffirm an existing communicative approach to ethical wrongdoing or call for new communication processes for resolving these issues. Ethics programs may also provide feedback concerning how best to communicate the organization's ethical stance, how to report perceived wrongdoing, or how to evaluate accounts. Most importantly, perhaps, metacommunication can instruct members concerning how the ethical issues associated with their organizational experiences should be discussed.

Kreps (1993) argued that metacommunication processes are critical in promoting long-term cultural change in organizations. He suggested that victims of sexual harassment, for example, "clearly and directly express their outrage at such treatment" (p. 316). As with whistleblowing, these expressions bring morally suspect behavior into the light of public scrutiny. "Unethical behaviors, such as sexual harassment," Kreps argued "are more likely to occur in the dark than in the light of public scrutiny" (p. 316). Metacommunication processes, in this case the statements of outrage concerning harassing communication, serve to alter the overall ethical culture of the organization. This metacommunication regarding the appropriateness, desirability, or form of various messages can serve as a powerful inducement for organizational change. The ongoing process of reducing ethical equivocality ultimately requires that members make public statements about ethics, including speaking out when ethical principles are violated or ignored.

LIMITATIONS AND CONSEQUENCES

Although dialogue and discussions about ethics through programs, quality initiatives, audits, and codes of ethics facilitate the process of enactment, selection, and retention they by no means ensure the ongoing development of an ethical organization. There are limitations to the ability of organizations to continually reconstitute themselves in relation to new information inputs, standards, and values. There are some organizations that are fundamentally unethical in their basic character. These organizations can only exist as long as informational inputs about ethics essentially go unattended or as long as interpretations are offered that downplay or obscure ethical questions. Tobacco companies, for example, will exist as profitable enterprises only as long as they deny the fact that their products make the customers sick. These companies also must continue to obscure this basic ethical issue. They do so by portraying the primary value issue as one of smoking as personal freedom to divert attention from the more salient issue of health. There are two other important limitations to the enactment of the organization's value environment. These include consistency of behavior and communication, and the ability of members and stakeholders to reach some level of consensus about ethics.

It would be naive to suggest that improved communication necessarily creates more ethical organizations. Consistency must also exist between the communication of members and their behaviors. Systematic and sustained inconsistency between statements about ethics and the ethics of behavior, even in the presence of codes, audits, quality initiatives, and programs, signals to members that ethics are not important and the language of ethics is to be ignored. The codes and programs are seen as merely a facade, window dressing, or public relations, designed to gloss over the organization's real values and conduct. Ethics programs and lofty codes become elaborate deceptions. This inconsistency is often cited as the primary reason many ethics programs and codes fail to substantively affect organizational behavior. Moreover, such inconsistency promotes hypocrisy, cynicism, and dishonesty and probably leads to even further moral decay. In the long run, maintaining consistency between communication and behavior, even at the expense of lower levels of ethical conduct, is probably more desirable than systematic and institutionalized hypocrisy, cynicism, and dishonesty. Rather than offering lofty statements of ethics that cannot be matched in behavior, organization members should seek first to integrate behavior and communication.

In his discussion of sexual harassment, Kreps (1993) pointed out that this form of unethical communication in organizations distracts members and "irrevocably decreases both the quality of organizational life and the productivity of organizational activities" (pp. 310–311). Institutionalized hypocrisy and cynicism, rooted in inconsistency between words and actions, coupled with failure to adhere to general standards of ethical conduct has the same affect. Employees are reluctant to affiliate and remain with irresponsible, unethical companies. Employee morale suffers and stress rises. The fundamental levels of trust necessary to effective work relationships will decay. Messages are no longer judged as credible. Under conditions of ethical and value inconsistency, the ability of employees and stakeholders to sustain high levels of commitment, creativity, and productivity is significantly compromised. Organizations constituted around ethical hypocrisy cannot function effectively.

Weick (1995) pointed out, however, that consistency is conceptualized from an enactment-based approach as "talking the walk" rather than the more traditional conceptualization of "walking the talk" (pp. 182–183). Weick noted, "People discover what they think by looking back on what they say, how they feel and where they walk. . . . The talk makes sense of walking. . . . How can I know what I value until I see where I walk" (pp. 182–183). Although Weick suggested that, in general, consistency in organization is a positive force, he is careful to reiterate the central enactment notion that (talk) sense-making interpretations follow (walk) behavior. Statements of moral principles, codes of conduct, and exhortations to do good that are not grounded in member history and experiences have little chance of helping members make sense of their environments.

A second limitation on enactment concerns the ability of members to reach some level of consensus about values and ethics and about which interpretations are most useful in reducing ethical equivocality. As noted in chapter 2, the diversity, interaction, and importance of values makes achieving agreement very difficult. This difficulty is accentuated by the fact that most managers lack the background and vocabulary to discuss ethics. Without some level of agreement, members cannot achieve coherence concerning equivocality reducing interpretations. Johannesen (1990) suggested that one approach to ethics involves agreeing first on the perspective or "ethical lens" that is most salient within a particular context. Some situations, for example, may be best suited for a political perspective emphasizing rational choice, analysis of facts, and unrestrained debate. Others may be more consistent with the humanistic perspectives of open and honest dialogue, unconditional regard, and empathy. Once individuals have agreed on the appropriate perspective, building consensus around a particular ethical judgment is more likely (Johannesen, 1990). Given the context-rich feature of organizations and organizational communication, this approach seems particularly fruitful. An effort to clarify and communicate the values that explain and make sense of organizational actions might provide the basic elements for building a larger consensus about what constitutes ethically desirable organizational conduct.

SUMMARY

Large complex organizations are the most powerful of human creations. They are also confounding, disorganized, confusing, and messy environments where making sense is necessary to structure an ongoing and highly diverse stream of informational inputs. The value- and ethical-based aspects of organizing too often go unexamined in part because these issues are divisive, lack clear yes-or-no answers, and because members lack a vocabulary for thinking about and discussing ethics. Stimulating discussion, debate, dialogue, and metacommunication among organizational members and stakeholders about ethics and values enhances the likelihood that organizations will take values and ethics into account in seeking to make sense of their informational environments. Three ways in which ethical questions can be placed on the organization's agenda include programs about ethics, ethical audits, and the development of codes of ethics. Codes and ethics programs are increasingly common in organizations. Audits are comparatively more rare, although they are gaining popularity as features of annual reports. These programs signal that ethics are important, help clarify the organization's values, and enhance the chance of members hearing what others say about ethics. They also facilitate discussions about what constitutes effective metacommunication regarding ethics.

It is also important to point out that there are substantive limitations to the effectiveness of enhanced communication about values and ethics. These limitations include consistency between behavior and communication and the ability of members to reach some levels of consensus about appropriate values, interpretations, and responses. Ethical consistency and consensus are both goals and processes. They are important not only in terms of serving particular individual, organization, and stakeholder values, but also in sustaining productive, healthy, creative, satisfying, and efficient organizing processes.

In the long term, ethics cannot be considered merely questions of good–bad, right–wrong, and desirable–undesirable. Ultimately, they also must be seen as fundamentally relating to quality of organizational life, effectiveness of organizational processes, competitiveness of organizational outcomes, and the organization's essential social worth.

CASE: CORPORATE CODES OF ETHICS

Codes of ethics have been widely used by many organizations. The following are reprinted sections of the Chrysler Corporation code of Ethical Behavior.

Obey the Law

Chrysler Corporation's base-line policy is to conduct all of its activities in full compliance with all relevant laws and regulations. It is expected that you will support this policy in every Company matter that comes to your attention. This is the starting point for the ethical behavior guidelines presented in this Code.

Chrysler's Code of Ethical Behavior

Individual actions project you not only as a person, but also as a representative of Chrysler Corporation. It is imperative that you do your utmost to maintain the highest level of integrity and ethics.

High standards of integrity and ethics require hard work, courage and sometimes difficult choices. Often it is necessary to determine a proper course of action and forego business or personal opportunities. This booklet, while not all-inclusive, provides standards of the ethical behavior expected of Chrysler employees.

The nature of certain operations of Chrysler may require standards of conduct more restrictive than those set forth in this booklet. In such cases, the managements responsible for such operations are free to publish local codes of ethical behavior. It is expected that employees involved in such operations will observe both the standards set forth in this booklet and any more restrictive standards

imposed by such local codes of ethical behavior.

Your Role

Each employee has a personal responsibility to observe Chrysler's Code of Ethical Behavior with attention to both the detail and spirit of each statement in this Code. This is *your* obligation.

It is also important that you encourage other employees to observe Chrysler's Code of Ethical Behavior and to report suspected instances of their failure to do so. The reputation and future economic viability of Chrysler may be at stake.

Work Environment

Chrysler expects all of its employees to be treated with dignity, their rights respected and their privacy maintained. This applies to all employees regardless of sex, race, ethnic background, religion, age, disability or membership in any other legally protected class. In addition, Chrysler will not tolerate harassment of or retaliation against any person in the workplace.

Personal Interests

You have a duty to avoid personal interests which may conflict or appear to conflict with

the interests of Chrysler, or which might
influence or appear to influence your
judgment or actions in performing your
Chrysler duties. Personal interests can cause
conflicts in numerous ways. Some of the
guidelines to be observed in order to avoid
such conflicts are set forth below.

■ **Outside Business Activities**
You are not to conduct any recurring private
business activities that inhibit in any way
carrying out your assigned Chrysler
responsibilities. Working or performing
services for suppliers or competitors while
employed by Chrysler is prohibited.

■ **Representing Chrysler**
You may participate in community, government and educational or civic organizations
and serve on boards of directors of nonprofit
private clubs, educational institutions and
hospitals. If participation is dependent upon
employment with Chrysler, the knowledge
and concurrence of the Executive Director —
Government Affairs is required. Chrysler
employees may not, without Chrysler's
approval, serve on boards of directors
of companies operated for profit.

■ **Personal Financial Interest**
You are not to engage in any personal
financial activities which could influence
your judgment or actions in performing
duties for Chrysler.

■ **Payment from Third Parties**
You, and members of your family, are
prohibited from soliciting and, except as
provided in the guidelines discussed below,
accepting personal benefits such as cash,
gift certificates, gifts, payments, loans,
special discounts, personal services, etc.,
from suppliers, customers, competitors,
or any third party as a result of a working
relationship.

Ethical Decision-Making Checklist

When you are confronted with a situation that is ethically troublesome to you, use the following checklist to help you determine the appropriateness of whatever action you are considering or are being asked to consider.

▪ Analysis

What are the facts?

Who is responsible to act?

When is the proper time to act?

What and whose rights are involved?

Which written guidelines and procedures should I consult?

▪ Solution Development

What solutions are available to me?

Have I considered all of the solutions which might permit me to reduce harm, maximize benefits, respect more rights, or be fair to more parties?

▪ Select the Best Solution

What are the potential consequences of my solutions? Of the options I have considered, which do the most to maximize benefits, reduce harm, respect rights and duties and increase fairness?

Are all parties treated fairly in my proposed decision?

▪ Implementation

Confirm your proposed decision with your supervisor or the Business Practices Office.

Implement.

Attention

This Code applies to Chrysler Corporation and each of its subsidiaries.

Violations of the Code of Ethical Behavior, or any other Chrysler policy or procedure, may result in disciplinary action up to and including discharge and, if warranted, legal proceedings. Chrysler reserves the right to amend, interpret and construe the Code. Nothing herein, however, shall constitute a contract of employment with any employee or conflict with Chrysler's right to terminate employment relationships at will.

Discussion Questions

1. What are the primary values manifest in this code?
2. How might this code serve as a mechanism for stimulating discussion and debate about ethics?
3. What repertoire of responses for reducing ethical equivocality does the code outline?

References

Aldrich, D., & Herker, D. (1977). Boundary spanning roles and organizational structure. *Academy of Management Review, 2,* 217–230.

Altman, I. (1976). Privacy: A conceptual analysis. *Environment and Behavior, 8,* 7–26.

Altman, S., Valenzi, E., & Hodgetts, R. H. (1985). *Organizational behavior: Theory and practice.* New York: Academic Press.

Andrews, K. R. (1989). Introduction. In K. R. Andrews & D. K. David (Eds.), *Ethics in practice* (pp. 1–13). Boston: Harvard Business School.

Bantz, C., & Smith, D. H. (1977). A critique and experimental test of Weick's model of organizing. *Communication Monographs, 44,* 171–184.

Bantz, C. (1989). Organizing and the social psychology of organizing. *Communication Studies, 40,* 231–240.

Barber, J. D. (1972). *The presidential character.* Englewood Cliffs, NJ: Prentice-Hall.

Barker, R. A. (1993). An evaluation of the ethics program at General Dynamics. *Journal of Business Ethics, 12,* 165–177.

Barnett, T. R. (1992, July). Will your employees blow the whistle? *Human Resources Magazine, 37,* 76–78.

Baron, D. P. (1993). *Business and its environment.* Englewood Cliffs, NJ: Prentice-Hall.

Batt, W. L. (1983). Canada's good example with displaced workers. *Harvard Business Review, 83,* 6–8.

Bennis, W. G., & Nanus, B. (1985). *Leaders: The strategies for taking charge.* New York: Harper & Row.

Benoit, W. L. (1995). *Accounts, excuses and apologies a theory of image restoration strategies.* Albany: SUNY Press.

Berscheid, E., & Walster, E. H. (1978). *Interpersonal attraction* (2nd ed.). Reading, MA: Addison Wesley.

Beyer, J., & Lutze, S. (1993). The ethical nexus: Organizations, values, and decision-making. In C. Conrad (Ed.), *The ethical nexus* (pp. 23–45). Norwood, NJ: Ablex.

Bok, S. (1979). *Lying.* New York: Vintage Books.

Bok, S. (1980). Whistle blowing and professional responsibility. *New York University Education Quarterly, 10,* 2–10.

Boulding, K. (1978). The legitimacy of the business institution. In E. M. Epstein & D. Votaw (Eds.), *Rationality, legitimacy, responsibility: Search for new directions in business and society* (pp. 83–99). Santa Monica, CA: Goodyear.

Bowen, H. R. (1953). *Social responsibilities of the businessman.* New York: Harper & Row.

Brummer, J. J. (1991). *Corporate responsibility and legitimacy.* New York: Greenwood Press.

Buchholz, R. A. (1990). The evolution of corporate social responsibility. In P. Madsen & J. M. Shafritz (Eds.), *Essentials of business ethics* (pp. 298–310). New York: Penguin.

Buono, A. F., & Nichols, L. (1995). *Corporate policy, values and social responsibility.* New York: Praeger.

Bureau of National Affairs. (1987). *Workplace privacy: Employee testing, surveillance, wrongful discharge, and other areas of vulnerability.* Washington, DC: BNA Reports.

Burelson, B. R., & Kline, S. L. (1979). Habermas' theory of communication: A critical explication. *The Quarterly Journal of Speech, 65,* 412–428.

Burgoon, J. (1982). Privacy and communication. *Communication Yearbook, 6,* 206–248.

Buttny, R. (1993). *Social accountability in communication.* Newbury Park, CA: Sage.

Cahill, C. M., & Haskins, W. A. (1984). The First Amendment issue of obscenity: A phenomenological analysis. *The Free Speech Yearbook, 23,* 30–42.

Carroll, A. B. (1975). Management ethics: A post-Watergate view. *Business Horizons, 17,* 75–80.

Centers for Disease Control. (1985). *CDC Guidelines for AIDS in the Workplace.* Atlanta, GA: Author.

Chaganti, R., & Sambharya, R. (1987). Strategic orientation and characteristics of upper management. *Strategic Management Journal, 8,* 393–401.

Chapman, R. (1985). The ruckus over medical testing. *Fortune, 112,* 57–58.

Cheney, G. (1991). *Rhetoric in an organizational society.* Columbia: University of South Carolina Press.

Cheney, G. (1992). The corporation (re)presents itself. In E. L. Toth & R. L. Heath (Eds.), *Rhetorical and critical approaches to public relations* (pp. 165-183). Hillsdale, NJ: Lawrence Erlbaum Associates.

Cheney, G., & Fernette, G. (1993). Persuasion and organization: Values, logics, and accounts in contemporary corporate public discourse. In C. Conrad (Ed.), *The ethical nexus* (pp. 49–75). Norwood, NJ: Ablex

Cheney, G., & Tompkins, P. K. (1987). Coming to terms with organizational identification and commitment. *Central States Speech Journal, 38,* 1–15.

Christians, C. G., Rotzoll, K. B., & Fackler, M. (1991). *Media ethics* (3rd ed.). White Plains, NY: Longman.

Clark, L. (1992, Fall). Ralph Nader presents national award to Gap's Louis Clark. In *Bridging the gap.* Washington, DC: Government Accountability Project.

Cobb, A. T., Wooten, K. C., & Folger, R. (1995). Justice in the making: Toward understanding the theory and practice of justice in organizational change and development. In W. A. Pasmore & R. W. Woodman (Eds.), *Research in organizational change and development* (Vol. 8, pp. 243–295). Greenwich, CT: JAI Press.

Collins, C. (1992). In defense of advertising. In M. Snoeyenbos, J. Milton, R. Almeder, & J. Humber (Eds.), *Business ethics* (rev. ed., pp. 420–429). Buffalo, NY: Prometheus Books.

Conrad, C. (1993). *The ethical nexus.* Norwood, NJ: Ablex.

Coulson, R. (1981). *The termination handbook.* New York: The Free Press.

Crable, R. (1978). Ethical codes, accountability and argumentation. *Quarterly Journal of Speech, 64,* 23–32.

Crable, R., & Vibbert, S. (1985). Managing issues and influencing public policy. *Public Relations Review, 11,* 3–16.

Cranston lashes out at Senate. (1991, November 21). *The Ann Arbor News,* p. A8.

Cressy, D., & Moore, C. A. (1983). Managerial values and corporate codes of ethics. *California Management Review, 25,* 53–77.

Cronkite, G., & Liska, J. (1976). A critique of factor analytical approaches to the study of credibility. *Communication Monographs, 43,* 91–107.

Cummings, T. G., & Huse, E. F. (1989). *Organizational development and change.* St. Paul, MN: West.

Cunningham, S. B. (1992). Sorting out the ethics of propaganda. *Communication Studies, 4,* 231–245.

Daniels, T. D., & Spiker, B. K. (1991). *Perspectives on organizational communication* (2nd ed.). Dubuque, IA: William C. Brown.

Deal, T., & Kennedy, A. A. (1982). *Corporate cultures: The rites and rituals of corporate life.* Reading, MA: Addison Wesley.

DeGeorge, R. T. (1986a). *Business ethics.* New York: MacMillian.

DeGeorge, R. T. (1986b). Ethical dilemmas for multinational enterprise: A philosophical overview. In W. M. Hoffman, A. E. Lange, & D. Fedo (Eds.), *Ethics and the multi national enterprise: Proceedings of the sixth national conference on business ethics* (pp. 39–46). Lanham, MD: University Press of America.

Delaney, J. T., & Sockell, D. (1992). Do company ethics training programs make a difference? An empirical analysis. *Journal of Business Ethics, 11,* 719–727.

Deming, W. E. (1982). *Out of crisis.* Cambridge, MA: MIT Press.

Dennison, D. S. (1978). Corporate image advertising and the FTC. In *Sourcebook of corporate image and corporate advocacy advertising* (GPO Publication No. 33-291-O, pp. 193–199). Washington, DC: U.S. Government Printing Office.

Dershowitz, A. M. (1994). *The abuse excuse.* Boston: Little, Brown.

Devine, T. M., & Aplin, D. G. (1988). Whistleblower protection: The GAP between the law and reality. *Howard Law Journal, 31,* 223–239.

Dill, W. R. (1958). Environment as an influence on manager autonomy. *Administrative Science Quarterly, 6,* 2–22.

Dirsmith, M. W., & Covaleski, M. A. (1983). Strategic external communication and environmental context. *Strategic Management Journal, 4,* 137–151.

Dixon, D. F. (1994). A day's shopping in thirteenth-century Paris. In J. W. Seth & R. A. Fullerton (Eds.), *Research in marketing: Explorations in the history of marketing* (Suppl. 6, pp. 13–25). Greenwich, CT: JAI Press.

Dowling, J., & Pfeffer, J. (1975). Organizational legitimacy: Social values and organizational behavior. *Pacific Sociology Review, 18,* 122–136.

Drucker, P. (1981). What is business ethics? *The Public Interest, 62,* 18–36.

Drucker, P. (1982). *The changing world of the executive.* New York: Times Books.

Duncan, R. (1972). Characteristics of organizational and perceived environmental uncertainty. *Administrative Science Quarterly, 17,* 39–47.

Edwards, R. (1993). *Rights at work.* Washington, DC: The Brookings Institute.

Elliston, F., Keenan, J., Lockhart, P., & Von Schaick, J. (1985). *Whistleblowing managing dissent in the workplace.* New York: Praeger.

Elliston, F., Keenan, J., Lockhart, P., & Von Schaick, J. (1990). *Whistleblowing research: Methodology and moral issues.* New York: Praeger.

Emery, F. E., & Trist, E. L. (1965). The causal texture of organizational environments. *Human Relations, 18*, 273–291.

Environmental Protection Agency. (1993, June 23). *Environmental Protection Agency Access EPA Toxic Release Inventory.* [Internet] Available: http://earth1.epa.gov:80/cgi-bin/waisgate?port=210&ip

Epstein, E. M., & Votaw, D. (1978). *Rationality, legitimacy, responsibility: Search for new directions in business and society.* Santa Monica, CA: Goodyear.

Evan, W., & Freeman, R. E. (1993). A stakeholder view of the modern corporation: Kantarin capitalism. In G. D. Chryssides & J. Kaler (Eds.), *An introduction to business ethics* (pp. 249–259). New York: Chapman & Hall.

Everett, J. L. (1994). Communication and social organization in organizations and organizational populations. *Communication Theory, 2*, 92–110.

Fairholm, G. W. (1991). *Values leadership toward a new philosophy.* New York: Praeger.

Fayol, H. (1949). *General industrial management.* New York: Pitman.

Federal Trade Commission. (1984, August 2). *FTC policy statement regarding advertising substantiation program* [Internet]. Available: http://www.webcom/~lewrose/article/absoubpol.html

Federal Trade Commission. (1992, July). *Green claims* [Internet]. Available: http://www.webcom/~lewrose/article/greencl.html

Federal Trade Commission. (1995, August 9). *History* [Internet]. Available: http://www.ftc.gov

Fernandez, J. P. (1993). *The diversity advantage.* New York: Lexington.

Ferrell, O. C. (1985). Implementing and monitoring ethics in advertising. In G. P. Laczniak & P. E. Murphy (Eds.), *Marketing ethics: Guideline for managers* (pp. 27–41). Lexington, MA: Lexington.

Filly, A. C., House, R. J., & Kern, S. (1979). *Management processes and organizational behavior* (2nd ed.). Glenview, IL: Scott Foresman.

Fischer, P. M., Schwartz, M. P., Richards, J. W., Goldstein, A. O., & Rojas, T. H. (1991, December, 11). Brand logo recognition by children aged three to six years. *Journal of American Medical Association*, pp. 3145–3148.

Fisher, W. (1987). *Communication as narration.* Columbia: University of South Carolina Press.

Frankel, M. (1989). Professional codes: Why, how and with what input? *Journal of Business Ethics, 8*, 109–115.

Fransiconi, R. (1986). The implications of Habermas' theory of legitimation for rhetorical criticism. *Communication Monographs, 53*, 16–35.

Freeman, R. E. (1984). *Strategic management: A stakeholder approach.* Marshfield, MA: Pitman.

Freeman, R. E., & Gilbert, D. R. (1987). Managing stakeholder interests. In S. P. Sethi & C. M. Fable (Eds.), *Business and society: Dimensions of conflict and cooperation* (pp. 397–422). Lexington, MA: Lexington.

French, P. A. (1984). *Collective and corporate responsibility*. New York: Columbia University Press.

French, W. L., & Bell, C. H., Jr. (1984). *Organizational development behavioral science interventions for organizational improvement* (3rd ed.). Englewood Cliffs, NJ: Prentice-Hall.

Freund, L. (1960). Responsibility-definitions, distinctions and applications in various contexts. In C. J. Friedrich (Ed.), *Responsibility* (p. 12). New York: The Liberal Press.

Friedman, M. (1962). *Capitalism and freedom*. Chicago: University of Chicago Press.

Galbraith, J. K. (1967). *The new industrial state*. Boston: Houghton Mifflin.

Galbraith, J. K. (1971). Matrix organizational design. *Business Horizons, 13*, 29–40.

Garrett, D. E., Bradfords, J. L., Meyers, R. A., & Becker, J. (1989). Issues management and organizational accounts: An analysis of corporate responses to accusations of unethical business practices. *Journal of Business Ethics, 8*, 507–520.

Gibb, J. (1961). Defensive communication. *Journal of Communication, 11*, 141–148.

Goldberg, J. (1990). Truth and consequences. *Omni, 13*, 72–76, 108–115.

Golden, J. L., Berquist, G. F., & Coleman, W. E. (1983). *The rhetoric of western thought*. Dubuque, IA: Kendall/Hunt.

Goldhaber, G. (1993). *Organizational communication*. Dubuque, IA: William C. Brown.

Goodman, P. S., & Kurke, L. B. (1982). Studies in change in organizations: A status report. In P.S. Goodman (Ed.), *Change in organizations new perspectives on theory, research and practice* (pp. 1–47). San Francisco: Jossey-Bass.

Gorden, W. I. (1988). Range of employee voice. *Employee Responsibilities and Rights Journal, 14*, 283–299.

Gorden, W. I., Infante, D. A., & Graham, E. E. (1988). Corporate conditions conducive to employee voice: A subordinate perspective. *Employee Responsibilities and Rights Journal, 1*, 101–111.

Gorden, W. I., Infante, D. A., Wilson, L., & Clarke, C. (1984). Rationale and development of an employee rights scale. *The Free Speech Yearbook, 23*, 66–80.

Gorden, W. I., & Mermer, D. (1989). *A conceptualization of workplace citizenship: A critique of freedom*. Unpublished manuscript.

Government Accountability Project. (1991). *Bridging the gap*. Washington, DC: Author.

Government Accountability Project. (1992). *Bridging the gap*. Washington, DC: Author.

Gray, R., Owen, D., & Maunders, K. (1987). *Corporate social reporting*. Englewood Cliffs, NJ: Prentice-Hall.

Greiner, L. (1970). *Organizational change and development*. Homewood, IL: Richard D. Irwin.

Grunig, J. E., & Repper, F. C. (1992). Strategic management, publics, and issues. In J. E. Grunig (Ed.), Excellence in public relations and communication management (pp. 117–157). Hillsdale, NJ: Lawrence Erlbaum Associates.

Grunig, L. A., Grunig, J. E., & Ehling, W. P. (1992). What is an effective organization. In J. E. Grunig (Ed.), Excellence in public relations and communication management (pp. 65–90). Hillsdale, NJ: Lawrence Erlbaum Associates.

Habermas, J. (1975). Legitimation crisis (T. McCarthy, Trans.). Boston: Beacon Press.

Heald, M. (1970). The social responsibility of business: Company and community 1900–1960. New Brunswick, NJ: Transaction Books.

Heath, R., & Nelsen, R. A. (1986). Issue management. Beverly Hills, CA: Sage.

Heller, T., & Van Til, J. (1986). Leadership and followership: Some summary propositions. The Journal of Applied Behavioral Science, 18, 305–414.

Herbeck, D. (1984). The regulation of pornography and free speech. The Free Speech Yearbook, 23, 92–109.

Herrick, J. A. (1992). Rhetoric, ethics and virtue. Communication Studies, 43, 133–150.

Hiam, A. (1992). Closing the quality gap. Englewood Cliffs, NJ: Prentice-Hall.

Hirschman, A. O. (1970). Exit, voice and loyalty. Cambridge, MA: Harvard University Press.

Holusha, J. (1994, April 1). Whistle-blower gets $22.5 million. New York Times, p. D1

Hoover, J. (1994, November). Postmodern ethics II: Lawrence Walsh's Iran-Contra report. Paper presented at the annual meeting of the Speech Communication Association, New Orleans, LA.

Hoerr, J. (1988, March 28). Privacy in the workplace. Business Week, pp. 61–68.

Iacocca, L. (1988). [Transcript of remarks by Lee A. Iacocca, chairman of the board, Chrysler Corporation, at a press conference in Milwaukee, Wisconsin.] Highland Park, MI: Chrysler Corporation.

Infante, D. A., & Gorden, W. A. (1985). Superiors argumentativeness and verbal aggressiveness as predictors of subordinates satisfaction. Human Communication Research, 12, 117–126.

Jablin, F. (1980). Organizational communication theory and research: An overview of communication climate and network research. Communication Yearbook, 4, 327–347.

Jackall, R. (1988). Moral mazes the world of corporate managers. London: Oxford University Press.

Jackson, J. H., & Morgan, C. P. (1978). Organizational theory. Englewood Cliffs, NJ: Prentice-Hall.

Jaksa, J. A., & Pritchard, M. S. (1988). Communication ethics methods of analysis. Belmont, CA: Wadsworth.

James, G. G. (1990). Whistleblowing: Its moral justification. In P. Madsen & J. Shafritz (Eds.), *Essentials of business ethics* (pp. 160–190). New York: Meridian.

Janis, I. (1972). *Victims of groupthink*. Boston: Houghton-Mifflin.

Jensen, V. J. (1987). Ethical tension points in whistleblowing. *Journal of Business Ethics, 6,* 321–328.

Johannesen, R. L. (1990). *Ethics in human communication* (3rd ed.). Prospect Heights, IL: Waveland Press.

Jones, B. L., & Chase, W. H. (1979). Managing public policy issues. *Public Relations Review, 7,* 3–23.

Johnson, W. B., & Packer, A. H. (1987). *Workforce 2000: Work and workers in the 21st century*. Indianapolis, IN: Hudson Institute.

Josephson, M. (1934). *The robber barons*. New York: Harcourt, Brace.

Kane, P. E. (1983). Public figure libel after Sullivan: Goldwater v. Ginsburg. *The Free Speech Yearbook, 22,* 43–51.

Katz, D., & Kahn, R. L. (1966). *The social psychology of organizations*. New York: Wiley.

Kernisky, D. A. (1992). *A critical analysis of the ethicality of organizational legitimation strategies: Dow Chemical's issues management bulletins, 1979–1990*. Unpublished doctoral dissertation, Wayne State University, Detroit, MI.

Kernisky, D. A., & Kernisky, I. F. (1994, November). *The good, and the paid: Countervailing forces in constructing American consciousness*. Paper presented at the annual meeting of the Speech Communication Association, New Orleans, LA.

Key, W. B. (1973). *Subliminal seduction*. New York: Signet.

Kincki, A., Bracker, J., Kreitner, R., Lockwood, C., & Lemak, D. (1992). Socially responsible plant closings. *Personnel Administrator, 37,* 116–117.

Kippen, A. (1990, February). GAPS in your defense. *The Washington Monthly,* 29–36.

Knight, K. E., & McDaniel, R. R. (1979). *Organizations: An information processing perspective*. Belmont, CA: Wadsworth.

Kohlberg, L. (1984). *The psychology of moral development*. New York: Harper & Row.

Kotter, J. P., & Schlesinger, L. A. (1979). Choosing strategies for change. *Harvard Business Review, 57,* 106–115.

Kreps, G. L. (1980). A field experiment test and re-evaluation of Weick's model of organizing. *Communication Yearbook, 4,* 389–398.

Kreps, G. L. (1990). *Organizational communication* (2nd ed.). New York: Longman.

Kreps, G. L. (1993) Promoting a sociocultural evolutionary approach to preventing sexual harassment: Metacommunication and cultural adaptation. In G. L. Kreps (Ed.), *Sexual harassment: Communication implications* (pp. 310–318) Cresskill, NJ: Hampton Press.

Laczniak, G. R., & Murphy, P. R. (1981). Marketing ethics: A review with implications for managers, educators, and researchers. In B. M.

Enis & K. Roering (Eds.), *Review of marketing* (pp. 251–297). Chicago: American Marketing Association.

Ladd, J. (1979). Morality and the ideal of rationality in formal organizations. In T. D. Donaldson & P. Werhane (Eds.), *Ethical issues in business a philosophical approach* (pp. 102–114). Englewood Cliffs, NJ: Prentice-Hall.

Laufer, R., & Wolfe, M. (1977). Privacy as a concept and social issue: A multidimensional development theory. *Journal of Social Issues, 33*, 22–42.

Lemos, R. M. (1986). *Rights, goods and democracy.* Cranbury, NJ: Associated University Presses.

Levine, A. (1980). Human rights and freedom. In A. S. Rosebaum (Ed.), *The philosophy of human rights: International perspectives* (pp. 137–151). Westport, CT: Greenwood.

Likert, R. (1961). *New patterns of management.* New York: McGraw-Hill.

Littlejohn, S. W. (1992). *Theories of human communication* (4th ed.). Belmont, CA: Wadsworth.

Lucas, J. R. (1993). *Responsibility.* Oxford, UK: Clarendon Press.

Macdonald, J., & Piggott, J. (1993). *Global quality: The new management culture.* San Diego, CA: Pfeffer.

Madsen, P., & Shafritz, J. M. (1990). *Essentials of business ethics.* New York: Meridian.

Makower, J. (1993). *The e factor.* New York: Times Books.

Marshall, J., Scott, P. D., & Hunter, J. (1987). *The Iran-Contra connection.* Boston: South End Press.

Matusewitch, E. P. (1981, January). Fear of lying: Polygraphs in employment. *Technology Review, 83*, 10–11.

Mauer, J. G. (1971). *Readings in organizational theory: Open systems approaches.* New York: Random House.

McBride, K. (1993). *Effective communication to minimize crisis in plant closings.* Unpublished master's essay, Wayne State University, Detroit, MI.

McDaniel, S. D., Hart, S., & McNeal, J. (1983). Subliminal stimulation as a marketing tool. *The Mid-Atlantic Journal of Business, 20*, 41–48.

McGregor, D. (1960). *The human side of enterprise.* New York: McGraw-Hill.

McGill, T. (1994). *Corporate public discourse: Exxon's accounts following the Valdez oil spill of March 24, 1989.* Unpublished doctoral dissertation, Wayne State University, Detroit, MI.

Meindl, J. R., Erlich, S. B., & Dukerich, J. M. (1985). The romance of leadership. *Administrative Science Quarterly, 30*, 78–102.

Mescon, M. H., Albrect, M., & Khedouri, F. (1985). *Management individual and organizational effectiveness* (2nd ed.). New York: Harper & Row.

Meyer, J. W. (1992). Organization factors affecting legitimation in education. In J.W. Meyer & R. Scott (Eds.), *Organizational environments: Ritual and rationality* (pp. 217–233). Newbury Park, CA: Sage.

Meyer, J. W., & Scott, R. (1992). *Organizational environments: Ritual and rationality.* Newbury Park, CA: Sage.

Miller, J. Z. (1992). Ethics and advertising. In M. Snoeyenbos, R. Almeder, & J. Humber (Eds.), *Business ethics* (rev. ed., pp. 431–420). Buffalo, NY: Prometheus Books.

Mintzberg, H. (1973). *The nature of managerial work.* New York: Harper & Row.

Moore, T. E. (1982). Subliminal advertising: What you see is what you get. *Journal of Marketing, 46,* 38–47.

Moritz, M., & Seaman, B. (1984). *Going for broke: Lee Iacocca's battle to save Chrysler.* Garden City, NY: Anchor.

Murphy, K.R. (1993). *Honesty in the workplace.* Pacific Grove, CA: Brooks/Cole.

Nader, R. (1990). The anatomy of whistle-blowing. In P. M. Madsen & J. H. Shafritz (Eds.), *Essentials of business ethics* (pp. 152–160). New York: Meridian.

Near, J. P., & Miceli, M. P. (1986). Retaliation against whistleblowing: Predictors and effects. *Journal of Applied Psychology, 71,* 137–145.

Newsom, D., Scott, A., & Turk, J. V. (1989). *This is PR* (4th ed.). Belmont, CA: Wadsworth.

Nicotera, A. M., & Cushman, D. P. (1992). Organizational ethics: A within-organization view. *Journal of Applied Communication Research, 20,* 437–462.

Nilsen, T. R. (1974). *Ethics of speech communication* (2nd ed.). Indianapolis, IN: Bobbs-Merrill.

Novak, M. (1982). God, man and the corporation. In D. G. Jones (Ed.), *Business, religion and ethics* (pp. 69–88). Cambridge, MA: Oelgeschlager, Gunn & Hain.

Occupational Health and Safety Act of 1970. (1970, December 29). *Public Law 91-596.* Occupational Safety and Health Administration [Internet]. Available: http://www.osha.gov.

Occupational Health and Safety Administration. (1986, June 26). *OSHA's Expanded Hazard Communication Standard Fact Sheet 89–86.* [Internet]. Available: http://www.osha.gov/oshfacts/policy/hazard.txt.

Osigweh, C. (1987). *Communicating employee rights and responsibilities.* New York: Quorum Books.

Parliman, G. C. (1987). Protecting the whistleblower. *Personnel Administrator, 32,* 26–32.

Parmerlee, M. A., Near, J. P., & Jensen, T. C. (1982). Correlates to whistleblowers' perception of organizational retaliation. *Administrative Science Quarterly, 27,* 17–34.

Parsons, T. (1956). Suggestions for a sociological approach to the theory of organizations. *Administrative Science Quarterly, 1,* 63–85

Pearlstein, S. (1992, July 16). Riches and wrongdoing: Whistleblowers go to court. *The Washington Post,* p. A1.

Pemberton, P. L., & Finn, D. R. (1985). *Toward a Christian economic ethic*. Minneapolis, MN: Winston Press.

Perrow, C. (1970). *Organizational analysis: A sociological view*. Belmont, CA: Brooks/Cole.

Peters, T., & Waterman, T. (1982). *In search of excellence*. New York: Harper and Row.

Petress, K., & King, A. (1990). Iran Contra and the defeat of accountability. *Communication Reports, 3*, 15–22.

Pfeffer, J. (1972). Size, composition, and function of hospital boards of directors: A study in organizational-environmental linkage. *Administrative Science Quarterly, 18*, 349–364.

Pfeffer, J. (1981). Management as symbolic action: The creation and maintenance of organizational paradigms. In B. M. Staw & L. L. Cummings (Eds.), *Research in organizational behavior* (Vol. 3, pp. 1–52). New York: JAI Press.

Pfeffer, J., & Salancik, G. (1978). *The external control of organizations*. New York: Harper & Row.

Preston, L. E. (1981). Research on corporate social reporting,-directions for development. *Accounting, Organizations and Society, 2*(1), 29–38.

Pritchard, M. (1991). *On becoming responsible*. Lawrence: University of Kansas Press.

Puckett, S., & Emery, R. (1988). *Managing AIDS in the workplace*. Reading, MA: Addison-Wesley.

Putnam, L. (1982). Paradigms for organizational communication research: Overview and synthesis. *Western Journal of Speech Communication, 46*, 196–206.

Putnam, L., & Cheney, G. (1985). Historical developments and future directions. In T. W. Benson (Ed.), *Speech communication in the 20th century* (pp. 130–156). Carbondale: Southern Illinois University Press.

Putnam, L., & Sorenson, R. L. (1982). Equivocal messages in organizations. *Human Communication Research, 8*, 114–132.

Ragsdale, J. G. (1993). Speeches of challenge and celebration: Lee Iacocca's 1980 and 1992 shareholder addresses. In M. Seeger (Ed.), *"I gotta tell you:" Speeches of Lee Iacocca* (pp. 67–96). Detroit, MI: Wayne State University Press.

Redding, W. C. (1973). *Communication within the organization*. New York: Industrial Communication Council & Purdue Research Foundation.

Redding, W. C. (1985). Rocking boats, blowing whistles, and teaching speech communication. *Communication Education, 34*, 245–258.

Redding, W. C. (1990). *Communication ethics: A case of culpable neglect*. Paper presented at the First National Conference on Communication Ethics. Gull Lake, MI.

Reich, R., & Donahue, W. (1985). *New deals: The Chrysler revival and the American system*. New York: Times Books.

Riahi-Belkaoui, A., & Pavlik, E. L. (1992). *Accounting for corporate reputation.* Westport CT: Quorum Books.

Rieke, R. D., & Sillars, M. O. (1993). *Argumentation: Critical decision making* (3rd ed.). New York: HarperCollins.

Rokeach, M. (1973). *The nature of human values.* New York: The Free Press.

Rothstein, M. (1989). *Medical screening and the employee health cost crisis.* Washington, DC: Bureau of National Affairs.

Sandage, C. H., Fryburger, V., & Rotzoll, K. (1983). *Advertising theory and practice.* Homewood, IL: Richard D. Irwin.

Sanders, W. (1983). The First Amendment and the government workplace: Has the Constitution fallen down on the job? *Western Journal of Speech Communication, 47,* 253–367.

Sanders, W. (1984). Common law tort and contract erosion of the at will rule: New paths toward freedom of speech in private sector workplace. *The Free Speech Yearbook, 23,* 1–13.

Schein, E. H. (1985). *Organizational culture and leadership.* San Francisco: Jossey-Bass.

Schlossberger, E. (1951). *Moral responsibility and persons.* Philadelphia: Temple University Press.

Schlenker, B. R. (1980). *Impression management: Self concept, social identity, and interpersonal relations.* Monterey, CA: Brooks/Cole.

Schlick, M. (1961). Causality in everyday life and recent science. In H. Moss (Ed.), *Freedom and responsibility* (pp. 292–303). Stanford, CA: Stanford University Press.

Scott, M. B., & Lyman, S. M. (1968). Accounts. *American Sociological Review, 23,* 46–62.

Seeger, M. W. (1984). Ethical issues in the communication innovation. *Michigan Journal of Speech Communication, 19,* 66–78.

Seeger, M. W. (1986). Free speech and institutional restraint. *The Free Speech Yearbook, 25,* 11–21

Seeger, M. W. (1987, November). *Father and founder: Henry Ford and the development of corporate paternalism.* Paper presented at the annual meeting of the Speech Communication Association, Boston, MA.

Seeger, M. W. (1993, November). *Responsibility in organizational communication: Individual, organization and environmental accounts.* Paper presented at the annual meeting of the Speech Communication Association, Miami Beach, FL.

Seeger, M. W., & Szwapa, C. (1989, November). *Justifications for legitimacy in the chemical industry.* Paper presented at the annual meeting of the International Communication Association, San Francisco, CA.

Sethi, S. P. (1975). Dimensions of corporate social performance: An analytical framework. *Pacific Sociological Review, 17,* 58–65.

Sethi, S. P. (1977). *Advocacy advertising and large corporations: Social conflict, big business image, the news media and public policy.* Lexington, MA: DC Heath.

Sethi, S. P. (1987). A conceptual framework for environmental analysis of social issues and evaluation of business response patterns. In S. P. Sethi & C. M. Fable (Eds.), *Business and society* (pp. 39–52). Lexington, MA: Lexington.

Shaw, M. E. (1981). *Group dynamics: The psychology of small group behavior.* New York: McGraw-Hill.

Siegel, B. (1981, January 4). The polygraph: In Ohio its lies raise doubts. *Denver Post–LA Times,* pp. B17–18.

Simms, M. (1991). *A critical analysis of workplace medical screening practices, privacy, and self disclosure: Assessing individual and organizational concerns in the 1990s.* Unpublished doctoral dissertation, Wayne State University, Detroit, MI.

Smirich, L. (1983). Concepts of culture and organizational analysis. *Administrative Science Quarterly, 28,* 339–358.

Smirich, L., & Morgan, G. (1982). Leadership: The management of meaning. *The Journal of Applied Behavioral Science, 18,* 257–237.

Smith, D. (1993). *Legitimation strategies of the A.H. Robins Corporation during the 21 year Dalkon Shield crisis.* Unpublished doctoral dissertation, Wayne State University, Detroit, MI.

Sniffen, M. (1994, October 13). Golden whistle. *Ann Arbor News,* p. A11.

Srivastva, S., & Cooperrider, D. L. (1988). Introduction: The urgency of executive integrity. In S. Srivastva & D. L. Cooperrider (Eds.), *Executive integrity* (pp. 1–29). San Francisco: Jossey-Bass.

Starik, M. (1995). Should trees have managerial standing? Toward stakeholder status for non-human nature. *Journal of Business Ethics, 14,* 207–217.

Steidlmeier, P. (1987). Business ethics: Reconciling economic values with human values. In S. P. Sethi & C. M. Fable (Eds.), *Business and society* (pp. 101–121). Lexington, MA: Lexington.

Stephens, C. U., D'Intino, R., & Victor, B. (1995). The moral quandary of transformational leadership. In W. A. Pasmore & R. W. Woodman (Eds.), *Research in organizational change and development* (Vol. 8, pp. 123–143). Greenwich, CT: JAI Press.

Stevens, E. A. (1992). *Corporate ethical codes: A study in competing values.* Unpublished doctoral dissertation, Wayne State University, Detroit, MI.

Stewart, L. P. (1993, May). *Ethical issues in diversity.* Paper presented at the annual meeting of the International Communication Association, Washington, DC.

Stogdill, R. M. (1974). *Handbook of leadership: A survey of the literature.* New York: The Free Press.

Stone, C. D. (1992). Toward legal rights for natural objects. In M. Snoeyenbos, R. Almeder, & J. Humber (Eds.), *Business ethics* (pp. 496–500). Buffalo, NY: Prometheus Books.

Stridsberg, A. B. (1977). *Controversy advertising: How advertisers present points of view in public affairs.* New York: Hastings House.

Subcommittee Hearings on Administrative Practice and Procedure of the Committee on the Judiciary of the United State Senate. (1978). *Sourcebook on corporate image and corporate advocacy advertising.* (Publication No. 33-291 O). Washington, DC: U.S. Government Printing Office.

Sullivan, L. (1987). The elimination of apartheid in South Africa. *Orbis, 31*, 3–6.

Sweet, D. W. (1989). *A managers guide to conducting terminations.* Lexington, MA: Lexington.

Sypher, B. D., Applegate, J. L., & Sypher, H. E. (1985). Culture and communication in organizational contexts. In W. B. Gudykunst, L.P. Stewart, & S. Ting-Toomey (Eds.), *Communication, culture and organizational processes international and intercultural communication* (Vol. 9, pp. 13–29). Sage: Beverly Hills.

Tabb, W. K. (1986). *Churches in struggle: Liberation, theologies and social change in North America.* New York: Monthly Review Press.

Taking the stand. (1987). New York: Pocket Books.

Thompson, D. F. (1987). *Political ethics and public office.* Cambridge, MA: Harvard University Press.

Thompson, W. N. (1975). *The process of persuasion: Principles and readings.* New York: Harper & Row.

Tompkins, P. (1984). The functions of human communication in organizations. In C. C. Arnold & J. W. Bowers (Eds.), *Handbook of rhetoric and communication theory* (pp. 659–719). Boston: Allyn & Bacon.

Tompkins, P., & Cheney, G. (1985). Communication and unobtrusive control in contemporary organizations. In R. D. McPhee & P. K. Tompkins (Eds.), *Organizational communication: Traditional themes and new directions* (pp. 179–210). Beverly Hills, CA: Sage.

Turkel, G. (1982). Situated corporatist legitimacy: The 1980 Chrysler Loan Guarantee. *Research in Law, Deviance, and Social Control, 4*, 165–189.

Valesquez, M. (1982). *Business ethics: Concepts and cases.* Englewood Cliffs, NJ.: Prentice-Hall.

Waters, J. A. (1988). Integrity management: Learning and implementing ethical principles in the workplace. In S. Srivastva & D. L. Cooperrider (Eds.), *Executive integrity* (pp. 172–197). San Francisco: Jossey-Bass.

Weick, K. (1969). *The social psychology of organizing.* Reading, MA: Addison-Wesley.

Weick, K. (1979). *The social psychology of organizing* (2nd ed.). Reading, MA: Addison-Wesley.

Weick, K. (1982). Management of organizational change among loosely coupled elements. In P. S. Goodman (Ed.), *Change in organizations: New perspectives on theory, research and practice* (pp. 375–409). San Francisco, CA: Jossey-Bass.

Weick, K. (1988). Enacted sensemaking in a crisis situation. *Journal of Management Studies, 4,* 305–317.

Weick, K. (1989). Organized improvisation: 20 years of organizing *Communication Studies, 40,* 241–248.

Weick, K. (1995). *Sensemaking in organizations.* Thousands Oaks, CA: Sage.

Werhane, P. (1985). *Persons, rights, and corporations.* Englewood Cliffs, NJ: Prentice-Hall.

Westin, A. (1968). *Privacy and freedom.* New York: Antheneum.

Wholey, D. R., & Brittain, J. W. (1986). Organizational ecology: Findings and implications. *Academy of Management Review, 11,* 513–533.

Will, G. (1989, December 18). Eurocentricity and the school curriculum. *Baton Rouge Morning Advocate,* p. 3.

Wolfe, D. M. (1988). Is there integrity in the bottom line: Managing obstacles to executive integrity. In S. Srivastva & D. L. Cooperrider (Eds.), *Executive integrity* (pp. 140–172). San Francisco: Jossey-Bass.

Woodward, J. (1965). *Industrial organizations: Theory and practice.* London, UK: Oxford University Press.

Yukl, G. (1989). Managerial leadership. *Journal of Management, 15,* 251–289.

Zeitz, G. (1980). Interorganizational dialectics. *Administrative Science Quarterly, 25,* 72–88.

Author Index

Subject Index

223

Organizational responsibility, 119-
133
communication, 130-132
defined, 120-122
environmental, 127-129
philanthropic, 124-125
product, 125
responsiveness, 121
to workers, 129-130
Organizational environments, 22,
23-26, 138

P

PACS, 15
Participatory management, 84-85
Persuasion, 150, 151
see also Ethics, Persuasion
Philanthropy, 120, 124-125
Philosophy, 13-14
Polygraph, 67-68, 71
Pornography, 79
Privacy, 17, 59, 62,63, 64-66, 71
Profit motive, 4
Propaganda, 152
Protestant work ethic, 13
Publics
external, 16-17
internal, 16-17
see also Stakeholders
Public relations, 140-141
and Stakeholders 137

Q

Quality Control Circles, 51-52, 85,
189

R

Rational decision making, 79-80
Religion, 12-13, 16
Responsibility
and authority, 42
corporate, 7, 8
definitions, 41-44
organizational, 7
personal, 40-41

see also Accountability, and
Organizational Responsibility
Requisite variety, 29, 146
Responsibility and freedom, 39,
40, 76-79
see also Organizational
Responsibility
Retention, 30
Rhetoric, 12, 111
see also Classical Rhetoric
Rights 59-74
defined, 59
human, 3, 59
individual, 7
organizational, 7
employee, 59-66, 63
see also Privacy

S

Scientific management, 9
Selection, 29
Sensemaking (see Enactment)
Sexual harassment, 194-195
Significant choice, 79-80
Social Responsibility Accounting,
132, 134
Social systems, 10, 11
Sophistry 11
see also General Systems
Theory
Speech codes, 79-80, 87-88
Stakeholders, 16, 17, 26, 107,
109, 111, 137-148
characteristics of, 140-144
defined, 139-140
identified, 141
management's role in, 143-144
Supreme Court, 64, 79
Surveillance, 66

T

Teams, 51, 81
see also Quality Control Circles
Testing, 65-66, 66-71

AIDS, 68-69, 70, 72-73
drug, 68, 70
problems with, 69-71
see also Privacy
Tobacco companies, 81, 108, 109,
110, 153, 154, 193

U

United Auto Workers (UAW), 107,
174
United Way, 112, 123
University of Michigan, 87-88
Unobtrusive control, 93

V

Values, 2, 3, 23, 26, 27, 104, 122
business, 4-5
of change, 166-167
democratic, 16, 76-77, 167
and leadership, 178-79, 181-
183

organizational, 26, 62
and organizational legitimacy,
104-105
values leadership, 181-182
see also Free Speech,
Legitimacy, and Virtue Ethics

W

Watergate, 14, 77, 90
Whistleblowing, 17, 89-101
characteristics of, 91
as communication, 95-96
defined, 90
ethical tensions in, 93-94
legal issues in, 96-99
motivational questions, 94-95
and retaliation, 91
see also Governmental
Accountability Project
Workforce 2000, 144